ANARCHISM

Anarchism/Minarchism
Is a Government Part of a Free Country?

Edited by

RODERICK T. LONG
Auburn University, USA

TIBOR R. MACHAN
Chapman University, USA

LONDON AND NEW YORK

First published 2008 by Ashgate Publishing

2 Park Square, Milton Park, Abingdon, Oxon OX14 4RN
711 Third Avenue, New York, NY 10017, USA

Routledge is an imprint of the Taylor & Francis Group, an informa business

First issued in paperback 2016

Copyright © 2008 Roderick T. Long and Tibor R. Machan

Roderick T. Long and Tibor R. Machan have asserted their moral right under the Copyright, Designs and Patents Act, 1988, to be identified as the editors of this work.

All rights reserved. No part of this book may be reprinted or reproduced or utilised in any form or by any electronic, mechanical, or other means, now known or hereafter invented, including photocopying and recording, or in any information storage or retrieval system, without permission in writing from the publishers.

Notice:
Product or corporate names may be trademarks or registered trademarks, and are used only for identification and explanation without intent to infringe.

British Library Cataloguing in Publication Data
Anarchism/Minarchism: Is a Government Part of a free country?
  1. Political science – Philosophy. 2. Anarchism. 3. Libertarianism. I. Long, Roderick T.
  II. Machan, Tibor R.
  320.1'1

Library of Congress Cataloging-in-Publication Data
Anarchism/minarchism : is a government part of a free country? / [edited by]
  Roderick T. Long and Tibor R. Machan.
      p.   cm.
  Includes bibliographical references.
  1. Anarchism. 2.Comparative government. 3. Legitimacy of governments.
  I. Long, Roderick T. II. Machan, Tibor R.
  HX833.A56943 2007
  320.5'7–dc22   2007007971

ISBN 978-0-7546-6066-8 (hbk)
ISBN 978-1-138-26546-2 (pbk)

Contents

Preface *Roderick T. Long and Tibor R. Machan*		vii
Notes on Contributors		ix

PART 1: MINARCHISM

1	Why the State Needs a Justification *Lester H. Hunt*	3
2	Libertarianism, Limited Government and Anarchy *John Roger Lee*	15
3	Rationality, History, and Inductive Politics *Adam Reed*	21
4	Objectivism against Anarchy *William R Thomas*	39
5	Reconciling Anarchism and Minarchism *Tibor R. Machan*	59

PART 2: ANARCHISM

6	Radical Freedom and Social Living *Aeon James Skoble*	87
7	The State: From Minarchy to Anarchy *Jan Narveson*	103
8	The Obviousness of Anarchy *John Hasnas*	111
9	Market Anarchism as Constitutionalism *Roderick T. Long*	133
10	Liberty, Equality, Solidarity: Toward a Dialectical Anarchism *Charles Johnson*	155
Index		189

Preface

Roderick T. Long and Tibor R. Machan

Libertarians seek a society in which people are free to do as they please with their own lives and peacefully acquired property, so long as they do not interfere with the right of others to do likewise with theirs. In such a society, much that governments currently do—all the myriad forms of forcible interference with their citizens' lives and property—would be abolished. But what would or should remain?

One libertarian tradition, drawing inspiration from classical liberal thinkers like John Locke, Adam Smith, Frédéric Bastiat, and the American Founders—and represented in the past century by, among others, Ludwig von Mises, Isabel Paterson, Ayn Rand, and Robert Nozick—calls for a constitutional government of strictly limited powers, which would be confined to the protection of everyone's negative (libertarian) rights. This position has come to be known as *minarchism*, the advocacy of minimal government. (Although some proponents and opponents of this position describe the government as "the state," arguably this latter term carries some baggage no libertarians wish to defend, given its use by such thinkers as Hegel and Marx who meant by it something like an organic society.)

Another libertarian tradition—inaugurated in 1849 by the Belgian economist Gustave de Molinari, further developed in the 1880s by the American journalist Benjamin Tucker and the circle of writers associated with his periodical *Liberty*, and represented more recently by Murray Rothbard, Morris and Linda Tannehill, David Friedman (son of economist Milton Friedman), Bruce Benson, Randy Barnett, and Hans-Hermann Hoppe, among others—proposes entirely abolishing government, in the Weberian sense of an institution holding a legal monopoly over a given territory, and replacing it with multiple providers of protection services *competing* on a free market. This position is generally known as *market anarchism* or *anarcho-capitalism*, to distinguish it from those forms of anarchism that oppose private property and the market. ("Market anarchism" is arguably a less controversial designation than "anarcho-capitalism," since libertarians disagree amongst themselves as to whether the term "capitalism" should be used to mean the unregulated free market that libertarians favor, or the pro-corporate regulatory regime that they oppose.) Outside of libertarian circles, the market anarchist position is best known via Robert Nozick's critique of it in his 1974 book *Anarchy, State, and Utopia*; ironically, academics unfamiliar with the libertarian tradition often assume (despite Nozick's footnotes) that the idea of competing protection agencies was Nozick's invention.

The purpose of the present volume is to examine the respective merits of minarchism and market anarchism from the perspective of several contemporary libertarian philosophers. The volume has been divided into minarchist and anarchist sections for the reader's convenience, although the nuances of particular contributors' arguments are such that some papers do not fit neatly into one category rather than another.

Notes on Contributors

John Hasnas is an associate professor at Georgetown University's McDonough School of Business, where he teaches courses in ethics and law. He is a Senior Research Fellow at the Cato Institute and an associated member of the Kennedy Institute of Ethics. Professor Hasnas has held previous appointments as an Associate Professor of Law at George Mason University School of Law, Visiting Associate Professor of Law at the Washington College of Law at American University, and Law and Humanities Fellow at Temple University School of Law. He has also been a visiting scholar at the Kennedy Institute of Ethics in Washington, DC and the Social Philosophy and Policy Center in Bowling Green, Ohio. He received his B.A. in Philosophy from Lafayette College, his J.D. and Ph.D. in Legal Philosophy from Duke University, and his LL.M. in Legal Education from Temple Law School. Between 1997 and 1999, Professor Hasnas served as assistant general counsel to Koch Industries, Inc. in Wichita, Kansas. His scholarship concerns ethics and white collar crime, jurisprudence, and legal history and his book *Trapped: When Acting Ethically is Against the Law* is currently available from the Cato Institute.

Lester H. Hunt is Professor of Philosophy at the University of Wisconsin, Madison. He has taught at Carnegie-Mellon University, University of Pittsburgh, and The Johns Hopkins University. He has written extensively on ethics, aesthetics, political philosophy, and the philosophy of law, and is the author of *Nietzsche and the Origins of Virtue* (1990) and *Character and Culture* (1998). He is currently working on a book on anarchy and justification of the state.

Charles W. Johnson lives and works in Las Vegas, Nevada. He is an alumnus of Auburn University, a Research Fellow for the Molinari Institute, and a member of the Industrial Workers of the World IU 640. He writes and maintains the Rad Geek People's Daily at <http://radgeek.com/>, and can be reached through his personal website at <http://charleswjohnson.name/>.

John Roger Lee (B.A., M.A. SUNY, Albany) (Ph.D. University of Southern California) is a retired professor of philosophy who taught at institutions in the State University of New York, the California State University, and the University of California systems. He lives in Los Angeles, California where he writes on philosophy and on political theory.

Roderick T. Long, B.A. (Harvard), Ph.D. (Cornell), is Associate Professor of Philosophy at Auburn University; President of the Molinari Institute and Molinari Society; editor of the *Journal of Libertarian Studies*; co-editor of the *Journal of Ayn Rand Studies* and *The Industrial Radical*; Senior Scholar of the Ludwig von Mises Institute; and author of *Reason and Value: Aristotle versus Rand* (Objectivist

Center, 2000) and *Wittgenstein, Austrian Economics, and the Logic of Action: Praxeological Investigations* (Routledge, forthcoming 2008). Long specializes in Greek philosophy; philosophy of agency; philosophy of social science; and moral and political philosophy. He blogs at Austro-Athenian Empire <http://praxeology.net/blog>, part of the Blogosphere of the Libertarian Left <http://libertarianleft.bravehost.com>.

Tibor R. Machan (R. C. Hoiles Professor of Business Ethics & Free Enterprise, Chapman University, CA) writes on ethics, business ethics, political philosophy, epistemology and philosophy of science. He wrote *Individuals and Their Rights* (1989) and *Libertarianism Defended* (2006), among other works. His most recent book is *The Right Road to Radical Freedom* (2007).

Jan Narveson, B.A. (Chicago), Ph.D. (Harvard), is Professor Emeritus of Philosophy at the University of Waterloo in Ontario, Canada. He is the author of more than two hundred papers in philosophical periodicals and anthologies, mainly on ethical theory and practice, and of five published books: *Morality and Utility* (1967), *The Libertarian Idea* (1989); *Moral Matters* (1993; 2nd ed. 1999), and *Respecting Persons in Theory and Practice* (2002); and, with Marilyn Friedman, *Political Correctness* (1995). He is also the editor of *Moral Issues* (1983); *For and Against the State* (with John T. Sanders, 1996), and *Liberalism: New Essays on Liberal Themes* (with Susan Dimock, 2000) He is or has been on the editorial boards of many philosophical journals; was also elected as a Fellow of the Royal Society of Canada, and is a frequent guest at colloquia and conferences around North America and in the U.K. and Europe. In 2003, he was appointed an Officer of the Order of Canada, which is Canada's next-to-top civilian distinction.

Adam Reed, Professor of Information Systems at California State University, Los Angeles, works in the philosophy and history of the cognitive and information sciences, and in both general philosophy and history. He wrote "Object-Oriented Programming and Objectivist Epistemology: Parallels and Implications," in the *Journal of Ayn Rand Studies*, and "From System Development to Information Infrastructure: The Shifting Technical Focus of Corporate IS Organizations," in the *Review of Business Information Systems*.

Aeon J. Skoble is Associate Professor of Philosophy and Chair of the Philosophy Department at Bridgewater State College, in Massachusetts. He is the co-editor of the anthology *Political Philosophy: Essential Selections* (Prentice-Hall, 1999) and author of the forthcoming *Deleting the State: An Argument about Government* (Open Court, 2008), as well as many essays on moral and political philosophy in both scholarly and popular journals. In addition, he writes widely on the intersection of philosophy and popular culture, including such subjects as *Seinfeld*, *Forrest Gump*, *The Lord of the Rings*, superheroes, film noir, Hitchcock, Scorsese, science fiction, and baseball, and he co-edited and contributed to *Woody Allen and Philosophy* (Open Court, 2004) and the best-selling *The Simpsons and Philosophy* (Open Court, 2000).

William R Thomas is Director of Programs at The Atlas Society. He has a Master's Degree in Economics from the University of Michigan, where he taught the economic history of the United States and China. He is a graduate of Oberlin College. Thomas is the editor of *The Literary Art of Ayn Rand* (2005), author of "Ayn Rand: Radical for Capitalism", and presenter of the recorded course "The Essence of Objectivism." He has published essays on topics in politics, ethics, and epistemology.

PART 1
Minarchism

Chapter 1

Why the State Needs a Justification

Lester H. Hunt

My Thesis

The point I wish to make here is actually fairly simple. As my title suggests, I wish to argue for the idea that the state is an institution that requires a justification. Some readers will no doubt feel that the fact that the state needs a justification is so obvious that arguing for it is a waste of time: it is best to move on forthwith to the real issue, which is what that justification (if there is one) might be. To others, the very idea that there is an issue here might seem baffling: why should government be any more in need of a justification than anything else? I would like to put forth a reason, a rather simple one actually, for thinking that it does need a justification; that it stands more in such need, perhaps, than any human institution of comparable longevity and persistence.

Hume's Challenge

Before I tell you just what this simple reason is, I would like to briefly set out a classic argument for the conclusion that there is in fact no issue here, that the state stands in no special need of justification. This will I hope motivate those who think that the state *obviously* needs a justification (so that discussing the issue of whether it does or not is a waste of time) to read on. I don't think that this classic argument does have an entirely obvious answer. To those who think that, on the contrary, the state stands in no special need of justification, I will just say, for the present, that there is indeed an answer to this argument and that the problem of justifying the state is a serious one.

The argument I have in mind shows up at the end of David Hume's essay, "Of the Original Contract," an extended criticism of John Locke's justification of the state. Locke of course is a social contract theorist, which in his case means that the state is made a legitimate institution (whenever it is such) by virtue of the fact that its subjects have in one way or another entered into an agreement to that effect: the only thing that can render a state legitimate is a certain sort of agreement among its subjects. After a lengthy discussion of historical examples meant to cast doubt on the idea that the governments that actually exist can have such a foundation, he turns his attention briefly to the idea that such an agreement, even if it exists, *could* justify the state:

> If the reason be asked of that obedience, which we are bound to pay to government, I readily answer, *because society could not otherwise subsist*: And this answer is clear and intelligible to all mankind. Your answer is, *because we should keep our word.* But besides, that no body, till trained in a philosophical system, can either comprehend or relish this answer: Besides this, I say, you find yourself embarrassed, when it is asked, *why we are bound to keep our word?* Nor can you give any answer, but what would, immediately, without any circuit, have accounted for our obligation to allegiance.[1]

Obviously, Hume is thinking that the answer to the second question, "Why should we keep our word?" is "because society could not otherwise subsist." Why not give that answer in the first place?

There is one feature of this argument that I think is a potential distraction. Hume assumes that what has to be justified, if anything does, in order to make the state a just or legitimate institution, is the idea that we owe it *obedience*. I doubt that this is how Locke frames the problem. In his treatment of the subject, the aspect of the state which seems to get the most attention is what one might call the "monopoly of force" aspect: specifically, the fact that the state backs up its edicts with threats of punishment (including, in his account of the matter, the death penalty) and forbids others from doing the same.

Further, aside from any issues involving the interpretation of Locke's theory, it seems to me that Hume's assertion, that society could not subsist without obedience to the state, seems rather doubtful in itself. For one thing, during the greatest part of the history and prehistory of the human species, life subsisted without any state at all. Our ancestors got along for many tens of thousands of years in small hunter-gatherer bands based to some extent on the extended family. During that time, they presumably lived together in relative peace by following customary rules of behavior. It is these features of a group of people – that they live together by following shared rules – that I would think make them a society. Society, understood in this way, antedates the state by a long, *very* long stretch of time. Further, one can doubt that, even in our times, society depends on *obedience* to the state. Over the years, I have asked undergraduate students whether they think that they have an obligation to obey the law, apart from any fear they might have of being caught and punished. Invariably, an overwhelming majority says that they do not, and a significant number even seem to find the question puzzling. For the most part, people seem to do what the law requires because of either a) the fear of being punished, b) the intrinsic wrongness of the act itself (for instance, stealing your neighbor's wallet) or c) what might be called the adverse natural consequences of the act itself (for instance, driving on the wrong side of the road). There may be certain advantages in a social system in which people obey state-made law just because it is the law – for instance, the system might thereby save on enforcement costs[2] – but it is *extremely* doubtful that society would collapse without such a feature.

---

1 David Hume, "Of the Original Contract," in *Essays Moral Political and Literary* (Indianapolis, IN: Liberty Classics, 1987), p. 481.

2 Of course, there could be a down side to it as well. People with an "obedient" frame of mind might be less exploratory and experimental in their view of life, and thus less inventive

However, Hume's focus on obedience is, as I have suggested, a distraction from the main point. One could probably reformulate his argument in terms of some other feature of the state in a way that would preserve its essentials. It would be prima facie plausible to say, for instance, that society, or at least a certain *kind* of society, the kind that we want to live in, could not subsist without (some) standing organisation that both deliberately manufactures rules and backs them with coercion (which is of course not the same thing as rules that one is somehow obligated to follow even apart from the coercion).

A potentially more serious problem with Hume's argument (a more serious problem than his apparent misinterpretation of Locke) lies in the fact that he rests his own argument on a debatable assumption. He is saying that if you are to complete Locke's defense of the state correctly, that is, in *Hume's* way, the most distinctively Lockean feature of this defense becomes a pointless extra step, one that actually weakens the case Locke seeks to make. Once we explain why we should keep our promises, we have an explanation that, it should be immediately obvious, also applies directly to the state. The problem with this is that Hume's way of completing the explanation is not the only way. He is assuming some form of utilitarianism, that the ultimate standard of right and wrong is social benefit. This is clearly not the way that Locke thinks about such matters. In his political philosophy he is a natural law theorist, not a utilitarian.

Nonetheless, Hume is making a point that goes well beyond his quasi-utilitarian assumptions, one that can be appreciated independently of whether we agree with him about the fundamentality of social benefit. Here is one way to look at it (there are probably others just as good, but this one brings out the aspect of the situation that I want to emphasise). Locke is concerned with the grounding of what we might call "the political realm."[3] A "realm" in this sense, is an array of *reasons* that people routinely give for either doing or believing things, in which these reasons are (sometimes very loosely) governed by a smaller array of fundamental principles. In this case, the reasons are of course *political* reasons. *Because the king said so* or *because he is the king* are political reasons for doing what the king said to do, or for believing that what the king did was right. Locke wanted to give an account of the circumstances in which these alleged reasons can become genuine reasons, can show that something is right or true. He thought that by doing so we can discover what the fundamental principles of the political realm are. The strategy by which he sought to achieve this end was to ground the realm of the political in the realm of the moral. *Because you promised* is a moral reason and not a political one. His theory is that the alleged reasons we encounter in the political realm become genuine reasons when

---

and productive. Admittedly, I am speculating here, but the point is that Hume is speculating as well, and very dubiously at that.

3 This is essentially the way Robert Nozick describes his own project in his *Anarchy, State, and Utopia* (New York: Basic Books, 1974) pp. 6-9. By importing the notion of reasons and principles into the definition of a "realm" I am giving it some content that it does not have in Nozick's discussion. But in view of the way he goes on to use these two notions in his later book, *The Nature of Rationality* (Princeton, NJ: Princeton University Press, 1993), Ch. 1, there is a chance he would have taken this in the spirit of a friendly amendment.

we can give good enough moral reasons why they should be accepted. By giving an account of what the relevant moral reasons are, he thought he could establish that the basic principles of the political realm consist of a small number of specific goals (the state is to pursue the general good and protect individual rights) and a tight set of constraints on state action: it must pursue these goals without violating rights.

The sort of theory that Locke is practicing is a very powerful one, in that (supposing we have a right to use it) it yields an abundance of results: namely, ideas, analyses, and principles about the political realm. Hume's point is to raise a doubt about whether we *do* have a right to use this method, or one that is *anything like it*. At bottom, the logical character of Locke's theory is that of an *explanation*: it purports to explain why the would-be reasons in the political realm are (sometimes) genuine reasons. Now, we only have a right to accept any particular explanation as long as we have no reason to think that there is a better explanation, one that explains the same phenomena but explains them with a more plausible set of assumptions, or a greater appearance of logical rigor, or explains these phenomena and others in addition to them, and so forth. Regardless of what one thinks of appeals to social utility, the deeper point of Hume's argument remains: that there might well be a better explanation than Locke's, better even than the general *type* of explanation that Locke gives. Hume's triumphantly italicised declaration, *because society could not otherwise subsist*, is obviously meant to bring home to us that there is indeed an explanation that is far more plausible than Locke's because it involves far fewer fanciful assumptions and appeals only to commonly available facts, and at the same time is clearly relevant to the issue at hand, which is: why is it a good idea to have such a thing as the political realm? This bare fact, that Hume *can* give the sort of argument that he does give, calls into question the need to ground the political in the moral, because it points up the possibility (which is so obvious once we notice it) that there can be other ways of explaining the political realm, aside from explaining it in terms of the moral realm. Why can't both these realms, the political and the moral, be explained in terms of the socially advantageous, or indeed in some other sort of reason? In fact, once we come to entertain such possibilities, why not go beyond Hume and consider the possibility that the realm of the political and that of the moral might both be completely autonomous, with their own sort of peculiar logic?

The Problem of the Double Standard

Hume's argument raises at least three questions regarding Locke's strategy. First, why should we seek to explain the political in terms of some other realm at all? Second, why should we explain the political in terms of the moral? Third, why must we explain it in terms of the particular moral reason that Locke chooses as the foundation of his theory ("because you promised"). I will only concern myself here with the first two issues. Although my own view is that on these two issues Locke was fundamentally right and Hume was fundamentally wrong, I think we can only see why Locke was right by taking at least one step beyond the ideas that his theory contains. Admittedly, Hume is right about one thing: Locke was rather too quick in supposing, without further argument, that the political needs to be explained in terms of some other realm. However, I think we can see the need for such an explanation if we add something to our notion of what the explanandum phenomenon, the thing to be explained, is.

The additional element I have in mind is something that might be called "the double standard." It is something that is actually quite familiar to us all. Consider what officers of the state are doing when they collect taxes. They are not passing a hat and asking for money. They are *telling* you to pay, and if you fail to give them the amount they demand, they have various ways, all more or less painful, to make you sorry you did not cooperate. Of course, private citizens sometimes act the same way, but when they do, we call them thieves and insist that they be stopped and punished. When ordinary individuals do it, it is called stealing, but when representatives of the state do what, in a perfectly straightforward way, seems to be the very same thing, it is called taxation. The same sort of thing can be said about what the state is doing when it practices military conscription. Here they are forcing people, in some cases very much against their will, to do work that is not merely unpleasant but may very well be fatal to them. If private individuals do such things, these practices are called abduction, kidnapping or perhaps something worse, and we stop them if we can. When done by representatives of the state, they are treated and spoken of completely differently, even by people who think such policies are unnecessary or ill-advised.

Finally, consider what officers of the state are doing when they try to keep individuals outside or, as it may happen, inside the nation whose state is represented by those particular officers. They are coercively preventing people from crossing an imaginary line on the ground, somewhat in the way you or I might prevent an unwanted guest from entering our homes. But of course the imaginary line on the ground in this case does not represent the boundaries of the officer's property. Further, even if the line does happen to coincide with the boundary line of some individual's property, that individual may have no interest in preventing the coerced person from crossing it. The officer's right to do this, if it exists, is not based on the sorts of consideration that could give a private individual a right to do something similar. In this case, what the officer is doing is something that private individuals, including criminals, don't do at all, but the same point can be made here as in the case of taxation and conscription: we do not treat or speak of the officers in anything like the way we would tread private individuals who did the very same thing.

Rather obviously, this process can be repeated in connection with a vast array of government activities. The questions thereby raised are accordingly also multifarious. Why isn't taxation theft? Why isn't conscription abduction? Such questions can be multiplied at great length. The problem I am pointing to here is accordingly rather large and amorphous, but there is one conspicuous feature that unites the examples I have given so far. In each case, we have individuals pursuing their goals by using force against others. Two simple facts are sufficient to make these questions real issues. First, according to the moral ideas we apply to our own conduct and that of our fellow human beings, we are not generally permitted to pursue our goals by the use of force. Ordinarily, it makes no difference how morally lofty my purpose is. I may know that you are about to spend the contents of your wallet by going to a movie, whereas I would donate the same amount of money, if I had it, to a highly effective charitable organisation, which might actually use it to save a human life. Still, taking the money would be stealing, and for that reason I do not do it. Second, the officers in my examples are individual human beings like you and me. There is no obviously good reason why the standard I apply to myself and my neighbors should not also apply to them. And yet we do seem to apply some completely different standard to them. What, if anything, might justify this? This is what I call this the problem of the double standard.

The problem, to generalise just a bit, is that by the light of moral ideas that we tend to find highly intuitively plausible, it is possible to see judgments we ordinarily make about activities of the state as counter-intuitive. So far, the problem is in a way like the problem of skepticism in epistemology: there is a simple, intuitively appealing argument in Descartes' *Meditations* that makes it possible for me to entertain the possibility that I am always dreaming. However, our current problem is much more serious than the problem raised by the dream argument. We know in advance what the outcome of the best analyses of the dream argument will be: you are not dreaming. It is as simple as that. But we cannot say that all the state activities I have described above are perfectly in order as they are. It is not that simple at all. This difference between these two problems is linked to another difference between them. The problem raised by the dream argument is of purely academic interest: there is no pressing *practical* problem of distinguishing dreaming from waking. On the other hand, there is a practical problem, as pressing as it can be, of deciding which of these state actions, or which forms and permutations of them, are right.

Even those readers who most stubbornly resist the idea that there is something morally problematic about the state are aware that the practices I have described are all, as we might say, morally explosive: when they go wrong they can go very wrong indeed. Americans who support tougher measures to keep Mexicans on one side of the Gadsden Purchase line were offended when the East German government coerced East Germans to stay on one side of the Berlin wall. Defendants at the Nuremberg trials were prosecuted for the crime of using conscript labor – by states that were at that very moment using conscripted military personnel. The idea that these functions of the state are simply legitimate as they are is not likely to strike anyone, on reflection, as very plausible. It would seem to commit one immediately to a particularly ugly sort of moral nihilism.

In that case, where is the solution to my problem likely to lie? Clearly, the most obvious way to avoid underwriting the actions of the state with an amoral blank check would be to find the elements of morality that we find intuitively gripping, and assemble an account that can explain not only why the officers of the state are acting within their rights in doing things that the rest of us may not do, but in addition why they are not acting within their rights when they are not. This answers the second of the three questions I said were raised by Hume's argument, namely: why must we explain the political in terms of the moral? The answer is that morality is more intuitively gripping than politics is. They do not stand on an equal footing, in the manner suggested by Hume's argument. Further, the political is by moral standards somewhat *counter*-intuitive. Part of what it is to understand the political realm, to produce an adequate theory of it (supposing that this can be done) is to resolve this counter-intuitiveness. And the most obvious way to do this is to explain the political in terms of the moral. Further, the search for such an explanation is not a merely academic exercise, aiming at understanding as an end in itself, but a practical one which aims at drawing a line between right and wrong.

The idea that the political needs to be explained in terms of the non-political is one of the most distinctive features of the social contract tradition. More exactly, it is the idea that lies behind one feature of this tradition: that it attempts to derive (in some sense of this word) the state from the state of nature. What, after all, *is* the state of nature? It does not, or at least does not necessarily, represent the "natural" aspect of human life in the sense of being purely animal or pre-social. It is arguable that in Hobbes and Rousseau it does represent the merely animal, or something close to it, but Locke makes it abundantly plain that people in his state of nature live together in (more or less) peace because they regulate their behavior (though with imperfect success) by basic rules that enable them to do so. What the state of nature always represents is of course the *pre-political*. What I have tried to do here is to exhibit the logic and plausibility of state of nature theory, interpreted as the project of explaining the political by grounding it in another realm.

The Asymmetry of the Moral and the Political

Having come this far, I am of course aware many will have failed to follow me for a variety of reasons: either they do not have the intuitions on which I have relied, or they will resist having them or (most interestingly) will have them but refuse to trust them. I will now turn my attention to this last source of resistance.

Of course, someone might say, there is a sense in which our intuitive, pre-theoretical use of our moral ideas clashes with our intuitive, pre-theoretical application of our political ideas. When I think about myself, my next-door neighbor, or my uncle Harry, I think that, whenever any one of us promotes his or her goals by using coercion against someone who is not bothering anybody, we are doing wrong. When I think about a tax collector or an immigration official, I think pre-reflectively that they are right to go after the tax-evader and the Mexican immigrant, even though the tax evader and the Mexican are not bothering anybody. I think of the immigration official as if they were on a different plane from me, from my neighbor, from my uncle Harry. But why isn't each way of thinking perfectly okay, on its own plane?

In a way, I have already responded to this line of thinking. If we *simply* accept our pre-theoretical immersion in the political at face value, without tempering it with skepticism, it seems to put the individuals who carry out state policy on a different plane from everyone else. And this seems to lead directly to the blank check problem, which I have already discussed. If the reason they can do what they do is that they are on a different plane from the rest of us, doesn't that mean that what they do is alright just because they (on this higher plane) are doing it? And wouldn't this mean they may do what they do, *whatever it is*? But there is a positive point to this line of thinking that is worth considering: Is there any *reason*, apart from the blank check problem, to be more skeptical about our political intuitions than about our moral intuitions?

I can give one such reason. It has to do with what I think is the most plausible sort of causal explanation of our intuitions, an explanatory story of their origins.

More exactly, it has to do with certain features that such an explanation would have to have. Our ideas of right and wrong, whether political or moral, no doubt evolved over a long period of time, much of which has left no record of itself, so any account of their origins is necessarily speculative. I don't wish to speculate about them here, but merely to point out that the nature of these ideas implies certain constraints on the possible ways in which they might have come about.

Morality and the state have certain features in common, which enable us to compare them in illuminating ways. Both are features of the social world which serve to regulate individual behavior, and both do so, to a very significant extent, by means of rules of conduct. But there are two enormous and obvious differences between rules by means of which they accomplish this regulatory function, between moral rules and state-made rules. First, moral rules are ones that people think they have reason to follow quite aside from the possibility of being caught and punished for not following them. This is in fact a necessary feature of a morality. It is one implication of any reasonable definition of a morality. Among state-made rules, it is not. Some people believe they have an obligation to follow state-made rules, others do not, and yet they are state-made rules just the same. Further, as I have suggested, such rules do not seem to need the support of such a belief in order to function. Whenever they require people to do things that might go against their current desires, state-made rules are backed by deliberate coercion. The second difference lies in the fact that, in the case of moral rules, there is no one who is in the position of making it true, simply by declaration, that a given idea is a rule in the system.[4] Moral rules that comprise the moral code of a given group of people – and here it should be remembered that I am talking about what might be called "positive morality," the source of our pre-theoretical moral impressions – are ones that exist simply because the members of the group (perhaps to different degrees) accept them as binding. Wherever these rules come from, whatever their content might be, they must be ones that everyone can accept as right and binding on them without their being coerced into accepting them. Though the content of these rules can obviously vary widely from one group of people to the next, there are limits to what sorts of rules could exist in this particular way. In fact, if we suppose that people are always influenced by their own self-interest in accepting rules, then it would follow that the rules of a morality are (to the extent that they are so influenced) beneficial to all members of the group.[5] Indeed, if we consider the sorts of moral rules that seem to exist in all cultures, it seems obvious that they are beneficial to all. All cultures seem to have

---

4 In those rare cases in which we seem to have an exception to this – perhaps the Pope has something like this sort of authority over Roman Catholic morality – that very fact indicates that the norm-making authority is state-like and that the resulting system of rules is as much a juridical one as a moral one.

5 Admittedly, I am leaving the idea of benefit obscure, other than that the standard of benefit is the interests of the person benefited as perceived by that person. In particular, I am leaving open the question of "beneficial compared to what?" Are the rules beneficial to each in that they are better than no rules at all? Or does it mean that each particular rule is better than any possible alternative particular rule? Clearly the former would be too low a standard of what constitutes a benefit, while the latter would be an arbitrarily high one. I don't need to settle these questions here, since my point is to contrast these rules with state-made ones.

rules that obligate one to keep one's promises, that protect property (of some sort), that protect the family (in one or more of the many forms the family can take), and it is obviously in everyone's interests to have rules that perform these functions.

In order to explain moral rules, and through them the moral intuitions that derive from them, we must create an explanation that shows the rules, and resulting intuitions, to be mutually acceptable to the individuals to whom they apply. If in addition we assume that this process is driven (to some extent) by self-interest, our explanation will predict that the resulting rules and intuitions will be (to that extent) mutually beneficial. As the reader has no doubt noticed, the situation with state-made rules is entirely different. Here self-interest has a completely different sort of significance, leading not to mutual benefit but to exploitation. Because they are coercive and need not be unanimous, these rules can be forced on people contrary to their perceived interests. This is something that others can indeed have an interest in doing. It is possible to have rules that transfer benefit *from* one person or sub-group *to* another, where such rules are in place *because* they do have that feature. We might call such rules "norms of exploitation."[6] Further, if we suppose that self-interest drives the formation of these rules to a significant extent, and in addition that peoples' interests are not (in some relevant sense) perfectly harmonious, then we can predict that systems of state-made rules *will* include norms of exploitation, unless by some clever device people prevent it from doing so.

The prospect becomes yet more depressing if we make one more assumption, a very plausible one I should think. Suppose that the state has a mystique of authority, such that people have to some degree a tendency to believe that its rules, whatever they might be, are right.[7] This would mean that the state has a significant tendency to corrupt the human intellect and conscience. People who are being exploited, if they possess this tendency, are apt to think that it is right that they be treated this way. Worse yet, those who are doing the exploiting, to the extent that they have the same tendency, will do so with a clear conscience: they too will believe that their victims deserve no better treatment.

Though I have made a number of unjustified assumptions in what I have said so far (that people are to some extent influenced by self-interest in creating or accepting rules of conduct, that they tend to accept state-made rules as right, and so forth), the point is of course that these are not implausible assumptions. And if they are true, then the ideas that we use in the political realm *deserve* our irony and skepticism in a way that moral ideas do not.

---

6 I take this felicitous expression from Nozick, *Invariances: The Structure of the Objective World* (Cambridge, MA: Harvard University Press, 2001), pp. 248-49.

7 We need not assume that this mystique is something that the state has intrinsically, nor that the rule by itself causes people to believe that it is right. Other causal mechanisms might be involved. We might say, for instance, that there is a class of "public intellectuals" who advocate various possible state actions by various arguments and that, when there is a new rule or policy that is because these intellectuals have convinced enough people. Because of the state's coercive nature, because it is perfectly adapted to serve as an instrument of exploitation, there will be a tremendous temptation to be influenced by discreditable motives in being swayed by the arguments of these intellectuals. The arguments would in that case serve only as "ideology," in the Marxist sense: they would be rationalisations.

I am aware, however, that the dichotomous distinction I have drawn between the moral and the political will seem artificial to some. They will want to raise something like the following objection. Clearly, morality too can include norms of exploitation. Racism and patriarchy are (or very, very recently were) part of our own positive morality. Slavery itself was, once, protected by moral norms as well as legal and political ones. The unanimous consent that arises within a hierarchical situation, in which some have power over others, will tend to be of this sort. In such a situation, the unspoken ground of the agreement will often be something like, "Unless you agree that your function is to serve me, I will use my power to make things very unpleasant for you." Rules that arise in this way will be rules of exploitation. Throughout history, a great many moral rules have been like this.

All of this is true, but it doesn't constitute an objection to the position I have argued for here. It is true that the moral *can* be contaminated in this way. The political on the other hand is *necessarily* characterised by the factors that cause this sort of corruption. The difference between the merely possible and the necessary is a profound one. Further, this objection admits, indeed insists upon, my own main point, which is that coercion – or if you prefer, hierarchy – is corrupting. If hierarchy is corrupting, then what human institution could possibly be more corrupting in its influence than the state?

Another possible objection would rest on a charge of circularity. The idea would be that I have argued for the primacy of the moral over the political on the basis of ideas that are actually moral in nature. What I have said, essentially, is that political ideas have a certain tendency to be unfair, and unfairness is a moral failing. According to moral ideas, moral ideas have more authority than political ideas. It is an argument that morality can't lose.

My answer to this objection would be that whether an argument is circular depends on what its conclusion is, and this objection mischaracterises my conclusion. I do not argue to the conclusion that political thinking tends to be unfair or immoral, but that it tends to be distorted thinking. It contains a bias in favor of ideas and principles that license hierarchical relationships, in that it tends to do so without good enough reason. It is a sort of thinking about which skepticism is a perfectly rational response. The objection to it is epistemic and not moral.

Evolutionary Explanations

I have already commented briefly on the similarity, and more importantly the difference, between the problem of the double standard, as I have called it, and the problem of skepticism raised in Descartes' *Meditations*. I will conclude by making some more general remarks about the difference between this problem and other core philosophical problems. Robert Nozick offered an interesting evolutionary explanation of the core problems of philosophy, an explanation of the fact that they are problematic. He suggested, as a "hypothesis," the possibility that the seemingly intractable problems of philosophy – including the problems of induction, of other minds, of the existence of the external world, of the justification of morality – "all mark assumptions that evolution has built into us."[8] Human beings, for example, are very good at "reading" faces. Children learn just a few days out of the womb to look at a smile and smile back. They nimbly leap from observed behavior to a conclusion about what is going on in the mind that goes with the face. Over many millennia, the capacity to make leaps like this was selected for and strengthened. One day, Descartes looks out his window at people walking by and realises that what he sees, strictly speaking, is "hats and coats, which may cover automatic machines" and he finds that he cannot construct a rational argument that starts with what he observes and ends with the idea that these are people and not automata.[9] The transition from the one thought to the other does not seem to have the right steps, linked in the proper way, to make it a genuine rational justification. Nozick's hypothesis is, in effect, that with regard to problems like this one, philosophy attempts to do, by means of rational thought, what evolution has designed us to do by instinct. His point (or part of it) is that, given the origin of the problem, we should not be too optimistic about the possibility that this can ever be done.

How does this apply to the double-standard problem? It seems to me that it does *not* apply to it, does not explain why it is a problem. But the reason why it does not apply, doesn't entail that it is any more tractable than the problem of other minds, rather the reverse. There is a big and directly relevant difference between the problem of the double standard and a problem like Descartes' problem of other minds. We are descended from hunter-gatherer bands and, before that, from group-dwelling primates who had a constant need to decipher each other's thoughts and emotions. Those who were able to leap to reliable conclusions about such things were more likely to pass their traits on to offspring than were their less intuitive neighbors. On the other hand, we did not descend from bands who constantly dealt with immigration officials and tax-collectors. A mere one thousand years ago, there were large areas of the earth where people had little or no contact with states at all, and those states that did exist were, by our standards, little more than brutal gangs of thugs. Even today, there are human beings here and there who still live beyond the effective reach of the states that nominally rule their territories.[10] Insofar as our evaluative intuitions can be explained by evolutionary means, they would have to be ones that can hold the individuals in a small band together: personal loyalty, tit-

---

8 *The Nature of Rationality*, p. 121. The explanation that follows, including the examples given, differs from the way that Nozick explains the idea, but I am fairly confident that my account is faithful to what he actually meant.

9 Descartes, *Meditations on First Philosophy*, "Meditation II," Haldane translation. Many editions.

10 I am assuming here that our physical evolution has not been nearly fast enough to catch up with the political evolution (really, revolution) of the past few centuries. This seems to be consistent with the views of the practitioners of the emerging discipline of evolutionary psychology. Though some (not all) who are competent to assess the evidence think that there might have been some significant developments in human evolution since the end of the Pleistocene (the last 10,000 years), on no account could our brains have evolved fast enough to have circuitry adapted to making sense of tax collectors and immigration officials. See David Buller, *Adapting Minds: Evolutionary Psychology and the Persistent Quest for Human Nature* (Cambridge, MA: The MIT Press, 2005), pp. 107-12.

for-tat notions of justice, fairness in the division of the proceeds of group efforts such as hunting and raiding, promise-keeping, property rights, obligations based on kinship and marriage. Clearly, bands of individuals who are disposed to learn these behaviors quickly and act on them reliably would be more "fit," in Darwin's sense, than bands that are constantly split and hobbled by greed, squabbling, and backstabbing. Our most deeply rooted moral ideas, this hypothesis would maintain, are ones that bind individual to individual.

This seems to immediately yield an explanation for the problematic status of what I have been calling the problem of the double standard. More precisely, it explains the asymmetry of intuitions that underlies the problem, the fact that moral intuitions are more gripping than political ones. The notions that I apply to my neighbor and my Uncle Harry are so gripping because they are these basic ideas that bind the band together. What we see in the problem of the double standard is that these notions are very poorly adapted to understanding the state as a legitimate institution. So far, the explanation of the problem sounds rather like the explanation that Nozick gives. The difference lies in the fact that his explanation takes the form of claiming that, in the contexts he is discussing, instinct outruns reason. His explanations include a certain assurance that we will continue to make the right inferences. I am not about to stop seeing my Uncle Harry as having a mind just because I cannot reconstruct the inferences involved as knock-down arguments. Nested inside this assurance is the additional assurance that there *is* a right answer, selected by the evolutionary process.

The difference between this and the evolutionary explanation of the problem of the double standard is that in the latter case, both sorts of assurance are missing. Here, the problem is not the difficulty of getting to a place, by means of reasoning, that we normally arrive at by means of intuition. The problem is that intuition seems unable to get there at all. In constructing a justification of the state, unlike in the problem of other minds, reason is really entirely on its own. And that, when you pause and think seriously about it, is quite disturbing.[11]

---

11 I would like to thank Imtiaz Moosa and the students in the University of Wisconsin-Madison Philosophy Department's First Year Seminar for helpfully discussing an earlier draft of this chapter with me.

Chapter 2

Libertarianism, Limited Government and Anarchy

John Roger Lee

Libertarianism is the political position that every individual should be free to do as he judges best, either individually or cooperatively with others, so long as nobody's action impedes a like liberty for other individuals or groups of individuals. The question addressed here is whether libertarianism envisions a government in human affairs, or whether human societies should flourish in the absence of government, in anarchy.

A Simple Story

Farmer A and Farmer B live and farm on Plots of land A and B respectively. Plots of land A and B are similar in size and fertility and a creek separates them. Farmer A and Farmer B each satisfy their water needs for farming and for life in general, from the stream with no diminution of the flow of the water and without polluting it.

Farmer A and Farmer B are at liberty relative to one another and as their situation has been described there are no legal relations between them and no government lording over them to enforce any further relations between them.

For example, Farmer A has no property right to Plot of land A and Farmer B has no property right to Plot of land B. Until now, it has just been a matter of custom and practice that Farmer A has always farmed Plot A and Farmer B has always farmed Plot B. Farmer A has never been tempted to set foot on Plot of Land B and Farmer B has never been tempted to set foot on Plot of land A. There are and have been no prohibitions of Farmer A stepping on Plot of land B nor of Farmer B stepping on Plot of land A. Rather, the matter has never come up.

Suppose now that Farmer B hears of a village across the creek and on the other side of Plot of land A. He decides to check the village out, crosses the stream and walks through some plantings that Farmer A has made. Farmer A sees this historic event and wants to hail Farmer B with a complaint. What should Farmer A say?

"Stop!" won't do because Farmer A and Farmer B are at liberty relative to one another and the presumptive order "stop" would, if successful impede Farmer B's liberty to move about as he would. Farmer A has no standing to issue the presumptive order "stop" for doing so would unjustly impede Farmer B's freedom.

Well maybe bare orders are out if we are to respect one another in speech; but surely the situation is different if an order or a request is coupled with a reason why the suggested action should be done. So maybe Farmer A should try something like:

Stop! You are walking on the plantings.

But how does the fact that Farmer B is walking on plantings give Farmer B *a reason* to stop doing so? Plantings are just as firm and suitable a surface for walking as is any other accessible portion of Plot of land A. A reason has not been given to Farmer B to stop walking as and where he is.

Well if Farmer A is as incensed as he seems to be at B's behavior he should want to complain:

Stop! You are walking on *my* plantings.

In saying this, Farmer A is accusing Farmer B of violating Farmer A's property rights in the plantings, through which Farmer B is walking. That is a complaint such that, if it registers on Farmer B at all, it provides a reason why Farmer B should stop doing as he's doing.

But this assertion of a property right, however, is something that Farmer A is in no position to assert. Farmer A and Farmer B live in perfect liberty relative to one another with no claims on one another. A property rights relationship has never been defined between them and so it cannot be asserted against Farmer B by Farmer A.

Well, such perfect liberty surely is limited by a provision that Farmer A should have a like liberty to wander through plantings and what-not on Plot of land B if he wants. But in the situation of this simple story, Farmer B has issued no pronouncements on the topic of Farmer A's possible perambulations on Plot of land B—he certainly has not tried to forbid them. Further, the prospect of such behavior has never occurred to Farmer A. So nothing in Farmer B's behavior has restricted a like liberty for Farmer A. So Farmer B's behavior is not illegitimate on grounds of not leaving a like liberty for Farmer A.

Farmer B is both a moral and a legal innocent in this story; although the latter, legal innocence, may just be because there are no laws extant in the community of the story.

Innocent as Farmer B may be in the story, the situation that the story describes is intolerable for any envisioned community which has the trade and commerce of a modern society. In transitioning from the simple model indicated in the story, to a satisfactory model of society, something would have to be added to the simple story, of the sort that Farmer A wanted to assert but did not have available—a system of rights and obligations—law.

How would Farmer A access a law? How could he bring it about that he has a legal protection against Farmer B wandering in Plot of land A, including among the plantings that Farmer A has made in Plot of land A? Could Farmer A secure this relief by posting signs on the Plot of land A side of the creek, signs that read:

No crossing! No wandering in Plot of land A, except by Farmer A.

It does not seem that such posting of signs would have the desired effect. The sign would be nothing other than a written version of the complaint that Farmer A tried earlier in an oral form:

Stop!

As Farmer A was in no position to issue an order to Farmer B then, so he is now not in such a position, even if the orders are in writing. Farmer A in this story cannot generate law all by himself, even by posting a written notice.

But a society without a system of rights and obligations—without law—is intolerable. As long as Farmer A and Farmer B acted independently from one another, as in the simple story, everything was all right—no law was needed. But when Farmer B's actions and expectations (that he could wander where he would, including in Plot of land A) clashed with Farmer A's expectations (that plantings he had made should be undisturbed and grow to maturity) the absence of law was first felt—through Farmer B's actions and through Farmer A's inelegant actions to stop them.

When people act freely they do so with expectations of what the outcome of their actions will be. When two people act their expectations for the future consequences of their action can interact. The expectations can interact harmoniously, or they can conflict. The simple story of Farmer A and Farmer B before Farmer B crossed the creek isolated the actions of Farmer A and Farmer B to the point at which their expectations and actions could not interact at all.

In that artificially isolated condition, nobody could do anything *with* another person without interfering with that person's liberty. But free people in free societies should be able to cooperate with one another; and to cooperate without interfering with others' liberty, people need a clear, prior specification of their rights and obligations relative to one another so they can gauge how the anticipated consequences of their actions will impact on the rights of others. Thus, people need a system of laws that specify the rights and obligations of people in diverse circumstances. How do they get such a body of law?

The Origin of Laws

In the account of the lack of consequence of Farmer A's posting a notice we saw that Farmer A's posting notice of the existence of a law had no effect on the fact that no law existed. Farmer A, and no individual by himself, can create law merely by proclaiming it,[1] nor could two individuals, nor twenty.

---

1 In history, certain individuals—Kings, Barons, and such—by the exercise of political and military skill have put themselves in a position where their proclamations served as law and were enforced by themselves or by their agents. This capacity owes more to their political and military skill than to any other features of these unique individuals.

American law comes from a constitutional convention[2] and from the ratification of the fruit of that convention by those entitled to vote in the prior government. But that was a solution to the problem of the origin of law that essentially requires government. And this chapter attempts to arbitrate between two different forms of libertarianism, one that countenances government, and one that is purely non-governmental—anarchistic libertarianism.

Anarchistic libertarians at this point imagine a free market on which private defense agencies announce and enforce alternative sets of laws and methods of enforcement, soliciting people who will contract for their services.[3] These private agencies will then enforce their announced laws for their subscribers,[4] earning whatever reputation they deserve by the quality of their actions. These agencies then will recruit new subscribers on the basis of their reputation. Some agencies will succeed handsomely contracting with a good percentage of individuals in the market for such services. Other agencies will fail as the rumors spread regarding the ineptness of their operations and as customers abandon them. Every individual is free to contract with whichever private defense agency has the most commercial appeal to them. Thus are laws promulgated and enforced according to anarchistic libertarians. Law arises out of a very broad class of contractual relations.

But, it is useful to ask: "under what contract law are these contractual relations formed? What court or agency is charged with enforcing them? If a party to the contract thinks the other party is in default, what forum is available in which he can make his case and seek redress?" In principle, none of these questions can be answered.

It is at this point that the conceptual incoherence of libertarian anarchy shines forth most clearly. Law is said to arise out of contractual relations but there can be no contractual relations without contracts and there can be no contracts without contract law in terms of which the contracts are drawn and through which they bind the parties to the terms contracted. Under what contract law are the contracts between individuals and private defense agencies drawn? Where there is no law prior to the imagined broad set of contractual relations between defense agencies and individuals, there is no law in terms of which any contractual relations can be drawn.

Anarchistic libertarianism illegitimately and self-defeatingly presupposes the prior existence of contract law in its account of how law and its enforcement would come to exist and have an ongoing role in an anarchistic society.

Intellectual difficulties of anarchic libertarianism have been pointed out in the past. Robert Nozick showed that the market alternatives of many competing defense

---

2   And a number of State Constitutional Conventions plus the incorporation of vast tracts of British Common Law, taken from our former colonial masters.

3   Murray Rothbard, *Power and Market* (Kansas City, MS: Sheed Andrews and McMeel, 1977); Randy Barnett, *The Structure of Liberty: Justice and the Rule of Law* (New York: Oxford University Press, 1998); Bruce Benson, *The Enterprise of Law: Justice without The State* (San Francisco, CA: Pacific Research Institute for Public Policy, 1990); David Friedman, *The Machinery of Freedom: Guide to Radical Capitalism* (New York: Harper and Row, 1973).

4   For the sake of efficiency, some free-riding non-subscribers may have laws enforced to their benefit by an agency in some cases.

agencies would tend, over time, to the rise of a monopoly defense agency that was in all respects the equivalent of a government.⁵ John Hospers wondered whether a defense agency headed up by Howard Hughes (an eccentric billionaire) and Edward Teller (a scientific genius active in the design and production of thermonuclear weapons) could be reined in by other defense agencies that had much less force at their disposal? Or would the Hughes-Teller Defense Agency work its will and impose its interpretation of the laws by overwhelming force and without regard to justice?⁶

It is however the conceptual difficulty, pointed out above, of presupposing the existence of law in its account of the origin of and viability of law under anarchy that shows the complete incoherence of anarchistic libertarianism.

A Brief Note on Natural Rights and Natural Law

Some readers may react negatively to the claim that Farmer A and Farmer B, in the basic story did not have rights to Plot of land A and Plot of land B or to the fruits of their labor on Plot of land A and Plot of land B. Some may think that Farmer A has a claim to Plot of land A and Farmer B a claim to Plot of land B as a matter of natural law.

The belief that humans have certain rights as a fact of nature has a long tradition going back, at least to Cicero in the Roman Republic. John Locke, for example, would have granted Farmer A a property claim in Plot of land A for having mixed his labor with that land, so long as as good and plenty land were available for others to acquire by hard work. Thomas Jefferson famously wrote that all men were endowed by God with rights to life, liberty and to the pursuit of happiness.

Not many people believe in a God that would do this for us, any more. And Locke's labor mixing, while leaving as good and as plenty for (all, some, present, future?) others, is notoriously difficult of application. But there is some truth that this tradition is commendable for urging on us.

As a fact of nature, people do have rights: legitimate normative expectations for the conditions that make cooperative co-existence possible.⁷ But it is metaphorical at best to say that people naturally have a right to life or to liberty, or to property.

Rather, what people have a right to is that there be a system of laws, operative in their environs, which system guarantees private property in some form, enforced by some mechanism, and guarantees life, for some period under some specification of conditions, and guarantees a full range of liberty of action and thought, compatible with a like liberty for all.

---

5   Robert Nozick, *Anarchy, State, and Utopia* (New York: Basic Books, 1974).
6   John Hospers, "Will Rothbard's Free Market Justice Suffice?" *Reason*, May 1973, pp. 18-21.
7   This definition of "right" is adequate for libertarian political theory. Some non-libertarian thinkers extend the scope of rights to include access to a minimal amount of those goods which are necessary for human flourishing. As this is an essay on the logic of the libertarian political theory, such farther reaching rights are not discussed here.

A right of life, liberty or property is meaningless unless it is seen as part of a larger coordinated whole which is the body of some legal system. A right of property, cut off from rights to contract, to bequeath, to use to secure a loan and clearly specified criteria of default on such ancillary agreements as well as clearly specified enforcement mechanisms and procedures, would be meaningless. A right to life needs to be specified and integrated into a body of law; but the way that it is integrated is open to differing formulations. One such formulation might mandate, as part of its specification of the right of life that all people must make whatever contributions of properties are needed to keep every other person alive for as long as possible, including in a persistent vegetative state.

To be sure, such an interpretation of a right of life is possible in a system of laws. It is not, however, the only interpretation possible; and it is not one that I would favor but one that I would work against, politically. The prohibition of murder, in the criminal law, is another implementation of a right to life in a body of law. But the mere prohibition of murder is not sufficiently nuanced to capture the ideal expressed when we speak of a right to life.

The normative requirement that is natural, that is imposed by nature, is: that there be a body of law in which life, liberty, property and the pursuit of happiness are possible to people who can cooperate with one another to pursue their individual and collective goals.

The metaphorical talk of rights of life, of liberty, of property and of a right to the pursuit of happiness serves as specifications of ideals that a decent body of laws must realise.[8] But it is only in the context of such a system of laws that they can be realised. What we naturally have a right to is such a system of laws operative in our community.

Farmer A in the simple story that opened this chapter had a right to a body of law that governed interactions among people in his environment, and had a right to that body of law meeting certain ideals. But Farmer A had no property rights in the simple story because there was no such body of law in the situation described in the story. So, a necessary condition for the existence of property rights (law) was not present.

---

8 I find this interpretation of natural rights and natural law, as ideal conditions that positive law should be held to realise, in the writings of Ronald Dworkin (e.g., *Taking Rights Seriously*, Cambridge, MA: Harvard University Press, 1977).

Chapter 3

Rationality, History, and Inductive Politics

Adam Reed

Disconfirmation

On 19 February 2006, *The Scotsman* reported the results of a poll of UK Muslims: 40 per cent want literal ("hard-line") Shariah Law to be the applicable legal system in "predominantly Muslim" areas of Britain. The article followed up with the usual details: Shariah Law specifies amputation of the offending part as a penalty for minor felonies, such as rape and theft; and death for major ones, such as homosexuality, atheism, blasphemy, apostasy, heresy, and fornication. These poll results are not atypical: there have been *no* results with significantly lower support for Shariah Law in *any* poll of Muslims worldwide. If the world were converted today to the "Enterprise of Law" system of Benson 1990, or any one of several similar "market law" systems widely advocated in the Libertarian community, then surely one such enterprise in this market would be the "Global Bin Laden Shariah Law Enterprise," with something like half a billion customers.

It is not necessary for me to list here the many books, from Spooner 1870 to Benson 1990, that explain "market law" (or, in earlier terminology, "market anarchist") systems, since Tibor Machan provides a comprehensive overview in his chapter of this book. I come to the question from different perspective. I hold, following Rand 1966-67, that all abstract knowledge, including philosophical knowledge, comes from inductive integration of observed facts of reality; that Man integrates "his percepts into concepts, his concepts into principles, his principles into sciences, and all of his sciences into a philosophy" (Rand 1969) With Rand, I reject the analytic-synthetic dichotomy, and hold that Politics—even as a branch of Philosophy—must be grounded in the observed and abstracted facts of psychology, economics, and especially history. Every science has seen in its history elaborate theoretical structures—one thinks of Ptolemaic epicycles—brought down by some disconfirming confrontation with observed facts. When this happens, it is time to switch to a theory that accounts for the facts, and to see where the disconfirmed theory went wrong.

Ethics and Interpersonal Ethics

Before getting into Rand's politics as an alternative to what I regard as empirically disconfirmed proposals for "market law," I will present a cursory outline of Rand's

(1964) foundation of objective politics in individual and interpersonal ethics, with additional inductive grounding from the literature of the human sciences.

Life, Purpose, and Happiness

We observe that man is—I observe that I am—a living organism. Living organisms do not exist unconditionally: an organism's existence is conditional on action that sustains its life (life is a process of self-generated and self-sustaining action). Organisms have specific ways of sustaining their lives. Man's main evolved instrument for sustaining his life is his ability to observe, think, judge, and act in accordance with his judgment. Judgment and action are faculties of the individual human organism. Man is the animal that lives by his individual judgment. To live and to thrive, man requires the absence of interference with actions by which his exercise of his individual judgment sustains his life. This is the pre-condition for being able to live by one's own judgment, that is, in the manner appropriate to man *qua* man. It is the single most fundamental and general human right, and for the purpose of politics—see below—the definition of what a right *is*.

The specific nature of every individual organism is the result of its biological evolution. Every organism that arises from biological evolution inherits traits that enabled and motivated its ancestors to survive and reproduce, and therefore is born with a purpose: to sustain and reproduce its life (Binswanger 1976, 1990: 89-95). This purpose is experienced by man as the *pursuit of happiness*. To optimise the pursuit of a goal—in the case of an evolved organism, the goal of sustaining and reproducing one's life—a cybernetic (teleological) system requires an ongoing scalar measure of *how well it is doing* at the pursuit of that goal (Wiener 1961, Ashby 1954). In human consciousness, the evolved measuring instrument (Rand 1964 [30] likens it to a "barometer") that measures how well one is doing at life is the faculty of *happiness*. Happiness is achieved by action that sustains and enhances one's life.

Overall happiness is the sum of two evaluations: how conducive one's current state and setting are to living long and well, and how efficacious one can expect to be at future actions that one will need to perform to sustain and enhance one's life. While the first component tends to change slowly and imperceptibly, the second will be frequently (and noticeably) affected by feedback from success or failure at achieving whatever goals one might have set for oneself. Even if one pursues a "value" (in the sense of a condition that one seeks, however erroneously, to gain or to keep) that is adverse to the first component (the objective of living long and well,) one's success at achieving this "value" will be automatically processed, and noticed, as evidence of one's effectiveness. Therefore success at achieving a value is experienced as happiness, even if that value is itself at odds with sustaining and enhancing one's life. This effect is a special case of a *cognitive illusion* due to the *availability heuristic* (Tversky and Kahneman 1973): a sharp increment in the success-based effectiveness estimate component of happiness can hide a greater but slower decline in the state-and-setting evaluation component. It is also the reason why many people believe, falsely, that values are subjective: they experience spikes of happiness from the achievement of *any* value, regardless of whether the achieved value is in itself objectively beneficial or harmful. The rational pursuit of happiness is the pursuit of values beneficial to one's life, not merely of values valued only because their achievement "makes one feel good."

The Trader Principle

To live and thrive, man requires the absence of interference with the actions by which the exercise of his judgment sustains his life. This is the pre-condition for being able to live by one's own judgment, that is, in the manner appropriate to man *qua* man. It is the origin of the concept of *rights*, which marks the component conditions of this general pre-condition as "conditions of existence required by man for his proper survival" (Rand 1961, 182). Rand's concept of rights is not a social or legal category, but rather a statement of fact that sets a boundary on what actions a rational individual will take and what additional values she will pursue: whatever other actions one takes and whatever other values one pursues, they must not compromise one's rights as a general pre-condition of life appropriate to (oneself as) man *qua* man.

Society begins with the realisation that one is better able to achieve values by cooperation and trade with others than alone. But the rational individual will take care that, in the pursuit of values by means of cooperation and trade, she does not compromise her rights. Therefore the rational individual will not deal with those who do not respect her rights. Similarly other rational persons, who as humans share the same pre-conditions for living lives appropriate to humans, will deal with me only if I respect their rights. In contexts in which one stands to gain values by cooperation and trade, the rational individual respects the rights of his or her potential trading partners.

Harmony of Interests

Is it possible to gain values more effectively by theft, fraud and extortion and in general by violating the rights of others, than by agreeing with them on completely voluntary cooperation and trade? However one endeavors to obtain values, one employs one's available resources—one's time, effort, brawn, intelligence, capital, social skills and so on—in this endeavor. Among voluntary trading partners who respect each other's rights, *all* of their resources are used for production of values. On the other hand, someone who tries to obtain values by depriving another of his, will face opposition from the prospective victim, who will rationally use some of his resources to try to thwart the aggressor's designs. Whatever fraction of his resources the aggressor expands on aggressive attempts that the prospective victim manages to thwart, will have been wasted. Thus, other things being equal, when we compare resources that have been used to obtain values rather than wasted on overcoming opposition, we find that those resources, and the sum of values obtained by their use, favor the man who employs his resources for production and trade over the one who attempts to gain values by violating the rights of other men. This is the principle of *harmony of interests*. On the average, the criminal will be poorer than if he had employed his resources for honest production and trade. It is not impossible for a very resourceful criminal to obtain significant values as a result of a relatively successful life of crime, but even the most "successful" criminal is unavoidably poorer than he would have been, had he used his resources and skills for production and trade—for activities in which none of his energy, capital and skill would have been wasted on overcoming the unavoidable resistance of his victims.

The "Prudent" Predator

What of the "prudent predator"—the one who manages to keep his crime hidden, so that his victims' resources are never deployed to thwart his schemes? If the victim is intelligent enough to have produced values worth stealing, then at some point she will notice the crime. And, once the nature of the potential crime is disclosed, future prospective victims will take precautions against it. The inventor of a novel swindle, however clever, has at most a one-time deal: even if there is as yet no law and no public warning against the newly invented crime, once the new crime has been carried out there will be. The inventive swindler will be a little richer, but not as rich as he would have been if he had employed his creativity to invent better methods of production and trade. The latter keep being productive and lucrative; the former are "shot" as soon as the first successful exploit becomes known. The rational man does not engage in predation, and the man who does engage in predation is not acting rationally—that is, is not acting in his own long-term interest.

Irrational "Values" and the Rational Man's Self-Defense

What of the man who seeks to gain or keep a condition that inherently or unavoidably violates the rights of another individual? We know from the trader principle, above, that such a value is generally inimical to maximal attainment of other values, including man's primary evolved value of preserving and enhancing his own life. Thus any contribution that the attainment of a predatory value might make to someone's current happiness will be illusory and transient. Yet it remains a fact that many men, because of envy, religious beliefs, or because of prior irrationalities and mistakes, sometimes persist in seeking false values. It is because of these facts—that some men are irrational in their choice of values, and some believe that predation is an effective means to attain their values—that rational men must defend their rights.

Foundations of Politics

The defense of one's rights may be either an immediate response to a present or imminent danger, a civil dispute over conflicting claims, or a response to an alleged crime that has already taken place. The first seldom places innocent parties in jeopardy, although householders have been known to shoot at their own spouses or children in the belief that they were dealing with a criminal invasion of their home. The second need not involve force at all, and reasonable parties may agree in advance to abide by the decisions of a mutually chosen adjudicator. It is the third case, of responding to an alleged crime that has already taken place, that puts innocent accused persons, as well as criminals, in jeopardy that needs to be minimised by a system of objective, uniformly enforced law.

The proper response to an alleged crime would not be a problem if men were omniscient. Unfortunately, men are not omniscient, nor even uniformly rational: if they were, there would be no problem of crime in the first place. Response to crime puts innocent, rational individuals in jeopardy because people make mistakes. Human experience includes evidence of wrongful jeopardy due to many categories of mistakes:

First, people can be wrong about whether some action is objectively a crime. For example, most alleged "crimes" under religious legal systems are not in fact crimes at all. They place innocent, rational people in jeopardy because believers subjectively, arbitrarily, and falsely believe themselves to be under threat of divine wrath that might be provoked by the mere presence of impiety, blasphemy, gambling, recreational drugs, or fornication in their midst. Nominally secular legal systems frequently also incorporate legal restrictions based on such arbitrary beliefs. To be secure in his rights, the rational person must insist on an objective code of law, one that would require objective proof of harm (or of some objectively demonstrable risk, or of a credible threat, etc.) rather than mere belief, or mere feeling, that some objectively harmless activity threatens or harms, by divine disfavor or other arbitrarily conjectured mechanisms, the well-being of believers.

Second, people tend to ascribe their misfortunes to the agency of others, and therefore to believe, falsely, that a crime took place when one didn't. A surgeon whose patient dies in spite of his best efforts may be accused of criminal negligence or manslaughter. A bereaved family may mistakenly see murder in an accident or a suicide. In the old west, horses and cattle that escaped from a corral sometimes were found, alive and well, days after some unfortunate Mexican or Indian had been hung as a horse thief or cattle rustler.

Third, a real crime that actually took place may be ascribed to the wrong person. A victim may pick from a lineup the person who most closely fits her memory of the perpetrator, but if the actual perpetrator was not in the lineup, the random person whom she picked will stick in her mind anyway. A witness may see the perpetrator of a crime briefly and in light too dim for her perception to be reliable, but if she is prejudiced against Blacks, she may believe that the suspect was Black anyway, whether or not he was. In cases where DNA evidence was available but could not be analyzed before trial, and was subsequently analyzed by the Innocence Project, approximately one in six defendants convicted "beyond a reasonable doubt" by American juries turned out to be innocent.[1] There is no reason to believe that, in cases where there is no DNA evidence, the incidence of false convictions is ever substantially different. When there is no reliable evidence of anyone's guilt, victims or prosecutors may nevertheless ascribe the crime to someone—anyone—"lest the crime go unpunished." "Confirmation bias," the tendency of ordinary persons to

---

1   Author's statistical analysis of data for capital convictions in the United States in 1986, counting and comparing cases listed on the website of the Innocence Project, http://www.innocenceproject.org, against totals from the United States Department of Justice Bureau of Justice Statistics, http://www.ojp.usdoj.gov/bjs.

give more credence to evidence that confirms their existing beliefs, and less credence to contrary evidence, often skews human judgment toward convicting the merely suspected and disregarding evidence that points to someone else.

Fourth, a victim or enforcer is likely to overestimate the degree of relative responsibility of the person accused or convicted of a crime, leading to the imposition of disproportionately severe punishment. In the zeal to punish, to set an example and provide a warning, prosecutors and judges often disregard evidence of the influence and of the contributions of other, sometimes uncaught and unindicted criminals to the crime; evidence of emergency conditions, and even evidence of innocent cognitive error.

All these factors mean that it would be unacceptably dangerous to innocent persons to leave the trial of people suspected of having committed a crime, and their punishment, in the hands of the putative victim or of the victim's agents. A victim of crime, when there is a crime, has a right to justice—but he does not have a right to impose on others, except to the least unavoidable extent, the risks of false accusation, false conviction, or disproportionate punishment. The safety of the innocent demands not only that those really proven guilty of real crimes suffer appropriate punishment, but also that the innocent be safe from the risk of being victimised by false accusations, false convictions, and disproportionate punishment. Their safety requires that the processes of determining what constitutes a crime, of whether or not a crime took place, and who was responsible, and to what extent, must be as *objective* as possible. The rational man understands that if he is a participant in a conflict, he cannot be also its objective adjudicant. To minimise the risk that he might inflict an unjust punishment on an innocent person, the rational man will delegate the adjudication of his disputes to the most objective, most impartial judge available. Only in the most unusual circumstances, in which a more impartial judgment is not available and the presumed criminal remains dangerous, will a rational man retaliate against a presumed criminal on his own. The rational man, even if he believes himself to be the victim of a crime, recognises that justice requires that the influence of subjective factors on the process of justice be minimised, and that to be just, *the retaliatory use of physical force must be placed under* **objective** *control* (Rand 1967, 19). This is the objective standard[2]—the proper criterion of optimisation—for judging proposals on how the process of justice ought to be organised.

Politics and Economics

In the design of any working system, on must begin with what Rand (1964, 19) called a "standard": a measure by which one can judge the relative merit of any alternative in the design. In engineering, this measure is called a "figure or merit," in economics a "criterion of optimization." This number measures how well a given system performs its function; in most cases it is simply a quantifiable statement of

---

2 In Rand, "a *standard* is an abstract principle that serves as a measurement or gauge to guide a man's choices in the achievement of a concrete, specific purpose" (Rand 1964, 19). In the applied sciences, a measurement that serves to guide choices in the achievement of a purpose is called a *criterion of optimisation.*

what its function *is*. The proper function of the political system is to *minimise the aggregate incidence of initiations of unjustified force*—whether initiated by criminals or by the political system itself—against innocent persons.

Can this be done by a market?

To answer this question, one must look at what a market in *force* would provide. The short answer is: whatever the customer is willing to pay for. In the market, a dollar paid by an atheist who wants freedom to live by the judgment of his own mind, and a dollar paid by an Islamist who wishes to force everyone to live under Shariah, are equally good to the seller, to whom the provision of law, and of its enforcement, are not a matter of objective justice but of giving every customer whatever that customer pays for. Similarly equal are a dollar paid by a criminal who wishes to shield himself from punishment for his crimes, and a dollar paid by his victim; or a dollar paid by a religious believer to avert the wrath of God that he thinks will fall on him if he fails to avert or punish consensual fornication among his neighbors, and a dollar paid by lovers who wish for nothing more than to be left alone to love each other. A market will produce whatever people subjectively want, in proportion to how much each is willing to spend to get it. *As long as some people are willing to expend resources to initiate force against others*, the aggregate incidence of unjustified force against innocent persons will not be minimised by a market. And, if everyone were optimally rational, then no one would initiate force against anyone else; the only reason why we *need* a political system is that some people are, in fact, not rational enough *not* to expend their resources on initiating force against others. Thus there is no reason to expect that the aggregate incidence of unjustified force against innocent persons will be minimised by a market. To see how this fact works itself out in practice, one needs to examine historical data on systems that approximated a regime of "market law."

History

Politics is not an experimental science, in the sense that one cannot carry out controlled experiments on human societies. It is, however, a *natural* science in that its theories can be compared with systematic observations of reality and, if contradicted, disconfirmed. There are at least two instances in the history of the Western world of systems of "market law." The more distant of the two was medieval Iceland. Isolated, and having a population small enough that most people were known to everyone they ever met by first name, and totally uniform in religion, language and culture, medieval Iceland was by far the best candidate, ever, for a successful market law polity. In that respect it eventually failed, but not before producing great sagas and many innovative solutions to general political problems (Friedman 1989, 201-08).

The more recent case was much more directly applicable to our reality today. It took place closer to our time, and even overlapped, in its last years, the first years of the United States. It was modern, diverse, and at its peak had the largest land area and the largest population among the countries of Europe. It was the Polish-Lithuanian Commonwealth, and it lasted formally from 1573 to 1795.[3]

The roots of the Commonwealth[4] were planted by Prince—from 1320 King—Vladislav IV Lokietek, who raised the military force with which he unified Poland by promising to "every man who joined the King's Military Estate (*Szlachta*) with a horse and an equerry, that he and his descendants would be forever free from taxes, except as levied by an assembly (*Seym*) elected by the hereditary *Szlachta*." Over generations the *Seym* refused to raise taxes to support internal government in Poland, and after Poland's union with Lithuania a similar process took place in Lithuania as well. In 1573 the Seym transformed the united Commonwealth into a republic; the office of King became elective and included command of the armed forces in foreign wars, and representation of the country in dealing with foreign powers, but without much actual power inside the borders of the Commonwealth.

As internal government evaporated, most of the wealthiest members of the *szlachta* obtained appointments as state officials (*wojewoda, kasztelan*) whose responsibilities included supervision of regional militias. These appointments authorised the office holder to maintain his own armed forces, funded and commanded by their owner, although nominally supplementing the dwindling armed forces of the state as supernumerary auxiliaries. The actual primary function of these private armies was to protect their employers' properties, since official instrumentalities of internal law enforcement were disappearing. The owners of private armies were called *magnaci* (singular *magnat*, thence *magnate* in English). Eventually, some magnates made arrangements to extend the protection of their private armies to other persons, clients from among commoners and less wealthy *szlachta*. This arrangement was codified as a legal contract in the case of commoners, and was practiced as an informal understanding between the magnate and his client if the client was a *szlachcic*. The client paid the magnate who protected him with services, with votes in the *Seym*, or in crops or commodities, or in cash. With the state administration progressively withering away, the magnates retained judges, adjudicated disputes and levied punishments among their clients, operated private prisons and executed convicts; negotiated, magnate to magnate, disputes among their respective clients, and operated, in every way, very much like the "Market Defense Agencies" or "Market Law Enterprises" projected by Rothbard 1970, Friedman 1989, or Benson 1990.

One of the services that the magnate expected of his clients was to keep arms and assist the magnate's private army with law enforcement duties when the client

---

3 According to the Rand Transcript (Sciabarra 1999) Ayn Rand would have been familiar with the history of the Polish-Lithuanian Commonwealth from the Russian History course of Sergei Fydorovich Platonov, a specialist in sixteenth- and seventeenth-century Russian history, and especially the "Time of Troubles," a period of frequent interventions in Russia by Polish-Lithuanian magnates.

4 The following historical account is based, except where more specific references are given, on four standard works of Polish history: Tymowski et al. 1986, Giertych 1986, Topolski 1995 and Lasociński 1995. Histories published in Poland under the Communist regime are not reliable and were not used. Giertych (1986) is a Catholic Libertarian, and his account favors the enforcement of Catholic norms by Catholic magnates and by religious orders, such as the Capuchins and the Jesuits, under their protection.

was called on. This system was very effective in nearly eliminating common crime. At a time when most of Europe still suffered from the presence of brigands and highwaymen, Poland's cities and highways were generally safe and free from violent criminals. Poland's diverse inhabitants developed elaborate systems for non-violent resolution of disputes (such as the Polish Jews' custom of *Din Torah*, in which each side appointed a representative, a chairman of the *Din Torah* was selected by joint consent of the two sides, and the three worked out a compromise acceptable to both parties; see Singer 1966, cited in Nozick 1974, 336n5) and for effective use of boycotts and ostracism (e.g., the Jews' *Yad Hazakah*, see Michałowska 1999).

The magnate system also led to the discovery of a new modality of national defense: there was no established order of internal government that an invader might use to impose his control. In 1655 Sweden, aided by Brandenburg and Transylvania, invaded the Commonwealth. Poland's vestigial official government quickly left. The invaders soon found themselves literally wandering around the country, with few of its inhabitants willing to do anything for the invaders except when literally forced to at the point of a Swedish musket. Unable to either govern or collect taxes on their own, the Swedes turned to the magnates, but only a few of the latter (Janusz and Bogusław Radziwiłł, Krzysztof Opaliński, Bogusław Leszczynski, Jan Schlichting, and Hieronim Radziejowski) were willing to be hired. Totally frustrated, at least in areas outside the reach of the half-dozen traitor magnates, unable to tax, harassed by "parties" of armed inhabitants (the first modern instance of "partisan warfare"), the Swedes eventually left, leaving behind them a trail of destruction and arson comparable, in previous Polish history, only to the Tatar invasion of 1241 (Giertych 1986, I/323).

Two of the traitors (Janusz Radziwiłł and Krzysztof Opaliński) died, of natural causes, before the end of the Swedish invasion. The other four, however, continued in the magnate business afterward as though nothing had happened. In an impressive display of class solidarity, for the entire duration of the Commonwealth no magnate ever took any action against another magnate's crimes, no matter how vile those crimes might have been. No magnate ever took up arms to protect anyone, even his closest clients, against the depredations of another magnate. The magnates did a creditable job of keeping their clients safe from minor (non-magnate) criminals, but no ordinary man was ever safe from the whims of a criminal magnate.

The extreme reluctance of magnates to confront each other manifested itself in other ways, beyond giving individual magnates absolute license to commit any crime at will. In resolving litigation among clients of different magnates, the judges' objective was not justice, but rather whatever compromise it took to defuse the risk of a potential armed confrontation. These compromises became the butt of jokes and of biting satire. The typical compromise paid far less attention to objective justice than to the balance of power between the litigants and their protectors.[5]

---

5 *Zemsta* (Revenge), by Aleksander Fredro, the most celebrated comedy of the classical Polish theater, was first staged in 1834 but was intended as a distillation of eighteenth-century satirical comedies of the Commonwealth period. To obtain revenge against a nobleman who insulted him, a lawyer sues for possession of the nobleman's ancient family castle. The lawyer's claim on the castle lacks even the most remote semblance of plausibility, but the

Like any class that ever managed to make itself immune to the law, the magnates were seldom openly corrupt and criminal. The most common form of covert corruption was for a magnate to increase a commoner client's obligations retroactively, putting the client into debt that the client had no power to contest. Debts were transferred by the magnate from a deceased client to the client's children, so that within a century the average man was saddled with unilaterally imposed debt that neither he nor his children could ever hope to repay—and no one was allowed to leave his magnate's jurisdiction without having paid off their debts. Thus a majority of the non-*szlachta* population of the Commonwealth were transformed from free men into near-feudal serfs, permanently attached by debt to one magnate or another.

Another form of corruption that became increasingly common among magnates was arbitrary enforcement of religious codes contrary to the custom and law of the Commonwealth. The population of the Commonwealth was more diverse in religious orientations than that of any other country in the known world. The Roman Catholic Church was always the largest denomination, followed by Orthodox and Uniate churches and some dozen varieties of Protestantism, Jews, Moslems, Zoroastrian refugees from Islamic rule in Persia, and eventually Unitarians. In its early history, the Commonwealth became the main destination for refugees from religious wars and religious bigotry elsewhere in Europe. By the mid-1600s, more than 90 per cent of Europe's Jews lived in the Commonwealth. Among the refugees from the Austrian Catholic conquest of Bohemia and Moravia who settled in Poland was Jan Amos Komensky (Comenius), bishop of Moravian Bretheren, inventor of the modern illustrated textbook and originator of the term "Enlightenment" (*Via Lucis*).

Lelius Socinius and his nephew Faustus Socinius, born in Siena in 1526 and 1539 respectively, were accused of heresy for denying original sin, the divinity of Jesus, and the Trinity. In the second half of the 1500s they took refuge in Poland, where they founded Unitarianism. Starting in 1638, Rome began to demand of the more extreme Catholic magnates that they act forcefully against the Unitarians, whom the Pope considered a revival of the ancient "Arian Heresy." An opportunity to do so arose after the Swedish invasion, during which Jan Schlichting, a Unitarian, was one of the six magnates who collaborated with the Swedes. Not understanding the praxeological mechanism of the Swedish defeat, many Catholic Poles ascribed it to a miraculous intervention of the Virgin Mary, and were willing to do the bidding of the Church in gratitude for the miracle. Although eager to slaughter the Unitarians in accordance with the wishes of Rome, the dozen or so extreme Catholic magnates drew back from the prospect of armed conflict with Schlichting, with a second Unitarian magnate, Jerzy Niemirycz, and with the majority of other magnates who might have come to the defense of the still prevalent principle of freedom of religion in the Commonwealth. In 1658 the magnates negotiated a compromise under which

---

judges, in the spirit of compromise that dominated the courts of the Commonwealth, give him half the castle and order the construction of an internal wall to separate the two halves. The adversaries settle their families into the two halves of the castle on either side of the internal wall. Their children fall into adolescent rebellion against their feuding fathers, expressed as forbidden love. After many misadventures the young couple manage to marry and eventually demolish the wall that separates the two halves of the castle.

the Polish Unitarians were forced to convert or to leave Poland within two years. Schlichting became a Lutheran, Niemirycz an Orthodox Christian. Those Unitarians who did not convert took refuge in Transylvania or in the Netherlands, where they were called the "Polish Bretheren." After the expulsion of the Unitarians freedom of religion in Poland, although officially never repealed, was unofficially at the mercy of the more extreme Catholic magnates, except for whatever limited protection adherents of other religions might obtain from other magnates in localities under their influence.

The enforcement of religious edicts was not the magnate's only motivation for departure from principled rule of law. Given the magnates' immunity from criminal law, manifest after the Swedish invasion in the lack of punishment even for treason, foreign powers were able to hire various magnates to protect their interests in the lands of the Commonwealth. With the protection of hired magnates, Prussian, Austrian and Russian governments were able to maintain agents, and sizeable military units, within the supposedly sovereign territory of Poland and Lithuania. Just as magnates shied away from confrontation with each other's forces, so they stayed out of the way of foreign forces and agents. The latter, just like the magnates themselves, enjoyed total impunity for whatever crimes they wished to carry out.

In historical perspective, the most significant crime carried out by foreign agents in seventeenth-century century Poland was the abduction of Christian Ludwig von Kalkstein. Von Kalkstein, an influential Prussian nobleman, was the leader of internal opposition, within Prussia, to the increasingly authoritarian and militaristic regime of the Prussian state. In 1669 Hieronymus Roth, speaker of the Prussian parliament, criticised rising tax rates that were imposed to pay for the growth of the Prussian military. Roth was imprisoned and tortured to death. His son fled to Warsaw, where in 1670 von Kalkstein joined him, hoping to obtain Polish support for the growing dissident movement in Prussia. Later that year, von Kalkstein was openly abducted by Prussian agents in Warsaw, bound, and taken by horse cart to Prussia, without any opposition from several Polish magnates whose forces would have been able to block the way. He was tortured for nearly two years, then in 1672 murdered in a Prussian dungeon. Having lost its leaders, the Prussian opposition withered. The consequences of von Kalkstein's unhindered abduction and murder—the henceforth unobstructed growth of Prussian authoritarianism, militarism and expansion, Hegel and Bismarck and Hitler, wars and genocides—included many of Poland's, and the world's, calamities for centuries after his death.

The most devastating consequence of the magnate regime was its effect on freedom of speech. The Catholic Church maintained an index of prohibited books, just as it did in countries where it was the established Church, and Catholic magnates enforced it. Every magnate felt free to seize and burn any book that he saw as offensive or inimical to his reputation or interests.[6] Other religious communities, and foreign powers from Russia to England, paid various magnates to police bookshops on their behalf.

---

6 This description of censorship in the Polish-Lithuanian Commonwealth is based on Bates 2001, except as referenced otherwise.

The magnate typically registered his objection to a book by seizing any copies that might be offered for sale and having them burned. In most cases this was enough for the author and publisher to excise the offending passages before reprinting the book and again offering it for sale. If a bookseller's stock was perceived as particularly offensive, the offended magnate might burn the store's entire inventory, sometimes together with the whole building it was housed in. A publisher's printing press might also be destroyed, often with the workshop. The range of works that could be considered offensive was extraordinarily inclusive. In 1788, a magnate named Mniszek suppressed, on behalf of his Russian clients, Jan Potocki's *Essai de Logique*, a book on logic written in French, the international scholarly language of the time. The Jesuits, acting under the protection of several magnates, also got directly into the act. Thus in 1611, following the death of a local magnate who protected a Calvinist publishing house in Kamieniec Podolski, the publisher's entire stock, printing press and workshop were destroyed by the local Jesuits.

Under the magnates, censorship was exerted against publishers and sellers of offending books, almost never against the author. This accounts for the fact that in the Polish-Lithuanian Commonwealth, unlike Italy or Spain or France, no one was ever burned at the stake, or beheaded, for heresy or blasphemy. Yet compared to those countries, or to Germany, England, or Scotland, all of them with much smaller populations than the Commonwealth, the Commonwealth's intellectual output during the Enlightenment was minuscule. In other countries, as long as the author avoided sedition against its regime and blasphemy against the one established Church he could write, and publish and sell, just about anything. In the Commonwealth, a publisher stood to lose his business if he printed or sold anything that might be contrary to the interests and whims of any of dozens of religions, foreign powers, or individual magnates. As long as the power of the magnates persisted hardly anyone, apart from dedicated religious fanatics, dared to challenge their total control over every word in print.

By 1772 the Commonwealth's neighbors, Prussia, Russia and Austria, learned the lesson of the failed Swedish invasion of 1655. Poland and Lithuania, lacking a stable internal administration that might be taken over and used by an invader, could not be successfully invaded all at once. Each invading power would need to extend its own internal administration to the territory it took over, and therefore each seizure would have to be limited to an area the invader could absorb. In the first partition in 1772, each power took a piece of Commonwealth territory closest to its own existing administrative centers, and thus easiest to integrate with its existing regime.

The partition of 1772 could not be effectively opposed by the magnates; the handful who tried included Casimir Pulaski, who soon thereafter left for America to participate in the War of Independence. Another Polish officer in that war, engineer Thaddeus Kościuszko, was a friend of Thomas Jefferson and a member of the American Philosophical Society. Kościuszko returned to Poland in 1784, and after the adoption of the U.S. Constitution in 1787 proposed for Poland a similar constitution to replace the rule of the magnates. On May 3, 1791, the Seym adopted the new constitution. Several magnates voted for the May 3rd Constitution, having concluded that a continuation of the magnate regime could only lead to further partitions, while a modern constitutional government—unlike the Russian, Prussian and Austrian autocracies—would end their impunity for crimes but would still safeguard their individual rights. The following year, conservative magnates tried to re-establish the magnate regime, formed the *Confederation of Targowica* and asked the Russian empress Catherine II for help in overthrowing the constitution. The Russians came, but when their forces overpowered the constitutional army they partitioned Poland again, in collaboration with Prussia, leaving only the center of the country to the restored rule of the magnates. Two years later, the rest was partitioned among Russia, Prussia and Austria, and the magnate regime was permanently over.

Conclusions from History

Given the historical evidence from the magnate regime in the Polish-Lithuanian Commonwealth, it is possible to conclude several things about what a system of competing "market law-defense agencies" is likely to produce in practice.

First, given the high cost of fighting against the trained armed force of such an agency, its owner or chief officer would be, in practice, immune from justice for crimes. While most leaders of law-defense agencies would, like most people in any position, act honorably, the exigencies of their business *qua* business will keep them from expending resources, and risking their employees' lives, on attempts to bring the heads of rogue law-defense agencies to justice. In their dealings with law-defense agencies, ordinary people will be at the mercy of their armed "hired servants." Publishers will censor their publications lest a law-defense agency CEO take offense and exact punishment, etc.

Second, given the potentially very high cost of conflict among "market law-defense agencies," in case of disputes those agencies will have an overwhelming incentive to compromise, rather than defend, the objective rights of their clients. Outcomes will reflect the balance of resources between agencies rather than objective justice.

Third, instead of being marginalised (as they are in a constitutional democracy), the adherents of religious cults and of extreme interpretations of various religions will exercise power proportional to the resources they commit to "defense of the faith." Those driven by religious fanaticism will commit to their cause, as was done in recent times by the Christianist anti-abortion underground and by Islamist organisations such as Al Qaeda, the sum of whatever resources they have, including their lives. While they will not be able to force the majority to conform to the entirety of their doctrine, their fanaticism and commitment will enable them to exact compromises significantly infringing the rights of non-adherents. The likely compromise will leave the fanatics with the ability to impose their version of religious law, such as Shariah, on their families, so that for example an Islamist father will be able to commit an "honor killing" of a "wayward" daughter with impunity. Christianist fanatics will be able to exact a compromise of the right to abortion, censorship of books and films that they find objectionable for religious reasons, etc.

Fourth, there will be little to stop foreign despots and other criminals from hiring, or even setting up their own "market law-defense enterprises." Awareness of history *might* motivate a common front against a foreign army or other large-scale criminal enterprise—or history might repeat itself.

From "Market Law" to a Constitutional Republic

In any society, a rational person will try to find ways to live his own life as well as one can. In a society in which individual rights were compromised by a system of competing "market law-defense agencies," there still will be women who will act to preserve their personal access to abortion as a backup for routine contraceptive failure—and physicians who decide to provide that service, regardless of what compromises the existing "market law-defense agencies" might enact. There will still be men who will reserve for themselves the right to love, by mutual desire, the woman of their choice—even if that woman's choice is to disobey and leave an Islamist family—and to defend that woman's life even at the risk of their own, regardless of what compromise their "market law-defense agency" might have made with the "market law-defense agency" of the Islamist fanatics. There still will be writers and film-makers who decide to tell in their books and films the truth they see, regardless of whom that truth might offend, and there will be book sellers and theatre owners who decide to show and sell those books and films, regardless of what compromise the relevant "market law-defense enterprises" may have arrived at, and regardless of the ability and willingness of their "market law-defense agency" to defend them if they did. All of those, and many others, if faced around them with a society based on "market law-defense enterprises," will need to decide: *what is to be done?*

The first step that those who seek to maximise their own objective freedom will need to take is find each other, organise for communication and planning of subsequent stages of action, and weed out from their company anyone who would join them with a religious or other repressive or subjectivist agenda in mind. The inclusion of owners or majority stockholders in "market law-defense enterprises" in this company will depend on their willingness to commit to the eventual integration of their forces with those of a new "law and defense enterprise" to be formed by the participants in stage 2. The first stage would conclude with a formal contractual agreement, among prospective citizens of a new community dedicated to optimal protection of their individual rights, on the future constitution of the legal and political system of their new community, the strategy for establishing it, and their commitment to a plan of cooperative action to implement this strategy. If their company does not already include a sufficient number of members with defense and law enforcement skills, and adequate experience in using those skills, progress to the next stage will depend on the development of effective law enforcement and defense capabilities among the prospective citizens.

In the second stage, the citizens will form a new "law and defense enterprise" in the existing market, but one formed as a cooperative organisation owned and controlled by its members, to prevent it from becoming (like the magnate forces in the old Polish-Lithuanian Commonwealth) an agency of the personal power of its owners or leaders. Membership-citizenship in the new cooperative-enterprise-community will require a contribution of resources from each member-citizen, in some combination of funds and of personal time and effort. The cooperative will probably accede to some temporary compromises with existing "market law and defense agencies," but will exclude its future sovereign territory, to be established in stage 4, from the scope of those compromises.

For stage 3, the cooperative will need to find an entrepreneur who recognises its members' *objective right* to protect all their other rights by establishing a government of objective law, and who will lease or sell to them a place—initially something like a gated community—in which they will be able to live under the protection of their cooperative's own law enforcement and defense force. After establishing its gated community, the cooperative will build a secure defense perimeter around it, and train its members to defend it against any future attempts, by competing religious and subjectivist "law-defense agencies," to compromise the freedoms of its members.

In the next stage, the citizens of the cooperative will proceed to exercise all their rights. Their gated community being their property, they will have a recognised right to restrict access to that property, and will deny access to forces of coercive, religious and subjectivist "market law-defense agencies." Those of the latter who persist in attempts to invade the community, and impose their arbitrary "laws," will be dealt with as enemies. The new constitutional republic will take all the steps that it may need to take to bring the use of retaliatory force within its borders under objective control. It will provide for the extension of its sovereignty to additional land that might be placed under its jurisdiction, by its rightful owners' decisions, in the future. The republic will attract rational people as investors, immigrants, and future citizens. It will make treaties with existing "market law-defense agencies" only on the basis of absolute inviolability of the rights of its citizens—and outside its borders it will continue to function as a "market law-defense agency" in protecting its citizens' right to mutually chosen association and trade with trading partners of their choice.

Historical Engineering

The problem for me and for other freedom-loving people today is also how to get there from here, to a constitutional republic dedicated to the unconditional protection of the rights of its citizens. This cannot happen in a society in which the average person fails to understand the nature of rights: even if someone agrees with me that individual rights are what governments are established to protect, still if he believes that rights are a matter of belief or of subjective preference, rather than *objectively necessary preconditions for living a life appropriate to a rational being*, then he will seek to impose on me a regime that will in fact infringe my real rights—for the sake of enforcing his arbitrary religious beliefs, or his subjective preferences. Therefore the first necessary step toward political freedom of the individual is to educate our fellow citizens in the nature of rights. When a majority of the citizens of the United States come to agree on this fundamental point, our laws will be adjusted accordingly, and the constitution amended along the lines suggested by Ayn Rand in the final pages of *Atlas Shrugged* (Rand 1957, 1168). Until a substantial majority of my fellow citizens agrees as to the nature of rights, my own rights will not be secure against a forcible imposition on me of restrictions grounded only in religious belief or in the subjective preferences of their proponents.

Once the laws and the constitution have been adjusted to assure me of maximum protection of my rights, a subsequent reversion of legal or defense authority to men whose vision of liberty *differs from the normative facts* can only infringe the rights that I already enjoy. What possible benefit could I, or any other rational person, derive from enabling anti-abortion Christianists, or Al Qaeda, or the Socialist Party, to operate their own "market law and defense enterprises" capable of enforcing, to whatever extent, the false beliefs of their members—and of compromising my rights in the process of doing so?

In a constitutional republic dedicated to the protection of individual rights, anyone might exercise his right to agree with others on living according to a different set of rules, and to form a voluntary organisation to do so. Some of the facts grounding the laws of the republic might not be known with total precision at a given time, or might need to be applied differently in different local contexts, and a constitutional republic could accommodate regional (e.g., "State") governments that may need to experiment with the details of the laws. But neither voluntary organisations nor subsidiary governments can be allowed to violate individual rights, and to do its job, a federal republic will need the authority and the means to prevent such violations. If, for example, a private gated community claims that it is imposing a penalty under rules that the person being penalised consented to, the validity of his consent may need to be adjudicated in government courts. If the criminal procedures of a subsidiary state could place innocent accused persons at *greater than the unavoidable minimum of risk* of false conviction and disproportionate punishment, then the Republic must have the authority and the means to correct (and justly punish) any resulting violations of individual human rights. Anything less would be itself a violation of individual rights and an infringement of liberty.

Bibliography

Ashby, W. Ross, *An Introduction to Cybernetics*, London: Chapman and Hall, 1956.
Bates, John M., Censorship in Poland: From the Beginnings to the Enlightenment, in Derek Jones and Jack Fritscher, *Censorship: A World Encyclopedia*, London: Fitzroy Dearborn, 2001.
Benson, Bruce L., *The Enterprise of Law: Justice Without the State*, San Francisco: Pacific Research Institute for Public Policy, 1990.
Binswanger, Harry, *The Biological Basis of Teleological Concepts*, 1976, reprinted Los Angeles: The Ayn Rand Institute Press, 1990.
Fredro, Alexander, *Major Comedies*, Princeton, NJ: Princeton University Press (Columbia Slavic Studies Series), 1969.
Friedman, David, *The Machinery of Freedom: Guide to Radical Capitalism, Second Edition*, Chicago and La Salle, IL, 1989.
Giertych, Jędrzej, *Tysiąc Lat Historii Polskiego Narodu, Volumes I-III*, London: Jędrzej Giertych, 1986.

Lasociński, David, *Historia Polski dla Zagubionych 960-1994*, Łódź: Oficyna Wydawnicza Lantra, 1995.
Michałowska Anna, *Władze wielkopolskich gmin żydowskich: Poznań i Swarzędz (połowa XVII – XVIII wiek)*, unpublished doctoral dissertation, Warsaw University, 1999.
Nozick Robert, *Anarchy, State, and Utopia*, New York: Basic Books, 1974.
Rand, Ayn, *Atlas Shrugged*, New York: Random House, 1957.
Rand, Ayn, *For the New Intellectual*, New York: The New American Library, 1961.
Rand, Ayn, *The Virtue of Selfishness: A New Concept of Egoism*, New York: The New American Library, 1964.
Rand, Ayn, *Introduction to Objectivist Epistemology*, New York: The Objectivist, 1966-1967.
Rand, Ayn, *Capitalism: The Unknown Ideal*, New York: The New American Library, 1967.
Rand, Ayn, *The Art of Non-Fiction*, lectures, 1969, in Ayn Rand (Robert Mayhew, ed.) *The Art of Nonfiction: A Guide for Writers and Readers*, New York: Plume Penguin Putnam, 2001.
Rothbard, Murray N., *Power & Market: Government and the Economy*, Menlo Park, CA: Institute for Humane Studies, 1970.
Sciabarra, Chris Matthew, The Rand Transcript, *The Journal of Ayn Rand Studies*, 1, 1-26, 1999.
The Scotsman (newspaper) "40% of UK Muslims Want Sharia Law," 19 February 2006.
Singer. B., *In My Father's Court*, New York: Farrar, Strauss, and Giroux, 1966.
Spooner, Lysander, *No Treason* (number VI) *The Constitution of No Authority*, 1870, reprinted Larkspur, CO: Pine Tree Press 1966.
Topolski, Jerzy, *Historia Polski*, Warszawa: Wydawnictwo Kopia, 1995.
Tversky, Amos and Daniel Kahneman, Availability: a heuristic for judging frequency and probability, *Cognitive Psychology*, 5, 207-32, 1973.
Tymowski, Michał, Jan Kniewicz, and Jerzy Holzer, *Historia Polski*, Paris: Editions Spotkania, 1986.
Weiner, Norbert, *Cybernetics, or Control and Communication in the Animal and the Machine*, Cambridge, MA: The MIT Press, 1961.

Chapter 4

Objectivism against Anarchy

William R Thomas

Ayn Rand was at once one of the foremost progenitors of the anarcho-capitalist movement in the second half of the twentieth century and one of its staunchest opponents within the classical liberal tradition. Rand's 1957 magnum opus, *Atlas Shrugged*, gave new life to the culturally moribund ideas of limited government. It also projected a compelling vision of a society without discernable government.

The novel's "utopia of greed" is an ideal society of the productive, the hardworking, the visionary, and the independent. It could also be plausibly seen as an anarchy. It has an arbiter (Judge Narragansett), but no police are mentioned. It has a leader (John Galt), but no head of state. It provides refuge to a pirate (Ragnar Danneskjöld), but has no military forces. Rand's libertarian Atlantis is "not a state, not a society of any kind— ... just a voluntary association of men held together by nothing but every man's self-interest" (Rand 1959, 747).

The Objectivist Conception of Government

Rand was not merely or even principally a political thinker. To be sure, Objectivism, the philosophical outlook she founded, has a politics, but Objectivism is a philosophical system in which politics plays a dependent role. As Rand said of herself:

> I am not *primarily* an advocate of capitalism, but of egoism; and I am not *primarily* an advocate of egoism, but of reason. If one recognizes the supremacy of reason and applies it consistently, all the rest follows. (Rand 1971, 1089, italics in original)

In Objectivism, political principles rest on the social ethics of justice and trade (see Thomas 2003a, for a summary). The purpose of government is to leave people as free as possible to live by their own rational judgment and productive effort. Since forcible threats against life, limb, and property deprive their victims of the freedom to act on their own judgment, society can only be fully in our interest when it is organised to ban the initiation of force against others by any individual. This is the normative basis for the individual rights to life, liberty, property, and the pursuit of happiness, and all their corollary and subsidiary liberty and procedural rights.

Rights are principles that only develop relevance in the context of government. A government is an institution that establishes social rules within a geographic area, enforces them coercively, and cannot be challenged with impunity.[1] Another way of

---

1 This definition is due to Roger Donway. Ayn Rand's definition is similar, but less precisely phrased: "A government is an institution that holds the exclusive power to enforce

looking at government is to note that whatever institution arises to predominate in the use of force in a region, that institution is a government. It may be a federal institution, or one of divided powers, or one that incorporates more or less competitive and/or for-profit provision of traditional government services such as courts and security forces. It may be elected, or it may not. It may be just or unjust. We need rights principles to prevent government from overstepping its proper function. And rights principles can only be fully developed in the context of establishing or reforming governmental institutions, because the relevant questions for fleshing out rights only arise in the process of making and applying law.

Classical liberals have traditionally restricted government to the functions of a "night watchman": providing defense against external enemies and domestic assaults, thefts, and murders. In addition to these defense and policing functions, Ayn Rand emphasised the important role of government in the provision of property and contract law and in tort claim adjudication. It is the development of these aspects of the law that has enabled the rise of industrial capitalism. In this context, Rand emphasised the need for "objective law," law codified and expressed in clear principles. Objective law has the great virtue of predictability, and the degree to which legal consequences can be rendered predictable is the degree to which irregularity and caprice can be removed from the actions of government.

The Problem of Government Financing

The founding right of a just government in the Objectivist conception is the right to live free from the initiation of force against oneself or one's property. As an absolute principle, this right should be respected by the government itself. Now, at a certain level of generality, it is easy to see how this would work for, say, police work or the courts. Police would investigate cases of initiation of force: theft, assault, murder, and the like. Police would not be entitled to initiate force against innocent parties. Arrest without cause, intimidation of witnesses, and arbitrary searches and seizures would be right out.

But what about taxes? In an essay that has been the source of ongoing debate, Rand argued against any form of tax:

> Since the imposition of taxes does represent an initiation of force, how, it is asked, would the government of a free country raise the money needed to finance its proper services?
>
> In a fully free society, taxation—or, to be exact, payment for governmental services—would be *voluntary*. (Rand 1964a, 116)

Rand offered, in the way of a suggestion, two ideas for replacing taxes with voluntary payments. The first was a government lottery. This idea, however, has been roundly criticised, since absent an enforced monopoly, the government lottery could not expect to earn more than a common market rate of return; the government in that case might as well run a drug store or go into any other line of business to earn a profit. And there is no reason to think that government officials, whose expertise

---

certain rules of social conduct."

presumably lies close to non-business tasks like law enforcement, diplomacy, and war-making, would be able to succeed in a competitive line of business.

Rand's second suggestion for funding the government was a fee for contract enforcement. This proposal is worth discussing in some detail, because, as we shall see, its problems can be generalised to a wide range of voluntary financing schemes, perhaps all.

> Suppose that the government were to protect—*i.e.*, to recognize as legally valid and enforceable—only those contracts which had been insured by the payment, to the government, of a premium in the amount of a legally fixed percentage of the sums involved in the contractual transaction.
>
> ... (If necessary, that percentage could be legally increased in time of war; or other, but similar, methods of raising money could be established for *clearly defined* wartime needs.)...
>
> The legal and technical difficulties involved are enormous: they include such questions as the need of an ironclad constitutional provision to prevent the government from dictating the *content* of private contracts (an issue which exists today and needs much more objective definitions)—the need of objective standards (or safeguards) for establishing the amount of the premiums, which cannot be left to the arbitrary discretion of the government, etc. (Rand 1964a, 116-17)

Larry Sechrest (1999, 91) has criticised this proposal on the grounds that it would fail to provide adequate funding of government services. Rand had proposed that the government provide the "night-watchman" functions of government to all, regardless of payment:

> It may be observed, in the example given above, that the cost of such voluntary government financing would be automatically proportionate to the scale of an individual's economic activity; those on the lowest economic levels (who seldom, if ever, engage in credit transactions) would be virtually exempt—though they would still enjoy the benefits of legal protection, such as that offered by the armed forces, by the police and by the courts dealing with criminal offenses. (Rand 1964a, 119)

In his critique, Sechrest notes that people who pay little or nothing to the government may still require costly police and court services. The problem, then, is excess demand. As government services come at no marginal cost to the user, it is reasonable to suppose that many people may respond to the incentive given by calling the police more than they would if they had to bear to the cost of the police visit, and troubling the courts more than they would if they had to bear those costs.

However, against Sechrest, it must be noted that if the source of government revenues is a fee on credit transactions, as in her example, there is no way without substantial further research to know whether the supply of basic government services will be adequate to the demand. There are still transactions costs involved in any call to the police and the courts: even the idle will lose time when they make such a call. So the number of calls will be finite. Indeed, calls to the police are free today, and in developed countries at least this does not cause a radical shortage of police services. But to return to the revenue side, note that contract fees are simply independent of the demand. It might well be the case that the government revenues would more than cover the maximum amount of police and court services demanded. Perhaps the pressing problem under Rand's example would not be a shortage of police, but excess revenue soaked up by feather-bedding in the police budget!

A different critique of Rand's example would be to deny that her contract fee is truly voluntary. To see this, consider the case of a handshake agreement, such as a friend selling a used computer to a friend. If the friends pay no contract fee on the transfer, the government will not recognise the contract. The seller now has money: could the buyer claim the money was stolen? The buyer has a computer: could the seller claim the computer was stolen? (Presumably, all this acrimony would be due to a falling out among the friends.)

The buyer might argue as follows: "My friend took my $500, and in return offered no legally recognised goods. In effect, he defrauded me and stole my $500." The seller might, for his part, appeal to the police as follows: "My friend gave me $500 as a gift, and borrowed my computer. I deserve to keep the money (as a gift), and I also deserve the return of my computer to me."

What should the courts make of this? The court could establish, perhaps, as a fact of the matter that the friends intended a trade. Normally, the court would recognise the informal contract. But in Rand's scenario, the court would be bound not to recognise that trade, wouldn't it? It might be consistent to accept the buyer's claim that the sale was fraudulent. It would also be consistent to return the money and the computer to the status quo ante. In either case, a trade unsanctioned by the contract fee could end up forcibly nullified, and perhaps one or more parties to the trade could be charged with fraud.

Indeed, no private property would be secure without the contract fee paid. Consider a second scenario to make this clear: Owner has bought a hand-crafted chair without paying the contract fee (and no dispute has arisen). Thief comes along and makes off with the chair in the night. If Owner puts the police on the case, to whom will they return the chair if they find it? There may be a general interest—perhaps enshrined in the criminal law—to apprehend thieves on principle (the thief's next victim could well have paid the fee). But perhaps Thief could plausibly claim to have made the chair himself. Might the courts return the chair to its actual maker? If the courts do recognise Owner's claim to the chair, they undermine the principle of non-protection of uninsured contracts. But if they do not recognise Owner's claim, then owners of property for which no contract fee has been paid would not receive full protection against even such a basic crime as theft. Fee-dissenters might well receive no real police protection beyond protection of their physical persons from assault and murder.

So, despite Rand's stated intention, the choice offered by her contract fee system would be stark indeed: the choice to pay the contract fee, or to not work for pay nor be secure in one's property. In this sense, it is obvious that a choice to pay the fee would not be wholly uncoerced.

The issue of the degree to which government financing can be made fully voluntary is one to which we will return when we consider the Objectivist critique of anarchism in the full context. For the moment, however, what we need to note is that Rand's essay on government financing left open a line of argument that would prove to be grist for Rand-influenced anarchists.

Rand and Anarchism

Rand's essay clearly links the principle of non-initiation of force with opposition to taxation. Yet Rand herself recognised that she did not have nor know of a well-developed theory for how government could be financed without taxation. She presents the contract fee, for example, "as *only* an illustration." And many critics have pointed out problems in those examples.

This left many Rand followers considering something like the following alternatives:

> If all voluntary methods of government financing should prove inadequate, then one has only three choices: either give up on the dream of a free society, concede that a free society is a society without government, or admit that taxation cannot be voluntary. (Sechrest 1999, 90-91)

Many former Rand followers have left classical liberalism behind, no doubt. Others have argued for taxation in the context of a classical liberal state, and have continued to support Rand's basic contention that a government is a necessary institution and that a just and properly limited government is achievable and sustainable. (Franck, 1994, is an example.)

Still others took the third fork: agreeing with Rand that "the imposition of taxes does represent an initiation of force," these questioned Rand's insistence on the need for a unitary government and offered, as an alternative, a market-anarchist vision.

Rand's first response in print to the idea of market-anarchism (which apparently had been subject of some conversation in her circle) appeared in her essay "The Nature of Government:"

> ... some people are raising the question of whether government as such is evil by nature and whether anarchy is the ideal social system. Anarchy, as a political concept, is a naive floating abstraction: for all the reasons discussed above, a society without an organized government would be at the mercy of the first criminal who came along and who would precipitate it into the chaos of gang warfare. But the possibility of human immorality is not the only objection to anarchy: even a society whose every member were fully rational and faultlessly moral, could not function in a state of anarchy; it is the need of *objective* laws and of an arbiter for honest disagreements among men that necessitates the establishment of a government.
>
> A recent variant of anarchistic theory, which is befuddling some of the younger advocates of freedom, is a weird absurdity called "competing governments." Accepting the basic premise of the modern statists—who see no difference between the functions of government and the functions of industry, between force and production, and who advocate government ownership of business—the proponents of "competing governments" take the other side of the same coin and declare that since competition is so beneficial to business, it should also be applied to government. Instead of a single, monopolistic government, they declare, there should be a number of different governments in the same geographical area, competing for the allegiance of individual citizens, with every citizen free to "shop" and to patronize whatever government he chooses.
>
> Remember that forcible restraint of men is the only service a government has to offer. Ask yourself what a competition in forcible restraint would have to mean.

> One cannot call this theory a contradiction in terms, since it is obviously devoid of any understanding of the terms "competition" and "government." Nor can one call it a floating abstraction, since it is devoid of any contact with or reference to reality and cannot be concretized at all, not even roughly or approximately. One illustration will be sufficient: suppose Mr. Smith, a customer of Government A, suspects that his next-door neighbor, Mr. Jones, a customer of Government B, has robbed him; a squad of Police A proceeds to Mr. Jones' house and is met at the door by a squad of Police B, who declare that they do not accept the validity of Mr. Smith's complaint and do not recognize the authority of Government A. What happens then? You take it from there. (Rand 1963, 112-13)

In response to these comments, Roy Childs offered a market-anarchist argument tailored to an Objectivist outlook in an open letter to Ayn Rand (Childs 1969). Childs's essay is a classic summary of a Rand-influenced approach to anarchism.

Childs's argument has two main pillars. The first is based on an application of the principle of non-initiation of force to government. Since, in effect, Rand's argument for voluntary government financing fails, even a limited government must initiate force.

> It is my contention that *limited government is a floating abstraction which has never been concretized by anyone; that a limited government must either initiate force* or *cease being a government; that the very concept of limited government is an unsuccessful attempt to integrate two mutually contradictory elements: statism and voluntarism.* (Childs 1969, 146, italics in original)

The second main pillar of Childs's argument is an appeal to the Objectivist moral view, rational egoism. Rand had asked her readers "What happens then? You take it from there." Childs responded directly:

> The main question at this point is this: do you think that it would be in the *rational self-interest* of either agency to allow this to happen, this fighting out conflicts in the streets, which is what you imply? No? *Then what view of human nature does it presuppose to assume that such would happen anyway?* (Childs 1969, 153, italics in original)

Childs argued that, *pace* Rand, human beings are capable of individually judging values: "an individual *must* judge, and evaluate the facts of reality in accordance with logic and his own rational self-interest" (150, italics in original). In effect accepting Rand's charge that market-anarchists see no difference in kind between the basic activities of government and industry, Childs argued that the burden was on Rand to explain why individuals would not be capable of objectively choosing defense agencies. Individuals rationally choose products: that's why commerce is efficient. Why shouldn't a similar process also serve in the case of law and government services? "It seems obvious that man needs objective rules in *every activity of his life, not merely in retaliation or the use of retaliation.* But, strange as it may seem, the market is capable of providing such rules" (151).

But is that right?

Objectivist Arguments against Anarchism

The argument against anarchism that Rand sketched out in "The Nature of Government" (and against which Childs responded) laid out the essentials of an Objectivist position that has endured among her followers. Rand revisited the issue of anarchism in print several more times (1964b, 1971, 1973), and by uniting these various comments with comments of other thinkers working within the system of thought Rand founded, we can see the full character of the Objectivist argument and the ways in which its critics have underestimated or perhaps misinterpreted it. I summarise it in what follows as three main arguments, and I will then give a quick look over the inductive evidence to which both sides appeal.

"Coercion is Different"

The first Objectivist argument is that *there is a fundamental difference in kind between a market interaction and a fight.* This is the difference between "force and production" that Rand mentions (1963, 112) and that she recalls again when writes: "Remember that forcible restraint of men is the only service a government has to offer. Ask yourself what a competition in forcible restraint would have to mean" (113).

The most developed explanation of this point in print is David Kelley's "The Necessity of Government" (1974).

Kelley notes that individual rights, which ban the initiation of "coercion" (i.e., the use of force) against others, leave people free to act on their individual, even "subjective," value judgments, without directly harming the life, liberty, or property of others. Thus, a fundamentally harmonious system of voluntary exchange to mutual benefit (i.e., *trade*) is possible among individuals. Competition among businesses and for jobs takes place in this context, and law and the system of rights constrains the means that economic competitors can use (or at least, those they can use with impunity: anyone can *try* to rob and defraud; but succeeding in the face of the law is another matter).

But, Kelley continues, "Coercion is different."

> Coercion, in this world, must sometimes be exercised. Given the existence of criminals, and the constant possibility that some men prefer criminal to honest means and ends, the existence of a power to prevent and punish this by force has a certain value. Its value is restricted, however, by the moral principle forbidding its use against persons who have not themselves used force against others. If this power is exercised improperly, if it is not used in accordance with the objective principles that define and delimit its value, then it violates rights—the rights of innocent people, or at least the right of the guilty to have their guilt objectively demonstrated before suffering punishment. This is true by the very nature of coercion, and it is true only of coercion. (Kelley 1974, 246)

To elaborate: Differences over business values lead to broken contracts, firings, failure to deliver goods, and the rise and fall of whole businesses and even the wealth of regions. But differences of legal standards, right of enforcement, the application of rights, and the very ownership of property, lead to war, insurrection, false arrest, theft, and murder. Differences over the best way to make gloves has left no glovers in Gloversville, NY, but those who once were glovers went on to live, and often flourish, in other lines of work, and their heirs live on. Differences over the best way to organise Beirut, Lebanon, devastated whole sections of the city and left thousands dead.

This was Rand's point in commenting that anyone who thought that force could be controlled through competition was "obviously devoid of any understanding of the terms 'competition' and 'government'" (1963, 113).

Childs counters this argument by proposing a thought experiment.

> Suppose that I judged, being as rational as I possibly could, that I could secure the protection of my contracts and the retrieval of stolen goods at a cheaper price and with more efficiency [than from the government]. Suppose I ... set up an institution to attain these ends. ... there are only two alternatives as far as the "government" is concerned: (a) It can use force or the threat of it against the new institution, *thus initiating use or threat of physical force against one who has not himself initiated force*. ... Or: (b) It can refrain from initiating force, and allow the new institution to carry on its activities without interference. If it did this, then the Objectivist "government" would truly become a marketplace institution, and not a "government" at all. (Childs 1969, 147)

It first must be said that Childs's argument, as far as it goes, is correct. It is deductively true that were the government to use force against individuals who had not initiated force, then the government would be initiating force. But knowledge is not derived by deduction alone. Crucially, Childs has failed to address the empirical question of what it would actually mean for a rights-respecting government to interact with another putative law-enforcing body within the government's own territory. Childs seems to assume that the legitimacy of the private defense agency's actions will be plain on their face.

A similar assumption is made by Nicholas Dykes in relating anarchism with Objectivism (2005). Dykes chides Kelley (1974) for claiming that anarchism amounts to "placing coercion on the market."

> Kelley's assertion is mistaken, because "placing coercion on the market" is *not* an anarchist position. An anarchist is one who wishes to *eliminate* coercion. What anarchists seek in fact is to open protection of individual rights, arbitration of disputes, and judgment of wrongdoing, to any person or persons who may choose to offer these services and, further, to allow anybody who wishes to offer or to avail themselves of these services to do so freely—without interference from any group calling itself "the government." (Dykes, 81)

The problem in both these cases is that no mechanism exists in a genuine anarchy to distinguish rights-protecting agencies from generally coercive agencies. Kelley is therefore not mistaken: what anarchist agencies offer will be coercion: they will arrest people and seize or not seize property; they may kill or injure people who resist them: will all these actions be justified? That is what everyone in society will need to know.

When one supermarket offers bad produce, there is nothing to stop customers from shopping at a competitor's. But note that even in this rights-based interaction, there can be, and often are, significant problems. A supermarket that dominates the local market may come under new and destructive management. A new and better source of produce may not instantly appear. Someone must identify the opportunity, decide that it is worth pursuing compared with other activities, acquire the means to build or buy supermarkets in the area, build the necessary vendor relations, tend to all the myriad aspects besides produce that make for a good supermarket, and so on. In short, this process can take years, *if it happens at all*, and it can be very lumpy. For my part, I'm still waiting for Whole Foods (or any store like it) to show up where I live.

Consider as another example the incomplete, haphazard roll-out of cellular telephone service in the United States (where standard-setting was largely left to the open market). The market can be expected in time to provide ever-improving service, but when networks must be built and rendered compatible and the products are complex and difficult to perfect, the development of the market can be and usually is very, very messy if it happens at all. And providing rights-respecting law is not easier than rolling out a network, to be sure.

My point here is not advocate Socialism: the messy market process is the best one, for a variety of reasons. Most crucially, being free from force, a free market is always open to improvement (albeit, often slow improvement) by anyone willing and able to improve it. And being free from force, individuals in a free market may act on their own judgment in choosing which goods are best for themselves and their interests and values, without preventing others from doing the same.

To take Childs and Dykes together, we can say that is a fantasy to imagine that a competitor to a government can simply show on its face its rights-respecting character.

In fact, anyone who judges the existing government's procedures as legitimate would have to demand that any putative "defense" agency show in its basic constitution, procedures, laws, structure, and method that its actions would be compatible with respect for individual rights as defined by the government's own laws, constitution, and legal traditions. The same would follow in the context of an existing anarchy: anyone who had judged their armed force as legitimate would need to ensure that all other significant armed forces were also ensured—as far as possible and practical—to comport themselves in cooperation with said legitimate force, including acceding—at minimum—its ultimate standards.

Objectivist philosopher Leonard Peikoff puts this point bluntly:

> "What if an individual does not *want* to delegate his right of self-defense?" the anarchist frequently asks. "Isn't that a legitimate aspect of 'freedom'?" ...
>
> The citizens of a proper society should reply ... as follows: "Don't delegate your right of self-defense, if that is your choice. But if you act on your view-point—if you resort to the use of force against any of us—we will answer you by force. Our government will answer you, in the only terms you yourself make possible." (Peikoff 1991, 372)

It is important to note that for an Objectivist, a proper government is whatever institution succeeds, in the current context of knowledge, in protecting individual rights and providing objective, rights-based law, secure from threats domestic and foreign. That institution might be federal; it might be a representative republic; it might incorporate checks and balances; in short, there are many plausible options for its design. Without more experience living in a free (or significantly freer) society, it will be difficult to know beyond some generalities what form the proper institutions of government should take.

Thus neither Peikoff nor any other Objectivist invests government as such with unwarranted objectivity or propriety. Rather, Objectivists recognise that it is precisely to the extent that it provides the institutions for upholding objective, rights-respecting law, that any government merits being regarded as proper. The Objectivist position does not presume that non-market methods will create a just government— that will require effort, planning, and learning from experience (it may even require the use of force against violent opponents of a rights-respecting regime). But it does note that the anarchist's corresponding faith in the efficiency of "competition" is unwarranted.

In this context, it is worth revisiting my earlier observation that the problems inherent in Rand's proposed contract fee to finance government apply to a wider class— perhaps all—voluntary government finance schemes. The contract fee, we saw, had, through its effect on the way the law would treat a case, substantial coercive implications. This is because of the nature of force: to expose oneself to competition over force simply is to expose oneself to the possibility of coercion. There is no way to live in society and not face some kind of threat of force. Stepping out from behind institutional protection therefore must mean stepping into a potentially dangerous situation.

This result can be generalised to the case of a generic citizenship fee: suppose the government was reconstituted by Objectivists, following Rand's suggestion and Childs's example, as a kind of dominant defense agency (Government A). To finance Government A, all taxes would be unified into a "citizenship fee" which would entitle the payee to the full force and protection of Government A. But no one is required to pay the citizenship fee, and Government A is constitutionally bound not to initiate force. However, this commitment must be hedged by the fact that Government A retains subpoena and search powers, and it does have a doctrine of forcibly neutralising imminent or intolerable threats. (College students, for example, are not allowed to build atomic bombs in their basements, not even for fun: the risk of catastrophic harm to their neighbors is too great.)

The only consequence of not paying the citizenship fee is that Government A will treat the non-payer as an alien: it will now protect him only insofar as it serves the interests of Government A's citizens. If the non-payer forms or joins another defense agency (Government B), Government A will need ensure that Government B comports with all relevant standards and that Government B does not pose a credible threat to Government A's ability to go about its business. Perhaps this is what Childs had in mind: "There could be contracts or 'treaties' between the competing agencies," he writes (1969, 153). Well, there are treaties, and then there are treaties. Government A treaties are, perforce, demands for total compliance. In any case, should Government A, through a proper process, determine that the non-payer was a rights-violator, or a threat, Government A would of course have to take coercive action immediately, as it would in dealing with any threat or criminal.

Though this kind of arrangement seems to provide for voluntary government financing, and seems to allow for competing defense agencies, it is hard to see how any alternative government of non-payers could really achieve independence from Government A, without a war. Meanwhile awaiting the revolution, the mere act of non-payment would likely expose one to thieves and other predators. (Of course, non-payers might self-select to be armed to the teeth. But this presumes that Government A would allow them to stay so well armed, which might not be prudent.) Life outside the embrace of Government A (and its approved ally governments B, C, etc.) could be precarious at best.

So it appears that one could reasonably doubt whether the citizenship fee of Government A is truly voluntary. Yet the problem is not lack of respect for the principle of non-initiation of force. The problem, rather, is inherent to the nature of force, and thus inherent to the nature of enforced law and government over force.

But why does Government A need to demand total compliance from competitors in its territory? Why can it not simply trust the people to ensure, as customers, that competing defense agencies will be rights-respecting? To see this, we need to look more closely at the two further arguments that Ayn Rand offered against anarchism. Each of these aims to show why a unified and formally structured system of law, defense, and law-enforcement is required. Or, one might say, these arguments show why genuinely anarchic provision of law and enforcement would be doomed to warfare and strife.

Rationality Cannot be Taken for Granted

The second Objectivist argument against anarchism is that *rational, productive individuals need government to guard against the irrational use of force*. Rand put it this way: "A society without an organized government would be at the mercy of the first criminal who came along …" (1963, 112). Childs rebuts this argument by appealing to the need of each individual to act by his own independent judgment in the cause of his own rational self-interest. And Objectivists agree that people *ought to* act for their rational self-interest. But there is a difference between a normative prediction (of what people ought to do) and a positive prediction (of what they will do).

One of the reasons Objectivism places *rationality* front and center as the prime virtue, is that people do not achieve it automatically. Indeed, people often fail, in one respect or another, to behave rationally. It is clear enough, for example, that drug abuse is not in the long-term rational self-interest of the abuser. Furthermore, drug abuse is morally condemned all over the world. Yet drug abuse has been and is likely to remain a condition into which many fall. There are reasons: moderate drug use of various kinds (medical and recreational) is rational and appropriate. The abuser slides down a slippery slope from there. Furthermore, most drugs provide some kind of short-term sense of well-being and even enhanced efficacy. The costs are usually long-term. It's a common failing to over-value the short-range and perceptually apparent against long-range effects, which can usually only be known abstractly, through a process of reasoning. The upshot is: It's not rational, it's not right, but people do it anyway.

In a future society where the Objectivist values of reason, individualism, achievement, and freedom are widely held and are applied in education, high culture, and moral counseling, we can reasonably expect that people will, on average, do better than they do today in living rationally. But even then, irrationality will be with us.

And that goes for crime, as well. The anarchist holds that somehow, the competition among armed agencies will ensure that no armed force committed to irrational ends can establish itself. But the history of the world up to now is a history replete with thieves and murders in every epoch, and one in which even in the best societies, substantial minorities (at the minimum) have been strongly committed to the use of force to attain pecuniary, moral, and religious ends. In chaotic and anarchic situations, family, ethnic, and religious ties often provide natural loci of established, trusting relations around which quasi-governmental institutions develop. Modern anarchic societies such as Afghanistan, Somalia from 1991, and Lebanon in 1975-90 show this process clearly. But this demonstrated process of competition in force-provision provides strong short-term incentives for individuals to embrace attitudes of ethnic and religious solidarity that are not rational in the full, long-range sense.

It is also notable that most anarchist discussions focus on local courts and police forces as the paradigm of government that must replaced. But throughout history, the greatest irrational threat to freedom has come from predatory conquerors. The absence of strong, unified defense forces for a territory gives predators (or predatory rebels) a tempting incentive to attack. Indeed, the absence of a dominant defense agency in an anarchy means that the anarchic society is far less able than one with a unified government to provide an effective, coordinated military defense. It is notable that in modern history, anarchic conditions have tended to survive only in places (e.g. Somalia, Congo) of little wealth or importance.

In economic life, it is not the end of the world when a company, a family, or a religious group acts in ways contrary to its long-range, rational self-interest. To be sure, it is not necessarily a trivial matter, either. Ignoring the threat they can pose to the underpinnings of liberal government—which Rand illustrated in *Atlas Shrugged* (1957)—there are the real problems they can cause for other, rational, people who interact with them—problems which Rand illustrated in *The Fountainhead* (1943), a novel which focuses on an independent innovator who struggles against an inimical culture despite living in an essentially free society. Nevertheless, because market interactions take place in the context of a legal system that respects rights, the irrationalities of others do not prevent, in the end, rational people from producing the values they need. But, as noted in the first Objectivist argument, "coercion is different." In the competition to provide and enforce law, irrational choices of others can have life and value-threatening consequences.

Thus it does not appear that the anarchist can explain away the threat that, absent government, it is likely that force will be used in ways an Objectivist would describe as irrational. Regardless of one's view of anarchy as an abstract conception, as a practical matter in the course of forming a free society, organisers of government institutions will need to keep strongly focused on preventing the formation of powerful force-using agencies that are motivated by predation (as in the case of thieves or conquerors), or by familial, ethnic, corporate, or religious solidarity.

Rational Conflicts Abound

The third Objectivist argument for government and against anarchy is that it is common for people generally committed to rationality to come into conflict over contracts, property, and moral issues due to natural differences in their contexts of knowledge, values, and abilities. For this reason, it is unrealistic to expect that anarchic armed forces—ones that lack established, institutionalised means of objectively arbitrating their mutual conflicts—will be able to resolve conflicts without resorting to force, however rational and committed to rights-respecting they might be. Ayn Rand put this point like so:

> ... even a society whose every member were fully rational and faultlessly moral, could not function in a state of anarchy; it is the need of *objective* laws and of an arbiter for honest disagreements among men that necessitates the establishment of a government. (Rand 1963, 112)

These "honest disagreements" include the innumerable conflicts and disagreements about contracts and personal injury that get handled in the courts as a matter of course today. These often involve projects or products worth a great deal of money and into which a great deal of time has been invested. Bankruptcy proceedings, as an example, often involve the fate of major industrial companies, thousands or tens of thousands of lives, and billions of dollars of invested capital.

Consider a company, say, an airline, in an economic downturn. The founder of the company may have concluded that the company can survive until business picks up in a year or so, if only the banks will be patient. But the bankers and their investors may have decided that that they cannot take the risk: they want to foreclose now. These are reasonable judgments each. But imagine this somehow occurring in the absence of established governmental procedures: the law enforcement is "whatever the market will bear." The founder has reason to contract with an armed force that embraces a generous doctrine on interpreting bank covenants and bankruptcy law. The founder may even reasonably conclude that in doing this he is serving the interests of the bankers as well as himself: they will, he decides, earn a better return from being patient than from selling the company assets at a knock-down price. And the founder's love of his company is itself rational, even if it is not universal (others don't have all the reasons to treasure this airline that the founder or the workers do). But the bankers' investors need an armed force that will attach a debtor's property on the instant the banks foreclose, and they reasonably don't want to earn the reputation of being weak in upholding their contracts.

Anarchists imagine that after a few short, salubrious experiences with low-grade warfare, these two armed forces will sort out their differences and get along as well as the U.S. and Canada now do. But the truth is that determining whether a private defense agency respects rights is probably no harder in the free market than ensuring that famous corporations don't cook their books. But wait: famous corporations have cooked their books, with no one the wiser. As for short, salubrious wars, it is as likely that with a small mistake, an overlooked datum, or a little "collateral damage," the warfare would spiral down into a cycle of attack and counter-attack that could draw in others, and create a lasting deterioration of societal trust and safety.

In addition to reasonable legal differences over facts, interpretation, and enforcement doctrine, there are a wide-range of other particular legal judgments and policies that might plausibly be construed as rights-respecting. Within this range, very serious ideological disagreements could easily arise. I've already mentioned subpoena power, searches, and action against probable threats, over which reasonable people could differ and which endanger rights. Now consider, for instance, abortion and foreign policy, two issues that have divided the American libertarian movement, just as they have divided American culture more generally. In both cases, each side of the debate has reasons for regarding the other side not merely as wrong but as murderers and/or oppressors.

Abortion kills fetuses that otherwise would likely have lived to become children. If those fetuses have rights, that is *murder*. Shouldn't a rights-respecting force prevent murder? On the other hand, preventing abortion by force obliges a woman to submit to outsiders controlling how she uses her body. Shouldn't she fight for her rights, if it comes down to it?

An aggressive, pro-liberty foreign policy could entail warfare with unjust and oppressive outside forces (Thomas 2003b, 11-13). War is ugly: at least some innocents die in every war: that's a reason to oppose aggressive wars even against unjust regimes. And furthermore, it might be reasonable to conclude that an aggressive foreign policy magnifies foreign threats: live-and-let-live might be a better policy for encouraging liberty over the long run. But how can one stop an armed force bent on war? Well, if boycotts and arguments fail, there's always (civil) war.

These kinds of disputes cannot be eliminated from the exercise of governmental power even in a society with firm and deep commitments to reason and liberty. What is required to eliminate the potential for such conflicts is a meta-commitment to the law and the government as just institutions. Key to this is the objectivity of the courts, the impartiality of the police forces in enforcing the law, and the existence of a responsive process for improving and rectifying the law. These features of governance will earn it trust even from those who dispute the current thrust of policy or who stand to lose from a particular court decision.

The Objectivist position on government is that achieving and maintaining a free, modern society requires that we consciously design governmental institutions to provide rights-based and objective law, rights-respecting law-enforcement, and robust regional defense against outside threats to our rights. If the anarchist position is that these goals can all be achieved through a "polycentric" legal system that allows for private provision of many subsidiary functions of government (Barnett 1998), then perhaps an anarchist position can be an Objectivist position on government (and, ergo, a practicable means of securing and enforcing freedom). But in that case, the anarchism-minarchism debate has been in part the result of a confusion about the meanings of terms like "government" and "state."

But I take it that most anarchists have something else in mind: a society where there is no over-arching legal and enforcement system—and hence, no *state* (Dykes 2005, 130-31 and Childs, 145). This would be a society where the enforcement of the law comes down to individual options just as acquiring clothing is a matter of individual options. You can make your own clothes, or buy them from any number of vendors and in any number of ways. In an anarchy, presumably, one is supposed to be able, at minimum, to take the law into one's own hands with some measure of impunity.

But this is exactly what an organised governmental system would forbid. Even a legal system that reserved room for acts of self-defense and preserved a robust right to arms would need to demand oversight of all legal decision-making to ensure that decisions authorising the use of force (to imprison or seize restitution from criminals, for example, and ex-post facto assessments of putative actions of self-defense), would be made objectively and in accordance with rights-respecting legal standards. In such a system, the law could not serve its full purpose were it to allow competitors to use force with impunity.

Evidence, Briefly Considered

In his case for an Objectivism-influenced anarchism, Dykes remarks: "Rand offered no evidence for her 'mob rule' assertions" (2005, 104). It is true that in "The Nature of Government" Rand did not offer many examples, but she returned to the subject of anarchy several times in her writing. One set of examples she appealed to were contemporaneous non-state, force-wielding institutions: mobsters and the pre-1990s PLO, which operated from various camps and communities first primarily in Jordan and later in primarily in Lebanon:

> [Anarcho-capitalists'] distance from reality may be gauged by the fact that they are unable to recognize the actual examples of their ideals in practice. One such example is the Mafia. The Mafia (or "family") is a "private government," with subjects who chose to join it voluntarily, with a rigid set of rules rigidly, efficiently and bloodily enforced, a "government" that undertakes to protect you from "outsiders" and to enforce your immediate interests—at the price of your selling your soul, i.e., of your total obedience to any "favor" it may demand. Another example of a "government" without territorial sovereignty is offered by the Palestinian guerrillas, who have no country of their own, but who engage in terroristic attacks and slaughter of "outsiders" anywhere on earth. (Rand, 1973, 44)

Presumably, Rand would have mentioned al Qaeda and other terrorist organisations were she writing today.

Another interesting example Rand mentions is the property status of the radio spectrum in the early days of radio:

> Collectivists frequently cite the early years of radio as an example of the failure of free enterprise. In those years, when broadcasters had no property rights in radio, no legal protection or recourse, the airways were a chaotic no-man's land where anyone could use any frequency he pleased and jam anyone else. Some professional broadcasters tried to divide their frequencies by private agreements, which they could not enforce on others; nor could they fight the interference of stray, maliciously mischievous amateurs. This state of affairs was used, then and now, to urge and justify government control of radio.

> This is an instance of capitalism taking the blame for the evils of its enemies.
> The chaos of the airways was an example, not of free enterprise, but of *anarchy*. It was caused, not by private property rights, but by their absence. It demonstrated why capitalism is incompatible with anarchism, why men do need a government and what is a government's proper function. What was needed was *legality*, not *controls*. (Rand 1964b, 125)

In reply, Rand-influenced anarchists have appealed to two major bodies of evidence. The first is international relations and trade, which take place in the anarchy that exists between governments (e.g. Childs, 154). This is a valid set of evidence to our concerns, since it concerns people acting with modern knowledge and modern technology. But there are major problems adducing international relations to the case for anarchy.

The international system of the late twentieth century was created out of the effects of two world-spanning and hugely destructive wars. Today, where international relations are most stable and trade most prosperous, substantial international institutions (NATO, the U.S. Pacific alliances, the European Union, the World Trade Organization, the Internal Monetary Fund) also exist that not only formalise detailed cooperation among governments, but in some cases effectively supersede national sovereignty. Objectivists, for their part, would like to achieve the benefits within a country of institutions that secure a measure of freedom, without requiring that we wait through a major war or two to establish them.

Another problem with adducing international relations as evidence for anarchism is that international interactions, even along peaceful borders, happen much less frequently than do domestic interactions. A domestic anarchy would raise points of governmental friction not merely along one clear, highly controlled, and (relatively) easily isolated border, but on every piece of property and in every interaction. The number of potential conflicts in a domestic anarchy would therefore be exponentially higher. This is one reason why anarchies, if not unified by a dominant force, often quickly break down into autonomous zones (another reason, in, e.g. Lebanon 1975-present is that communal forces were a source of the collapse of general government in the first place).

Dykes synthesises a variety of anthropological and historical research to provide further evidence for the plausibility of anarchism. The primary examples he mentions are:

> ninth-century Anglo-Saxons, Medieval Irishmen and Icelanders, sixteenth-century Iroquoians, or the twentieth-century Kapauku, for all of whom individual freedom and private property were as natural and necessary as breathing, and for whom domination by a state lay in the future. (Dykes 2005, 130)

The problem with historical examples of social behavior is that as the distance in institutions, technology, culture, and context of knowledge generally, from the present increases, the relevance of the experience for modern times declines. For example, Anglo-Saxons, Medieval Irishmen, and Medieval Icelanders are all representatives of people of primitive technology, relatively little use of money and writing, with war-making as a key component of the average "free" man's life. They were also societies that were conquered or ultimately controlled by outside forces of comparable technological level. These were people who could not even grasp the controlling concepts of modern political and economic life. It is dubious indeed that these societies embodied anything like the freedom that industrial capitalism requires.

The same goes for the sixteenth-century Iroquoians, and the twentieth-century Kapauku, who were a primitive New Guinea tribe (originally discussed in some detail in Benson 1990, 15-21). Without going into each of these cases in more detail, the relevant question to ask would be: how easy would it be to start and run a business in these societies? What evidence do we have of outsiders being able to acquire property and settle peacefully among these people? Did one need approval to trade or travel? These societies, like Somaliland 1991-present, are basically tribal societies.

Advocates of minimal government can appeal to the history of the U.S.A. and Britain, world-beating economies in their hey-day of economic freedom. They can show economic studies correlating economic freedom with wealth and economic growth, in modern conditions. Where advocates of limited government appeal to the case of Hong Kong, anarchists are reduced to appealing to Somaliland—and ignoring examples of disastrous anarchies such as twentieth-century Afghanistan and southern Somalia (post 1991). When a Somaliland that may still described as meaningfully anarchic shows itself to be the economic tiger of Africa and merits comparison to, say, Chile, then the anarchists would have a piece of solid evidence. But, for the reasons that we have surveyed in this chapter, there is better reason to think that by the time Somaliland is truly thriving (right now, it merely recovering from tyranny, chaos, and collapse), it will have a functioning state.

Conclusion

In the foregoing, I have discussed the Objectivist argument for government (laid out essentially in Rand 1963) and compared it with some Ayn Rand-influenced arguments for anarcho-capitalism. In essence, the Objectivist position is that 1) Competition in force provision is and would be warfare and should not be equated with interaction in the market; 2) The fact the people are often irrational implies that unregulated armed forces would be dangerous; and 3) Even reasonable, freedom-loving people are likely to have innumerable disputes over rights and force involving serious moral, personal, and financial commitments, providing further reasons why unregulated armed forces are highly dangerous. Real examples of unregulated armed forces are not encouraging, either.

Rand's heart with anarchy even though her head was not? But then, How else can Galt's Gulch, the stateless "Atlantis" of *Atlas Shrugged*, be "just a voluntary association of men, held together by nothing but every man's self interest"? How can it function without a government? Well, here is one interpretation:

Galt's Gulch is a secret valley, and only the select few in the novel know of its existence. In effect, every member of this small community has been selectively chosen. It is more like a tribe (an intellectual one, to be sure) than it is like a large, diverse modern society. Only the most rational people with the greatest integrity and the strongest predispositions to create and produce are invited. Thus, there are no irrational actors: no thugs, no thieves, etc. There is no need for a military force because the valley is kept hidden from the outside world. And what about the inevitable disagreements to which even rational people are prone? These are held in check through the moral suasion of Judge Narragansett, the valley's arbiter of disputes, and the moral example of John Galt, the leader of their intellectual tribe. No one in the valley expects to be able to apply this model to society at large. So *Atlas Shrugged* holds no hidden brief for anarchy.

In any case, it wouldn't matter much if it did. It is my view that anarchy vs. minarchy is hardly the most pressing issue before us. The political challenge that faces Objectivists and lovers of freedom more generally is the real and practical project of increasing freedom in the world. While the goal of creating a society founded on protection of individual rights provides a clear direction in which to move the current political institutions, many, many questions of practical implementation and theoretical elaboration remain to be answered. Whether the government of a practical free society will have substantial elements of private or polycentric law provision, or whether it will have more expansive powers than most minarchists predict, or both, will only be something we can know with any certainty when we have more institutional and cultural experience. What the philosophical arguments I have covered here are intended to do is indicate, most of all, that the institutions of the free society must be consciously designed. The free society, to use a market metaphor, must have a business plan. Freedom will not simply evolve. We will have to create it.

Bibliography

Barnett, Randy E. 1998. *The Structure of Liberty: Justice and the Rule of Law.* Oxford: Oxford University Press.

Benson, Bruce. 1990. *The Enterprise of Law: Justice without the State.* San Francisco: Pacific Research Institute for Public Policy.

Childs, Roy. 1969. "Objectivism and the State: An Open Letter to Ayn Rand." *The Rational Individualist* 1, no. 10 (August, 1969); reprinted in Joan Kennedy Taylor, ed., *Liberty Against Power: Essays by Roy A. Childs, Jr.* (San Francisco, Fox and Wilkes: 1994) 145-56.

Dykes, Nicholas. 2005. "The Facts of Reality: Logic and History in Objectivist Debates about Government." *The Journal of Ayn Rand Studies* 7, no. 1 (Fall, 2005), 79-140.

Franck, Murray I. 1994. "Taxation is Moral." *Full Context* 6, no. 10 (June, 1994), 9-11.

Kelley, David. 1974. "The Necessity of Government." *The Freeman* 24, no. 4, 243-48.

Peikoff, Leonard. 1991. *Objectivism: The Philosophy of Ayn Rand.* New York: Dutton.

Rand, Ayn. 1943. *The Fountainhead*, 25th Anniversary Edition. New York: Signet, 1993.

Rand, Ayn. 1963. "The Nature of Government." In *The Virtue of Selfishness*. New York: New American Library, 1964, 107-15.

Rand, Ayn. 1964a. "Government Financing in Free Society." In *The Virtue of Selfishness*. New York: New American Library, 1964, 116-20.

Rand, Ayn 1964b. "Check Your Premises: The Property Status of Airwaves." *The Objectivist Newsletter* 3, no. 4 (April, 1964). Reprinted as "The Property Status of the Airwaves" in *Capitalism the Unknown Ideal*, 122-29.

Rand, Ayn. 1971. "Brief Summary" in *The Objectivist* (September, 1971), 1089-90 in bound volume.

Rand, Ayn. 1973. "The Missing Link—Part II." *The Ayn Rand Letter* 2, no. 17 (May 21, 1973). Reprinted in *Philosophy: Who Needs It*. New York: Signet, 1984, 35-45.

Sechrest, Larry. 1999. "Rand, Anarchy, and Taxes." *Journal of Ayn Rand Studies* 1, no. 1 (Fall, 1999), 87-105.

Thomas, William. 2003a. "Ayn Rand: Radical for Capitalism." In Frost and Sikkenga, eds, *History of American Political Thought*. Lanham, MD: Lexington, 2003, 617-32.

Thomas, William. 2003b. "Weighing War." *Navigator* 6, no. 4 (April, 2003), 11-18.

Chapter 5

Reconciling Anarchism and Minarchism[1]

Tibor R. Machan

Libertarianism and Anarchism

Libertarian political philosophy has become one of the competing live options among serious students in the field. Not all have equal respect for it, of course, but undergraduate and graduate courses and seminars, as well as texts and readers in political philosophy, theory, and economy now explore it diligently, unlike when it had been relegated to near-obscurity in the academic world, prior to the publication in 1974 of the late Robert Nozick's *Anarchy, State, and Utopia*.[2]

Nozick began his famous book with a discussion of whether a libertarian country or society[3] would be anarchist, as Murray N. Rothbard (as well as some others) had claimed. Nozick concluded that even with full respect for everyone's basic negative individual rights, a society would "back into" a minimal state. He argued that this backing into a minimal state—or minarchy, as I call it, since "state" suggests an idea of society as a large organism with government as a very powerful ruling agency the way the mind is for a person[4]—comes about even if those in a "society without a state"[5] who are in the midst of private efforts to defend—or punish culprits for

---

1 This chapter draws heavily from Tibor R. Machan, "Anarchism and Minarchism: A Rapprochement," *Journal des Economistes et des Etudes Humaines*, Vol. 12, No. 4 (December, 2002), pp. 569-88.

2 New York, NY: Basic Books, 1974. The publication of this work brought about a rather sudden elevation of libertarianism to the status of a palatable political alternative, in the mode of a change of attitudes hinted at in Thomas S. Kuhn's *The Structure of Scientific Revolutions* (Chicago: University of Chicago Press, 1962), namely, not because of the sudden improvement of the arguments supporting the position but because of its acceptance by someone at a highly prestigious institution, namely, Harvard University. Of course, Nozick's arguments for libertarianism were ingenious and novel but as far as their philosophical merit is concerned, they were not exceptional.

3 I use "country" or "society" to designate a society with any kind of government or legal order, which means that there could be anarchist libertarian countries even in the terms of Rothbardian anarchists.

4 Political philosophers such as Plato, Hobbes, Hegel, Rousseau, Karl Marx, T. H. Green, Bosenquat, et al., come to mind as contributors to that tradition as evidenced by the innumerable criticisms offered in support of dismissing it as unfounded! (See, for example, Thomas Nagel, *Libertarianism Without Foundations*, 85 YALE Law Journal 147 [1975].)

5 For the most recent publication of Murray N. Rothbard's libertarian-anarchist essay, "Society Without a State," see Aeon Skoble and T. R. Machan (eds.), *Political Philosophy, Essential Selections* (Upper Saddle River, NJ: Prentice-Hall, 1999), pp. 488-99. It also appears

violating—individual rights are compensated for their worries about the possible side effect of private defensive actions. He claimed there would still be serious concern about those side effects. So, Nozick concludes that in the resulting system, which I call a minarchist society, one legal order alone would prevail within a given, contiguous geographical area with a single administration of this legal order.

This is contrary to what Rothbard and other libertarians have claimed, namely, that in a fully free society, one that respects and protects individual rights of the sort Nozick (and Locke, Rand and Rothbard each) regards as basic, there would be competing providers of legal services—courts and police and whatever is needed for maintaining a libertarian legal order—within the same geographical or similarly homogenous realm. Or, to use as a clue the title of one well-known book promoting this view, law would become an *enterprise*,[6] just as is any other provision of services that people might want.

Nozick was not the first libertarian who had confronted the issue of whether libertarianism requires anarchism. Such early individualists as Lysander Spooner, Josiah Warren, and Benjamin Tucker, and, more recently, Murray Rothbard, Roy Childs, Jr. (until just before he died), Morris and Linda Tannehill, John Hasnas, John Sanders, Jan Narveson, Nicholas Dykes, Walter Block, Roderick Long, and Jan Lester—including, in the background, Eric Mack and other less explicit champions—all have advanced the anarchist libertarian case.[7]

Against these have stood, recently, Ayn Rand, and most of her students, such as David Kelley and myself, as well as other libertarians, such as John Hospers, Douglas B. Rasmussen, and Douglas J. Den Uyl, all of whom have denied the alleged anarchist implications of libertarianism. More precisely, *they have*—as I have understood them—*denied that the free society would need to abolish government*. Instead, they have argued that such a society could and even should have a government that would *consistently uphold and protect individual rights*, at least as its official, constitutional policy.[8] This means that the infractions government allegedly must commit against a system of individual rights would not be required.[9]

---

in J. R. Pennock and J. W. Chapman (eds.), *Anarchism*: Nomos XIX (New York: New York University Press, 1978), pp. 191-207, and in T. R. Machan, *The Libertarian Reader* (Totowa, NJ: Rowman and Littlefield, 1982), pp. 53-63. Originally the work was published in *The Libertarian Forum*, January 1975, pp. 3-7.

6 Bruce Benson, *The Enterprise of law: Justice without the state* (San Francisco, CA: Pacific Research Institute for Public Policy, 1990).

7 See the Bibliography for details.

8 Some libertarians belong among those who defend government as a necessary evil but others hold that properly constituted, government is a positive good (based on the objective value to anyone of having his or her rights clearly identified and competently, expertly protected). For the latter most governments may well be corrupt, just as a body guard who has become a bully would be, but this need not be the case. In my view Randy E. Barnett, *Restoring the Lost Constitution* (Princeton, NJ: Princeton University Press, 2004), is a most sophisticated development of how the legal system of such a minarchist government would not have to involve rights violations.

9 Nicholas Dykes criticises Objectivists for not embracing anarchism in his "The Facts of Reality: Logic and History in Objectivist Debates about Government," *The Journal of Ayn*

This minarchist position may be put rather simply: When living in communities, dangers from others exist and it is *ethically* imperative to address these dangers; government, rightly understood, is the institution that specialises in proper protection of individual rights, thus it would be ethical to establish government instead of leaving the task of rights-protection to individuals and agencies lacking the special training to protect rights properly—that is, *via* due process, which means, without violating rights in the process of this protection. This institution, government, is, moreover, unique in free human communities because protecting individual rights isn't like other tasks (such as producing and selling bread or insurance) because its genesis isn't peaceful interaction but the initiation of force and the required response. This is why politics *cannot* be reduced, without remainder, to commerce, contrary to what individualist anarchists maintain, although chronologically both would emerge side by side.[10]

I will reconsider this dispute here and show that both individualist anarchists—those who reject government but embrace law and order for a society—and minarchists—those who support a properly limited government as the agency for administering it—are right and their differences are mostly apparent.[11] In one respect

---

Rand Studies, Vol. 7, No. 1 (Fall, 2005), pp. 79-140. As a brief comment, Dykes doesn't seem to realise that monopoly in the use of retaliatory force is not the same as a legal or coercive monopoly in that use. He persists in this equivocation. Yet, one can have a monopoly that comes about naturally, because it is freely granted to one by people—as, say, they effectively granted the Beatles a monopoly status in rock music or Fred Astaire in dancing or IBM in computers and Microsoft in software (for some time)—without keeping anyone else out by force. Furthermore, if people freely select a group of specialists to protect them by way of a long-term, binding contract [or compact], that's not to establish an objectionable, coercive monopoly, merely an exclusive but binding relationship. If you marry someone and promise, via contract, never to cheat on them, your refusal to fool around may make it appear that someone has a coercive monopoly on your spousal services but, in fact, it has come about voluntarily and so there can be no moral objection to the exclusivity of that relationship.

It is along such lines that Rand's notion of the "monopoly" of retaliatory force needs to be understood. And it is along lines of Randy Barnett's view of the US Constitution that her understanding of instituting government is best understood. Just as I may hire an exclusive body guard—write a long-term contract with one—and thus set up a monopoly, so one may become a citizen under a government on a purely voluntary yet exclusive basis. (Rand may have misunderstood what competition among governments amounts to, although I suspect what she really found unpalatable is that two governments could service the same citizenry, akin to having two airlines service one's single flight from LAX to JFK.)

One cannot do Dykes' piece justice with any kind of brief reply. But his equivocation is a serious flaw in it. The paper also ends on a dubious note, from a scholarly standpoint, when it suggests that those defending minarchism suffer emotional or psychological problems (like having an affinity for paternalism from their childhood). Such psychologising is very bad form—how can one defend oneself against it when there is no proof or evidence for the thing other than its having been suggested in a respectable forum?

10 Commerce requires law—e.g., protection of property rights—and law's implementation requires commerce—the buying and selling of the tools and equipment it must use.

11 I had given indication of my stance vis-à-vis this issue in my essay, "Ethics vs. Coercion: Morality or Just Values?" in Llewellyn H. Rockwell, Jr., et al., ed., *Man, Economy*

no competing legal orders would exist in a fully free society while in another sense competition among different legal orders would be the natural libertarian—and even non-libertarian but relatively liberal—situation of the multitude of countries that can co-exist.

What is the anarchist case for the libertarian society's approach to adjudication and law enforcement? What about it suggests that it is truly anarchistic? And what is the minarchist case for the libertarian society's approach to law? What indicates that it is anti-anarchist? I'll show that the two positions only appear to be different because of certain preconceptions about what a legal order must involve.

Why Bother About All This?

Some might wonder why this topic is of general interest and should concern any political philosopher? In other words, why is this not some sectarian issue, relevant only to those who find libertarianism promising?

The fact alone that Nozick's treatment of it received such close attention throughout the community of political philosophers and theorists—as well as economists and public policy scholars—should suggest that there is more at stake here than merely settling an intra-libertarian squabble. The dominant principles of Western liberal democracies are of two distinct types. One stresses personal autonomy, individual sovereignty. The other stresses some more or less extensive collectivism or, more recently, communitarianism. In this position all who are able naturally owe provisions for those who are in dire straits—the poor, helpless, injured, etc. These provisions are to be obtained via taxation or universal service, both of which are, to use Nozick's words, "on par with forced labor" and therefore rights-violating.

Whether either system can be stable, coherent, orderly, non-contradictory and just in the policies it precipitates has been the subject of numerous debates.

Arguably one motivation for incorporating a serious, maybe even substantial, welfare provision into an essentially liberal order is that without it no reason can be found for supporting the traditional configuration of countries as political entities. In other words, only if there are enforceable positive duties all citizens have toward one another may a government be justified at all. If no such duties are involved in maintaining justice, perhaps the need for government could not be established. So, in a sense, one promise (or threat?) of consistent classical liberalism, namely, libertarianism, is that it would require the abolition of government altogether, including the very idea of a country. But not all libertarians consider this a sound inference from their agreement that all individuals have unalienable rights to life, liberty and property.

---

and Liberty (Auburn, AL: Ludwig von Mises Institute, 1988). The main difference is that anarchists believe government can be a floating institution, not requiring homogeneity, while minarchists believe government must (at least within the context of contemporary technology) involve a homogeneous jurisdiction.

A Brief Statement of the Positions

Let me now restate, as neutrally as I can, why anarchism seems to follow from libertarianism. And I will also give the minarchist response to this as briefly as possible, at first.

The libertarian view is that each individual is a sovereign person, in possession of basic negative rights to life, liberty and property (and whatever other rights are implied by these). None may violate these. If one needs to protect these rights, the option exists of doing so oneself or hiring others.

As with all services human beings may offer to others, various parties may offer provisions and none may acquire a protected, legal monopoly. So the protection of basic rights may be provided to different individuals by different organisations or agencies (including business firms) specialising in such provisions. Ergo, no exclusion of competing providers can be justified on libertarian grounds. This, in essence, supports the anarchist libertarian idea of the provision of legal adjudication and enforcement.

The response to this has often been that such a system would in principle be chaotic and could more easily than would a minarchist system lead to a failure of providing decisive results. This is because dissatisfied parties could always seek yet another trial court, employ yet another police department, switch to yet another appellate court, etc., so there would be no "court of last resort" so as to issue a genuinely *final* or *decisive* judgment. Such a situation would basically render the legal system non-functional in a variety of cases where those involved wish to press on with their claims. Although some court-like organisations could operate in societies, in sufficiently large numbers of cases, when much is at stake, there needs to be a system of law with a court of last resort.[12]

---

12 There is an analogy to how a government ought to be conceived in the following: In nearly all sports, they are played without referees at a certain level but when the stakes are high, then referees are hired to make sure the rules are followed. Take tennis. Millions of people play the game without referees but at Wimbledon or the US Open, the games are played with close supervision by a team of expert referees. Similarly, many agreements are made by people without the benefit of formal contracts but when the stakes are big, contracts and courts that will adjudicate them are needed should a dispute arise. Many disputes can be handled without the benefit of legal adjudication—arbitration boards or private courts can deal with these. But when someone is accused of a serious crime, this raises the need for a formal court, adhering to due process, involving officers of the law who can arrest people, judges, etc.

Now libertarian anarchists claim that because in ancient Iceland and some other places there was a good deal of dispute-settlement without the benefit of an integrated system of government—traveling courts handled some, etc.—there is, in principle, no need for any government at all, any formally integrated, homogeneously operating law courts, appellate courts, etc., etc.

Yet just because millions of people play tennis without the benefit of a referee, it doesn't follow that when the stakes are high referees aren't needed.

Of course, this analogy is just that, an analogy. And as such, it is not identical to the case of a legal system administered by a government since such an agency would have to have the power to issue arrest warrants, send out the police to arrest suspects, etc., whereas in sports

It has also been argued that a legal system is essentially different from other kinds of provisions because (a) it involves the use of force against those who haven't authorised this use (alleged criminals); (b) there is a need for law prior to market transactions, so law itself is in a different category (politics versus economics), and (c) one should not be a judge in one's own case (vis-à-vis self-defense in complex cases).

It is my contention that, contrary to appearances, the two camps of libertarians aren't real opponents but emphasise different issues, ones regarding which a common ground (and system of justice) can be found.

What is Government?

Government is, rather broadly put, a legal service institution the actions or policies of which are backed by allegedly justified physical force and its threat. Since it is just the definition of government that's in dispute in this discussion, I will only give this rough characterisation rather than a formal definition for the time being.

Government has been rejected by anarcho-libertarians on grounds that its very nature involves fundamental injustices (such as taxation or exclusive legal jurisdiction).[13] Legal services consist of enforcing laws, and laws are supposed to uphold justice. If, as libertarians hold, justice consists of respecting and protecting individual rights, then legal services involve the adjudication of disputes about rights violations, overseeing conviction of criminals, and providing for some of the police protection and military defense for people who live within the relevant jurisdiction, all in the effort to give freely consented-to protection to these rights.

Rights are the objective criteria by which just adjudication is to be conducted, so far, at least, as libertarians understand them. This, as they tell it, fulfils the requirement of a civilised legal system whereby the rule of law rather than of (the will of) human beings (as rulers) is followed. So government is criticised by libertarian anarchists because it is considered impossible for it to pursue and achieve justice without also breaching it.

If the provision of legal services is to be just, the argument goes, not only must government enjoy the full consent of the governed (which may be explicit or, some have argued, implicit—based not only on overt but tacit agreement implied by one's actions[14]) but refrain from establishing a monopoly in the provisions of its

---

there would be no need for such organised legal machinery unless players became unruly, in which case the referees would call in the law.

13 Rothbard discusses the issue in *The Ethics of Liberty* (Atlantic-Highlands, NJ: Humanities Press, 1982), pp. 162-63. For his definition, see p. 171, where he says, "The State may therefore be defined as that organisation which possesses either or both (in actual fact, almost always both) of the following characteristics: (a) it acquires its revenue by physical coercion (taxation); and (b) it achieves a compulsory monopoly of force and of ultimate decision-making power over a given territorial area."

14 Arguably though, everyone's consent may not be needed. (See, op. cit., Barnett, *Restoring the Lost Constitution.*) Consider this: I hire a bodyguard who consents to become my defender against all aggressors. Some person then attacks me and my bodyguard defends

services. This second reason for why government is coercive by its very nature is often explained by reference to Max Weber's definition of it: "A state is defined by the specific means peculiar to it, the use of physical force. The state is a human community that successfully claims the monopoly of the legitimate use of physical force within a given territory. Politics, then, means striving to share power or striving to influence the distribution of power, either among states or among groups within a state."[15] In short, government is supposedly an imposed monopoly.

Notice, however, that Weber talks here of the state as a human community in the fashion of Hegel, Marx, Green, and Bosanquet rather than of classical liberals such as Locke, Mill or Spencer. Still, many do make use of this conception of the state to characterise government as an organisation that monopolises the use of force within some geographic area and raises its revenue through coercive taxation.[16] Tyler Cowen gives a slightly different definition of government or state, characterising it by "finance through taxation, claim of sovereignty, ultimate decision-making authority, and prohibitions on competitive entry."[17] And John Hasnas tells us that "What appears to be essential for an organisation to be considered a state is that it monopolises the basic policing, rule-making, and adjudicative functions in an identifiable area and funds these functions through taxation."[18]

What is of concern to me here is not the nature of the state as it is closely linked to Hegel's or Marx's ideas—as a holistic, organic community of human beings—but the nature of government, which is the institution that may be established to provide legal services for human communities. As the United States Declaration of Independence refers to it, such "governments are instituted among men, deriving their just powers from the consent of the governed." Here government is not a state,

---

me from this attack, a course of conduct that may become violent toward the aggressor. Now, does it matter that the aggressor did not give consent to my bodyguard defending me? No. If you like, the aggressor, in effect, gives consent by taking an action that has as its natural, rationally-to-be-expected result, my defending myself either personally or through an agent. (See, for more, Tibor R. Machan, *Individuals and Their Rights* [LaSalle, IL: Open Court Publishing Co., Inc., 1989, especially Chapter 7, "Individualism and Political Authority.") So, *does it matter that a government that acts purely defensively isn't consented to by, say, criminals or foreign aggressors?* This would be a government that does not coercively collect taxes or such, so consent would only be relevant to its getting hired and being paid freely, voluntarily, by those whom it defends. Payment could be in the form of premiums, as with insurance, or per service, as with some attorney or dentist fees, or bundled with prices for various goods and services, as with payments for newspapers that also provide magazines on Sundays. For dealing with the free rider problem, see note 22.

15 Max Weber, *Economy and Society: An Outline of Interpretive Sociology* (1978), p. 56.

16 See, e.g., Murray N. Rothbard, *For a New Liberty* 49-50 (1973); John Hospers, "What Libertarianism is," in *Liberty for the 21st Century* 14 (Tibor R. Machan & Douglas B. Rasmussen, eds., 1995); David Boaz, *Libertarianism* 187 (1997); Robert Paul Wolff, *In Defense of Anarchism* 1 (1970); Ludwig von Mises, *Liberalism in the Classical Tradition* 35 (1985).

17 Tyler Cowen, *Law as a Public Good* 8 Economics and Philosophy 249, 250 (1992).

18 John Hasnas, "Some Reflections on the Minimal State" (unpublished MS).

meaning a human community of a certain type, but an institution *within such a community*.

The libertarian controversy concerns whether governments need to be in violation of basic individual rights or might they exist and function without doing violence to those rights. And that is my concern here as well.

In the broad field of political theory—apart from the various schools that defend various configurations of human politics—there is much controversy about the scope of legal services or governments. Some, as already noted, would include the provision of a wide set of goods and services apart from the protection of individual, negative human rights. Indeed, some deny that such rights exist and conceive of government in a pro-active, affirmative mode, whereby the laws mandate conduct that produces goods and services for various segments of the citizenry. Indeed, some argue that government comes before any rights, government being the grantor of rights, not their protector.[19]

Others, especially in the classical liberal political tradition, see the protection of individual rights as the sole service that a properly conceived government or legal order provides. It is "to secure these rights" that governments with just powers are established. And among libertarians there is a further, more specialised controversy, namely, about whether within some region of inhabitation only one or several governments or providers of legal services might properly or justly exist.[20]

So, to begin with, must there be an insidious, rights-violating monopoly afoot when legal services are being delivered by governments? Or might government not be a monopoly at all or one of the benign sort that we find in the provisions of all goods and services: even a barber shop has a monopoly, at the exact place where it is located, as does a grocery store, an amusement park, an apartment complex, a gated housing community or a department store? Or, is it a prominent monopoly that happens to have emerged without anyone having forcibly imposed it?[21]

In certain cases of providing goods and services no monopoly of even the former, benign sort, is involved, as in the purchase of, as already noted, take-out pizzas. One need not go anywhere to get the benefit of competing providers, only make a phone call to different establishments. Trash pickup is also provided in this fashion, as is mail delivery and satellite television reception. Must a provider of legal services be like this in order to avoid being coercive as libertarian anarchists charge it is?

---

19 See, Cass Sunstein and Stephen Holmes, *The Cost of Rights* (New York: W.W. Norton, 1999) and Liam Murphy and Thomas Nagel, *The Myth of Ownership* (New York: Oxford University Press, 2002).

20 For a succinct account of the matter, see Aeon Skoble, "The Anarchism Controversy," in Tibor R. Machan and Douglas B. Rasmussen, eds., *Liberty for the 21st Century* (Lanham, MD: Rowman and Littlefield, 1995), pp. 77-109.

21 This is the kind of monopoly that Robert Nozick envisions as the dominant legal authority. See, Nozick, op. cit., *Anarchy, State, and Utopia*, p. 109.

May Governments Exist?

I have in the past argued that governments may serve communities without any degree of coercion, involving no coercive monopolies.[22] Jack Sanders, who argues for a society without government, discusses whether the view proposed by me qualifies as anarchist or archist.[23] He claims that in the position that I hold the concept "government" is used idiosyncratically since it proposes that one can have such an institution without any measure of coercion. Sanders argues that history shows that no government has ever existed that did not engage in extensive coercive activities.

One response to this point[24] is that the concept of "government," not unlike that of "marriage," is rarely—perhaps never—instantiated flawlessly, fully consistently. These are both normative concepts and while it is important to learn whether instantiating them is realistically *possible*, it is not always decisive that they are rarely or even never fully or perfectly instantiated. So the *history* of governmental conduct is not decisive as to the *nature and morality* of government, any more than the history of actual marriages is decisive as to whether marriages can exist *as they ought to*, whether as usually conceived they could be a proper arrangement between couples.

Another, perhaps more direct, response, hinted at earlier here, is that in the relevant tradition, namely, classical liberal political theory, the concept "government" is used in a way that suggests that it has been held to be compatible with at least nearly-full respect for individual rights. John Locke, for example, not only deemed government compatible with such respect but believed it was needed to provide effective protection of such rights.[25] And the U. S. Declaration of Independence, as already noted, sketches a characterisation of the function of government that also suggests such compatibility. And, more recently, Ayn Rand and her students have argued that government *can* exist without taxation, a practice that Murray Rothbard and others have seen as one that is decisively anti-libertarian.[26]

It also bears noting that anarchist libertarians are very different from the usual type of anarchists since they defend various arrangements in society that serve the sole purpose of protecting individual rights, calling these "defense agencies," "protection agencies," "justice services," or whatever.[27]

---

22 See, Tibor R. Machan, "Dissolving the Problem of Public Goods, Financing Government Without Coercive Measures," in Tibor R. Machan, ed., *The Libertarian Reader* (Lanham, MD: Rowman & Littlefield, 1982). I have also advanced some points in support of this position in op. cit., Machan, *Individuals and Their Rights*.

23 Jack Sanders, "The State of Statelessness," in Jack Sanders and Jan Narveson, eds., *For and Against the State* (Lanham, MD: Rowman and Littlefield, 1996), p. 286.

24 See, op. cit., Machan, "Individualism and Political Authority."

25 For a discussion of Locke and anarchism, see Stuart D. Warner, "Anarchical Snares: A Reading of Locke's Second Treatise," *Reason Papers*, No. 14 (Spring, 1989), pp. 1-24.

26 Supra note 7. I am not maintaining, however, that Locke or the American Founders were even minarchist libertarians. My point pertains to the logic of their position.

27 Murray N. Rothbard, Morris and Linda Tannehill, Bruce Benson, Walter Block and most other recent or contemporary libertarian anarchists favor such—what they regard as market-based—approaches to defending individual rights. See, as a seminal statement of this

David Kelley notes one matter, mentioned at the outset of this discussion, which anarcho-libertarians rarely discuss.[28] It is that market institutions, such as corporations, partnerships, private businesses and even plain, ordinary one shot trade, presuppose a background of some kind of law enforcement, including protection of property rights and the integrity of contracts. The category of such enforcement would appear to have to be different from the provisions of other goods and services. J. Roger Lee has also raised this issue, in terms of the charge that anarcho-libertarians are committing a philosophical *category mistake* as they attempt to reduce all politics to economics. This may be symptomatic of some economic approaches to understanding human (social) life.[29]

It might be argued, of course, that "politics" is a category that's inherently coercive and thus inherently incompatible with justice. The idea here is that, all along, the belief that human community life requires politics has rested on a misunderstanding, namely, that the use of initiated force is sometimes proper. Anarcho-libertarians see ample evidence for this belief among out and out statists and tend to think that minarchist libertarians simply haven't gone far enough in distancing themselves from this very bad habit of associating community life with necessary coercion.

However, the anarchists who hold this view have got this wrong: the distinctive aspects of politics in part concern, for minarchist libertarians, *the need for using force against unwilling persons* who have, if you will, *implicitly asked for it by way of their criminal conduct*. It is not that politics rests on *the acceptance of initiated force* as sometimes justified but on *the need to cope with (defend and retaliate against, and adjudicate disputes involving) such force* in special, appropriate ways (suggested by the concept of *due process* in criminal law enforcement). Unlike addressing market interactions, politics, at its base, addresses the proper organisation of dealing with involuntary or coerced human interactions—crimes, wars, and other forms of rights violation (or violence, for short).

To this libertarian anarchists have replied that even today there are arbitration agencies that carry on with the provision of legal services, so clearly it must be possible to do so. However, all such agencies are still subject to legal scrutiny by governments if their customers file complaints against them. They can be sued in regular courts.[30]

It might also be of concern here that with the reduction of all politics to commercial enterprises the very idea of limited government—that is, the limiting of the providers of rights protection and adjudication to the tasks aiming for this goal—will be impossible. After all, why should an ordinary business enterprise not expand its activities, perhaps to providing social security services, unemployment

---

view, Morris and Linda Tannehill, *Liberty Via the Market* (Self-published, 1969) and *Market for Liberty* (Lansing, MI: 1970; New York: Laissez-Faire Books, 1993). For a more recent exposition of this view, see, op. cit., Benson, *The Enterprise of Law*. Cf., Tibor R. Machan, "Market for Liberty Reviewed," *Reason*, March, 1971, pp. 13-17.

28 David Kelley, "The Necessity of Government," *The Freeman 24* (April, 1974).

29 See, for a recent example, Eric A. Posner, *Law and Social Norms* (Cambridge, MA: Harvard University Press, 2000).

30 See, note 12, above.

compensation, and wildlife preservation, old age security, the building of dams, etc.? Such an enterprise might do this even if no profit is involved, provided other of its provisions garner a large enough profit.

Thus Sander's claim, that the concept of government proposed by me, both here and elsewhere, is idiosyncratic, is open to serious doubt.

What is a Monopoly of the Legal Use of Force?

The question over which there is perhaps the greatest controversy among those who want legal services provided solely for the protection of individual (and, of course, derivative, including contractually instituted) rights, is whether governments need to be a *coercive* monopoly—as is, say, the US post office's first-class division—rather than a benign monopoly, like that of a privately owned apartment house or an air carrier (once airborne).

In order for the US postal service to retain all first-class mail service, a legal authority must prohibit anyone from offering this service for sale. This monopoly, then—of the USPS—is indeed coercive.

A monopoly, as I have said, is not coercive if it exists by virtue of overwhelming customer support—for example, Microsoft's dominance in the software industry may well not be coercive although it could reach the level of a monopoly, namely, a firm that's the sole provider of the relevant goods and services.[31]

A privately owned apartment house is a *de facto* monopoly in the same way as any particular ownership constitutes such a monopoly, especially to someone else who wants just that item but cannot have it since it is now owned by another. The owners may exclude those they do not wish to deal with from utilising the provisions, just as anyone may set terms of use or non-use for others, by, say, evicting renters. As to monopolies in provision of services, a passenger air carrier becomes a *de facto* monopoly between ports of embarkation and disembarkation. Flying American Airlines from LA to NY, one has no access to competitors *en route* over, say, Kansas.[32]

---

31 Max Weber's definition of "the State" does not specify coercive or non-coercive monopoly as characteristic of states or governments. Even Hasnas claims of the state only "that it monopolizes the basic policing, rule-making, and adjudicative functions in an identifiable area." This is ambiguous: the issue that is crucial is *how* it comes to monopolise these functions, coercively or by the consent of those to whom they are provided. Only when he adds taxation to the definition of the state or government does the coercive nature of such an institution become evident. But that is begging the question no less so than did Murray N. Rothbard when he made taxation a defining element of government.

32 It is instructive to note that dealing with travel providers is often frustrating in nearly identical ways to dealing with government agencies; once one is on board or has signed up, changing carriers is very cumbersome and given one's plans, nearly impossible and financially prohibitive. Those providing the service seem to be well aware of this, given how they tend to conduct themselves toward their customers. Not in all cases, of course. One can disembark from a London cab and find another easily enough, although doing the same from one hired to transport one to some remote region of the city (let alone some village in New Mexico)

In short, some domains and some service providers, given the nature of the dominion or service, may only appear to be coercively monopolistic. However, since customers are aware of this and prior to entering the exchange have every chance of seeking out actual or potential competitors (who have every chance, in turn, to enter the market), the apparent coercive monopoly is not in fact such even if and when it is the sole provider of the service for a long period of time. Arguably, then, becoming a citizen of a country can amount to consenting to an unusually long-term securing of rights protection from a given government that provides services in a reasonably homogeneous region so as to make access to citizen-clients possible, convenient, and swift.

Surely the service envisioned to be provided by so called (non-coercive) legal service agencies—as well as by governments envisioned to only protect individual rights by operating within the terms of such rights—appears to have some of the characteristics of services provided via coercive monopolies. Citizenship, as noted above, is a condition that runs over the long term. One of its great benefits is, indeed, that it offers a substantial measure of predictability and objectivity—that is, the rule of law.

But is not one of the signs of non-coercive monopolies that potential competitors are not legally excluded, prohibited from entry into the market? Can there be *bona fide* competition among governments—for citizens, businesses and such—so that despite retaining some characteristics that resemble those of coercive monopolies, they are in fact non-coercive? Governments of this only apparently monopolistic type would be unlike postal monopolies in first-class mail provision but like air carriers between ports of embarkation and disembarkation?

Why Any Kind of Monopoly at All?

There are those who challenge this by maintaining that no such, even apparent, monopoly is needed for the provision of legal services. That is, one could simultaneously gain those services from competing agents—shop for them on the model of shopping for home-delivered pizzas or plumbing services. The idea is that one could gain legal service in, say, a court from one agency but then decide, no, that's not an agency one likes and so, without having to change location, gain the service by simply subscribing to another legal agency or enterprise (or, in plainer language, up and change one's citizenship without having to move).

One might put the question another way: Could there be legal service provisions without countries? Could legal service provisions overlap, be delivered to citizens without their having to move and even be divided whereby some agency offers police service, another prisons, and yet another adjudication? Or is this impossible along lines that it is impossible that during a flight from LA to NY one could enjoy the benefits of both competent service and instant change of the service provider? Perhaps even the separation of distinct parts may not work, just as it wouldn't work

---

may be far less manageable. There is also the analogy of being married and trying to be divorced—the process can be excruciatingly difficult. Or switching life insurance and related long-term coverage providers.

for a patient in a hospital to get a bed from one agency, blood tests from another and nursing from yet another, without some common provider that coordinates it all?

Is then Government Necessarily Coercive?

Arguably, the anarchists among those who would limit legal services to individual rights protection believe that government *cannot* be justified in terms invoking the principles of individual (negative) rights. The idea is that by excluding alternative providers, a government would practice restraint of free trade. It is as if one pizza delivery service were to prevent others from reaching the same customers.

Minarchists dispute that governments must be coercive. This is so even though they hold that governments would naturally govern (and ought to) within a homogeneous region, in a given jurisdiction (or country). They even admit that throughout history governments that have had jurisdiction over homogeneous regions have been coercive, to a greater and lesser extent. But they contend that this isn't unavoidable or necessary.

Even by the reconstituted—non-Hegelian—conception of Weberian government, government is only a monopoly, not a *coercive* monopoly. Weber said that government "successfully claims the monopoly of the legitimate use of physical force within a given territory." This does not imply that such a successful claim must itself issue in a legal or coercively maintained monopoly. It is a monopoly, of course, but not necessarily a coercive one.

Does libertarian anarchism, as Kelley has argued, presuppose the existence, recording and protection of private property rights—that is, government? If so, then before there can be a market, there must be law and its enforcement. If, however, law and its enforcement are themselves subject to trade and exchange, this puts the cart before the horse.

Of course, law and its enforcement presuppose a market, as well. To hire those who guard and enforce the law, there must at least be a labor market. All of the tools of law and its enforcement need to be produced and sold to those who will make professional use of it. Thus, again, markets must come before law and its enforcement.

Yet it is arguable that the two, law and its enforcement and trade or exchange emerge side by side, simultaneously as far as their chronology is concerned. Conceptually, however, *there must be some idea of the right of ownership and its institutional recognition and protection prior to the development of market exchanges*. What Rasmussen and Den Uyl call the meta-normative framework of law and law enforcement is presupposed by market exchange.

It is, then, not a chronological priority of law and order but its conceptual priority that is at issue. For libertarian, free market anarchists an extensive and complex market system is part and parcel of civilised society. And they cannot have that in a purely anarchist community in which everything is up for sale, including law and order. These must have a security, at least conceptually if not actually, prior to the commencement of market transactions.

They indeed do, even as libertarian anarchists see matters, since they have not given up law and order but only the sort of law and order that is imposed upon citizens without their consent. If libertarian anarchists claim that they want law and order, wherein private property rights, contracts, and the basic criminal law are secured, they want what amounts to a free government roughly in the classical liberal tradition minus some of its coercive elements (e.g., taxation).

The Morality of Self-Defense

We need now to advance this examination by noting that arguably human beings *ought to* defend themselves against criminals and foreign aggressors. This is a view not shared by old-fashioned anarchists, those who reject all law enforcement. As a matter of ethics, this seems to be uncontroversial among those involved in the debate about the nature of limited government or legal services. Furthermore, if the division of labor is a sound principle, not everyone ought to do his own defending—it is quite complicated to do so, with due process constraints, especially. We ought, instead, to employ specialists in law enforcement and adjudication.

Government could be construed to be at least a would-be specialist in the professional of securing justice—just as the dentist is a specialist in securing dental health. The significant difference is that government is, at least in complex communities, a pre-market institution. It is required for the maintenance, elaboration and protection of individual, including private property, rights.

A Certain Kind of Competition

What is in dispute is whether the competition that libertarians see as natural in the delivery of most if not all services could be obtained in the provision of legal systems while the traditional geographical homogeneity of countries is retained. Or would such competition or non-exclusion make room for overlapping—layers of Swiss-cheese type—legal jurisdictions. Would it not then be a violation of individual rights to establish and maintain governments that aren't competing *within a given geographical region*, akin to how different pizza delivery providers compete in the same neighborhood?[33]

The answer that non-anarchists would be inclined to give is that there can be competition between governments just as there can be competition between different apartment houses and gated communities—or airlines *while in flight*—but not the

---

33 There are some cases of Swiss-cheese type countries that might be pointed to as quite peaceful and operational, such as Baarle-Nassau/Baarle-Hertog. History has left us here with a territory composed of two municipal jurisdictions. The shape of this realm is unique: it belongs, in part to Holland and in part to Belgium. The people until recently have been quite comfortable with the situation, even though it raises so many complicated and difficult problems that even the most brilliant jurists are puzzled. See, for more on this, http://wings.buffalo.edu/philosophy/faculty/smith/baarle.htm. Arguably this shows their viability, workability and even survivability, although not necessarily their superior efficiency for purposes of administering a system of just criminal law. See note 11 above.

kind that takes place within the same territory, as is the case with pizza delivery services. But one could not have some crucial legal services—mostly involving the criminal law—provided in the fashion of pizza deliveries.

This answer disputes the viability, at least until the availability of transporter type machines familiar from *Star Trek*, of crisscrossing jurisdictions in criminal law, that is, the predominantly Swiss-cheese conception of governments. It is arguable that such a way of providing legal services runs the serious risk of generating *in principle irresolvable legal conflicts*.

As noted above, though, libertarian anarchists object by noting that if the competition is not within the same area, analogous to the pizza delivery business, then one is coerced to take one's legal "business" elsewhere, which would be a violation of basic rights. They also claim that there is no risk of accused or convicted criminals switching jurisdictions mid-way through legal proceedings because it would not pay, in the long run, for courts in adjacent or even remote jurisdictions, to go against the judgments of competing courts.

This analysis is, I believe, mistaken. It rests on the (economic?) assumption of the universally agreed to utility of common standards in market services. Indeed, in free markets providers do often converge on the standards they deploy for their customers, so that after the initial conflict between, for example, different VCR services, the market eventually settled for one over the other.

Justice, however, is not a utilitarian but rights based objective, aiming at settling disputes *in individual cases*, not over the long run. Even if in time the various courts would see the utility of adhering to common standards, at any given time they may well not do so, and this would be an obstacle to justice that is supposed to be swift and efficient *for individual citizens*.

Furthermore, to reiterate, one needs to consider that although pizza delivery does occur within the same territory, competing dentists and even department stores do so while occupying at least slightly different localities. Even at a mall or the traditional market place, competition occurs among those who occupy different locations, so reaching out to a new provider involves some measure of cost. One needs time to move from, say, *The Gap* to *Abercrombie & Fitch*, from *Sears* to *J. C. Penney's*, or from a *Shell* to an *Exxon* gas station—one cannot have it all brought to one's doorstep where one can stay put and just point and thereby obtain different goods.

Yet it could be replied to this that in fact all those providers could compete in the fashion of pizza delivery providers. With the proliferation of on-line merchandising this has become a familiar process: Nearly everything is brought to the stationary customer. So it is not always necessary for customers to go to providers—they can stay at home or stationary somewhere else. And anarchist envisions the same as far as legal services are concerned.

However, in response to this, arguably the delivery system itself benefits from the un-libertarian coercive monopoly status of roads, something that a completely free society would not have available. Governments, however—or, as libertarian anarchists call their legal systems, "justice services" or "defense agencies"—require a homogeneous sphere of jurisdiction, if only because their customers would ordinarily live and work in different localities. To come together for at least some of the usual legal services, the legal authority or government would have to be stationary, not the customers.

Yet—and this is a crucial point in the attempt to reach a rapprochement between minarchist and anarchist libertarians—none of the above considerations preclude a certain kind of competition among governments. Even now, in a roughly analogous circumstance, New Jersey competes with New York, Holland with Belgium, or Denmark with Norway and Sweden, and so forth, in the task of providing persons with legal services, attracting business firms, citizens, and so on to where their respective governments are located. This suggests that there could be—indeed, is already—competition among stationary governments in the sense that once one finds the services provided by one of them unsatisfactory,[34] one can move to the jurisdictional region of another analogously to moving from one apartment house to another.

Thus it seems that both the traditional conception of a homogeneous country and free and open competition could be secured, satisfying the demands of minarchists and anarchists among libertarians.

It has always been my impression that there is some misunderstanding about this matter among supporters of the free society—they need not be divided on it; so long as the commitment to respecting individual rights is unwavering, a resolution between the anarchists and minarchists, along lines sketched above, makes good sense.

Could Law be just Another Business?

Now I wish briefly to turn to a subdivision of the argument between minarchist and anarchist libertarians, namely, the issue of whether law ought to be an enterprise, just as other enterprises that operate in the market place.

Among those who have been studying the structure of a free legal system there are several who model the nature of all law on enterprise. Bruce Benson's aforementioned book, *The Enterprise of Law*, stands out as a clear example. The subtitle of Benson's book, "Justice without the State," provides a clue to the difficulty with the idea of law as enterprise. The alternative Benson poses is that between freedom of enterprise and statism. Others seem also to have posed this choice, yet there is a third option, namely, free enterprise within the framework of a system of legal administration that identifies and protects freedom rights.[35]

As noted already, the concept "state" is a complex one in political and legal theory but usually it means a society conceived as an organic whole. Hegel, Marx, Green, and Bernard Bosanquet all worked with such a meaning of "state," as do many others who advocate a more or less powerful authoritarian political system.

---

34 By "unsatisfactory" I am not here talking of tyrannical or oppressive, merely of less than competent, sloppy, sluggish, etc., governments that provide only the services that governments ought to provide.

35 See, Randy Barnett, *The Structure of Liberty* (London: Oxford University Press, 1998), especially Part III, where Barnett explores the liabilities he associates with the minarchist position. But see, also, op. cit., Barnett, *Restoring the Lost Constitution*.

Indeed, Bosanquet might even be said to argue for a minimal *state*, given the context of his discussions and arguments with the British socialists and social democrats. (He, for example, opposed the welfare programs of the state in part on the ground that they are demoralising. He agreed that government couldn't make people morally good, etc.[36])

Despite some (relatively) minimal-statists in the history of political theory, the concept that seems to be the best candidate for a more benign substitute without losing certain distinctive political components is not "enterprise" but "politics." There are some fairly clear-cut reasons why the enterprise model of law has problems.

First, enterprises presuppose property rights. In order to invest, trade, hire, fire, contract and what enterprises as such are likely to do, those who embark upon an enterprise must have their right to private property and freedom of trade/contract *clearly (enough) defined and well (enough) protected* so as to carry on with their tasks. And the definition and protection of private property and related rights within a complex society can require objective law and its impartial maintenance and enforcement, as well as the closure for cases of dispute resolution and criminal prosecution. While the realm of politics may not be capable of yielding fully objective results, even by way of the judiciary of a free society, nor produce fully impartial enforcement of the law, it is arguably not explicitly committed to serving various private interests that—quite rightly and justifiably—prevent such objectivity and impartiality.[37]

There is then a serious threat of an institutional infinite regress if law itself is understood as just one more form of enterprise. There is your barbershop, your auto factory, farm, insurance agency, and brokerage firm and next on the block is your adjudicating institution. Whereas with the others there can be several on the same block, almost literally, with the adjudicating agency several different ones serving the same community will pose problems. Here is a hypothetical troubling example:

Suppose one justice agency is hired by the barbershop, another by the factory and a third by the insurance firm. And suppose some of these come into legal dispute among themselves, criminal or civil. How is the adjudication to ensue? Will the plaintiff be able to secure the presence of the defendant in the same courtroom? Not if the defendant refuses to deal with the same adjudicating agency as the plaintiff.

---

36 Bernard Bosanquet, *The Philosophical Theory of the State* (London: Macmillan and Co., Ltd.; New York: The Macmillan company, 1899).

37 For why the goal of objectivity and impartiality is thought to be impossible to achieve, see James M. Buchanan and Gordon Tullock, *The Calculus of Consent, Logical Foundations of Constitutional Democracy* (Ann Arbor, University of Michigan Press, 1962), the work that advanced the theory of public choice in line with which public servants are no less utility maximising than are market agents.

I dispute that this is a necessary feature of public service in *any* type of political order. It is, of course, typical behavior of public servants in what economists call a "rent seeking" welfare state. However, in a free, libertarian government such servants may well carry out their oath of office to defend the constitution because the constitution does not sanction special interest legislation and regulation. For more on this, see Tibor R. Machan, *Private Rights and Public Illusions* (New Brunswick, NJ: Transaction Books, 1995).

More importantly, suppose there is a dispute between the adjudicating agency and some other enterprise regarding contract violation or private property rights (titles, deeds, etc.). Who will adjudicate this dispute? And how will jurisdiction over the parties be determined?

Benson & Co. have some answers to these questions, mainly along lines of interagency contractual agreements. This solution resembles international law. In the international arena we have no binding court of last resort, yet often the World Court and similar bodies function quite successfully as adjudicators of disputes between parties with different citizenship and, indeed, between different countries. Why so? Because there are various motivations that impel the parties to come to a resolution, usually involving business disputes.

The International Model: Problems and Possibilities

There are also some serious problems with the international adjudication process, especially where criminal law is concerned. Here compliance is not so readily come by. Different countries hold different standards of justice and reciprocity is often resisted. When an international court indicted Yugoslavia's past president, Slobodan Milosevic, compliance wasn't initially forthcoming because the government of Yugoslavia did not then grant the authority of the court, not at least within its jurisdiction. When the presence of ex-Chilean dictator Augusto Pinochet in the Spanish courts was sought, he had to be captured in England where he went for medical treatment. Chile did not cooperate with the Spanish authorities. And when Bertrand Russell and Jean-Paul Sartre established the international court in which the United States of America was indicted and convicted of war crimes in Vietnam, the US government refused to respond. Indeed, in our day the US government objects to any world court overriding its legal system's final authority.

And these are only the more visible cases. Thousands of others where international cooperation in criminal adjudication is absent understandably go unnoticed. Those, I think, may be deemed failures of the enterprise of law or at least the model of law as a sort of competitive enterprise.

On the other hand, one can embrace the enterprise model with some modifications that will leave intact the idea that systems of adjudication need to be broadly integrated in order for them to be functional. If we consider, say, the USA, Canada, Mexico, New Zealand, Australia, Japan and all other countries as forums of dispute-adjudication, the possibility of changing one's residence or citizenship affords one something akin to benefiting from competition. Even within countries with a substantial federalist political organisation there is the opportunity for benefiting from competition. New York versus New Jersey, Pennsylvania, and so on, each a state of the USA, all compete for customers of their adjudication services. Certainly we see such competition functioning vis-à-vis taxation, which in this context could be viewed as court fees. They vary and parties to potential disputes will shop to find the most efficient process at the lowest cost.

In this scenario, however, the forums wherein adjudication can proceed are large habitations, with thousands or millions of potential disputants signed up within the same homogeneous system. They are usually committed fairly long term and may leave only if they have a clean record and no adjudication pending that involves them. Moreover, within the system various layers of authority operate, so that the appeal process is integrated and there is in principle a court of last resort.

In this sense adjudication service resembles some other business enterprises wherein one signs up for the long haul. Insurance services are like this, as are apartment rentals, car leasing and, yes, marriages. Midway through the duration of the long-term contract the option to exit does not exist or exists only at great cost. And this is because the very idea underlying these kinds of relationships, between customers and service providers or trading partners, is that reliable, ongoing and predictable arrangements are of benefit to all of the parties.

Is Law Enterprise or Not?

So in one sense the idea of the enterprise of law (meaning a business, not just an endeavor) is a mistake—if it is modeled on the shopping mall, where one can conduct trade fast and furious and switch trading partners without much loss—or on pizza delivery, where one need but call for the service and it'll be provided for a price to one's own location.

In another sense, however, law that involves enterprise is already the norm. Different legal jurisdictions are already offering different services and so there exists competition. Sadly, of course, much of the competition is between adjudicating agencies that offer not just different levels of efficiency and competence but, actually, fundamentally different goods. Some are in the business of providing what is pretty close to a just adjudicative and punitive service, while others are offering subjective, arbitrary decisions and services (i.e., what's on the shelves of welfare states). But we can easily imagine this to be different, so that the competition involved ensues among agencies that could well all be limited to aim for just resolutions of conflicts.

To reduce all human institutions to enterprises runs the same risks as any other type of artificial reductionism; it suppresses significant elements of what is being reduced. Governments—and, indeed, defense agencies, justice agencies or what have you—are political institutions. They pertain to the ancient human search for the right answer to the question, "How should we organise our human communities as such?" The question doesn't concern commerce but the nature of what Aristotle called the *polis*, the organised human community.

What Ought Versus What May be Expected to be

Few libertarians of any variety believe that in some near future a fully free society will materialise anywhere around the globe. Just as those who believe in marriage do not think perfectly good marriages are very likely, so libertarians do not hold that fully free countries are very likely. But neither are these utopians, ones who believe their idea is an impossible ideal.

A risk with advocating anarchist libertarianism is that its misleading language, namely, advocating "societies without governments," will sound utopian, meaning impossible, so much so that the more reasonable version, minarchism, will also be rejected. Libertarian societies are far from impossible, even if they are unlikely to come about because so many people thinking and acting properly about political matters is improbable.

If I am right and anarchist and minarchist libertarianism is nearly the same thing, with but the precise contours of jurisdiction posing an obstacle to their full reconciliation, those on both sides of the debate can get down to business and work in support of a libertarian country, no qualifiers necessary.

A Critic Answered

Walter Block has penned a response[38] to my paper in which I argue that there isn't much more than a verbal difference between limited government (minarchist) and defense-insurance agency (anarchist) libertarians. The gist of my case is that the anarchists' defense-insurance agencies or justice services are a version of non-coercive governments.[39] Admittedly such governments are rare but they have existed in human history and could exist where there is the will to establish them.

Block disputes my thesis for one reason: He defines government as necessarily coercive. He follows Murray N. Rothbard here, saying that "One sufficient and arguably necessary condition [for something being a government] is taxation" (p. 3), although he does not argue for this definition.[40] To simply assert this definition of "government" is unavailable to Block since the concept "government," as are many other concepts—e.g., liberty, love, marriage, law, justice, human being—is essentially contestable.[41] There are, in other words, ongoing debates about the right definition of these concepts and just to assert that one definition is arguably sound while the others are all misguided is itself misguided. Why are we to accept that the concept "government" necessarily implies coercion (e.g., taxation)? That most governments have been coercive is no more a defense of this position, as already noted, than that widespread adultery defines "marriage" necessarily implies adultery because

---

38 Walter Block, "Anarchism and Minarchism; No Rapprochement Possible: Reply to Tibor Machan," *Journal of Libertarian Studies* JLS 21, no. 1 (Spring, 2007), pp. 61–90.

39 In contemporary political philosophy the most direct advocacy of this view may be found in the volume *Society Without Government*, published by Arno Press and *The New York Times*, which contains Morris and Linda Tannehill, *The Market for Liberty* (1970) and Jarret B. Wollstein, *Society Without Coercion* (1969). Earlier there was Morris and Linda Tannehill, *Liberty Via the Market* (Self-published, 1969). See, also, Richard and Ernestine Perkens, *Precondition for Peace and Prosperity: Rational Anarchy* (1971). For several statements of classical anarchism, see Robert Hoffman, ed., *Anarchism* (New York: Atherton Press, 1970). For early discussions of mine, see Tibor R. Machan, "A Note on Neff's Anarchism." *Reason*, Vol. 2, no. 10 (January, 1971), and "Market for Liberty Reviewed," *Reason*, Vol. 2, No. 12 (March, 1971).

40 "Arguably" means that "a statement is open to dispute but could be defended in an argument." I assume he believes his definition could be defended but does not in fact defend it.

41 http://www.strike-the-root.com/4/machan/machan44.html

most marriages throughout human history have involved adultery or that the concept "game" necessarily implies competition because most games are competitive. Quite possibly other aspects of government are part of its definition.

Here is how I see the issue of how to define government: When classical liberals began to reexamine the nature of human community relations and started to undercut the view that such relations must involved the coercive ruler and the passively ruled—with government representing the rulers and the rest the ruled—this signaled the gradual emergence of a conception of government that began to preclude coercion. Locke already characterised government as concerned primarily with securing our natural rights, something the American Founders also accepted as explaining the existence of government with just powers (in the Declaration of Independence).

Eventually libertarians, those who took classical libertarianism to its proper conclusion, developed a concept of government that involved no coercion at all. Some of these libertarians chose to retain the term "government" for the institution that would maintain law and order in society, others came up with new terms such as "defense-insurance agency." But both meant the same thing, namely, legal authorities who would proceed to establish, maintain, and uphold justice via a legal order without ever officially using coercive force.[42]

Walter Block—along with several other self-described anarcho-libertarians, such as Roderick Long—refuses to accept the above sketch of intellectual history and insists on identifying libertarians who wish to retain the term "government" as advocating some measure of coercion. I, for one, deny that he is correct in this—as would have Ayn Rand, perhaps one of the most effective and influential defenders of a polity that precludes anything but defensive and retaliatory force from its proceedings—whose lead I follow closely enough in this debate—or John Hospers, John Nelson, Robert Nozick and several others. Rand explicitly advocated funding government without coercion, as have I.[43]

Let me now address some of Block's specific points.[44]

First a small matter. Block makes reference to the view that "The essence of libertarianism is private property rights based on homesteading and the non-aggression axiom" (p. 3). Given that he later criticises me for claiming that all libertarians agree with the view that people have unalienable rights, citing a debate about this among some, he should also have noted at this point that several libertarians base their position on different premises and that the so called "non-aggression axiom" is for

---

[42] We have the legal concept of "due process" signaling this idea quite clearly, namely, that *at its best*, government would secure our rights without every violating them. As an aside, I have used "coercion" to mean "force that violates rights," while using "force" to mean "violent means that may or may not be justified." Not all follow this usage, so I am here indicating what I mean by using the expression "coercion or coercive force."

[43] See note 47, below.

[44] Before I do this I wish to object to his repeated use of polemics and hyperbole, as when he characterises my efforts as an "attempt to paper over the differences between right wing anarchism and the classical laissez-faire limited government libertarian position" (p. 2). I am aware that in debates the parties will often stray from substance and deploy terms that have as the central if not exclusive function to emotionally injure opponents. But I believe this temptation is best resisted.

many a *derivative* principle, based on more fundamental norms, and not an axiom at all.⁴⁵

Block asks, rhetorically, "What are the necessary characteristics of government?" and answers it with the claim already cited above, that "One sufficient and arguably necessary condition is taxation" (p. 3).⁴⁶ He doesn't defend this claim but moves on to note the well-known fact that taxation "is a *compulsory* levy" (p. 3). He does say that "Some have denied this," but then mentions those who do not have anything to do with my own position, namely, ones "attempting to model a nation on the basis of a voluntary club" (p. 3). The position that I present, namely, that governments can exist that do not involve taxation—a position that's not idiosyncratically mine at all but is shared by many libertarians—is left, surprisingly, untreated by Block. Instead we read him making the following claim several pages after he offers his definition of government:

> If "government" collects no taxes, and does not use coercion to preclude the competition of other "governments" in "its" geographical area, then it is not a government at all, but rather a private defense-insurance agency, very much a part of the legitimate marketplace (p. 11).

There is no reason to invent the term Block deploys in the above paragraph—I have made that point in several of my earlier discussions, including in my review of *The Market for Liberty*.⁴⁷ Defense-insurance agencies are governments of a certain type.⁴⁸ The only interesting question is whether competition among them can take place within the same geographical area, in what I have characterised the "crisscross" fashion (the way pizza and newspaper delivery services can all operate within the same geographical area) or would have to service citizen-clients within a homogeneous region (the way electrical, water-supply or flood-control services are provided within such regions). If the former, then there can be competing governments (or defense-insurance firms) servicing people in the same region, if the latter then governments (or defense-insurance firms) would have to provide their services in separate regions. Whatever competition were to take place would follow

---

45 For a discussion of axioms, see Tibor R. Machan, "Evidence of Necessary Existence," *Objectivity*, Vol. 1 (Fall, 1992), pp. 31-62. An axiom is a concept or statement the truth of which cannot be denied without also assuming it. For a detailed case for rejecting aggression as a proper means for dealing with human beings, see Tibor R. Machan, *Individuals and Their Rights* (LaSalle, IL: Open Court Publishing Co., Inc., 1989). See, also, Tibor R. Machan, *Ayn Rand* (New York: Peter Lang, 2001), Chapter 2.

46 It is incredible that taxation could be a *sufficient* element of an organisation for it to amount to a government, regardless of the political framework in which the definition emerges. Taxation is the admittedly extortionist means of funding government in most political systems. Yet, *what* is being funded must be independently intelligible without reference to *how* the funding is to be accomplished.

47 Op. cit., Machan, "Market for Liberty Reviewed."

48 Classical anarchists, by the way, would reject the libertarian version of anarchism on the grounds that *no legal authority can escape corruption into despotism*. For more on this, see: http://www.black-rose.com/articles-liz/intro-@.html. See, also, the essays in op cit., Hoffman, ed., *Anarchism*.

the requirements of the services in question. My view is that the latter type of situation is suited to the services provided by a government (or a defense-insurance firm) and that the appropriate form of competition would involve emigration and immigration, as it does even today, although with far less difficulty. (Block keeps insisting that citizens are captives; this is wrong: only in countries such as the one from which I escaped, communist Hungary, is one forbidden to leave.) The situation would resemble the competition evident among gated housing or apartment complexes.

Block brings up an issue I do not address, namely, world government, so since I didn't introduce it I will only mention that I am not in principle against world government any more than Block could be against, using his own terms, a naturally emerging (say, via giant mergers) world-wide defense-insurance agency.[49]

Block goes on to allege that the "second fatal flaw in the limited government libertarian viewpoint concerns secession" (p. 4). Nothing in the limited government position I hold conflicts with secession, so I do not understand why he raises this topic. If one has honored all of one's contracts under the jurisdiction of a given government, emigrating to another is certainly unobjectionable. One could even remain in the same territory and reject citizenship, so long as this does not involve blocking services to others with whom one has signed up for the services of government, that is, fellow citizens. Changing citizenship may not be so simple as changing pizza delivery firms but it may actually be simpler than, say, leaving the teaching profession and entering farming—the opportunities for farming may be thousands of miles from where one did the teaching. Extricating one's involvement with some businesses in entirely free markets can be cumbersome, especially if one has signed up for long-term relationships (such as health or life insurance services, earning university degrees, etc.). In short, the secession issue in this discussion is not on point.

Block makes a great deal out of my being "the leading libertarian advocate of minarchism" (p. 6), which is really an exaggeration. I have spent most of my energies on other topics, although, as noted already, the one paper of mine on the topic with which Block should have dealt he leaves unmentioned.[50]

---

49 As an aside, it is interesting that if nothing of the nature of government is retained in the types of agencies that Block and his fellow anarchist-libertarians propose, they could easily become totally unlimited in the scope of their business operations: why should a defense-insurance agency not also get into the business of bakery, auto-manufacture, faming, education, etc.? The classical liberal and modern libertarian idea that an agency that addresses the problems of justice should remain separated from organisations in society such as churches, educational institutions, scientific research centers, art museums, the theater and so forth seems to be obsolete in Block's conception of such agencies. They could easily merge with all these others and come to address all the issues that totalitarian or welfare states do. Perhaps this would not involve them in any kind of coercive endeavors but it would very probably jeopardise the impartiality that the administration of justice requires, exactly as modern welfare states, with their myriad involvements in society, fail in this respect.

50 This is where I argue, following Rand's lead, that government may be funded without taxation. See, for more, Ayn Rand, "Government Financing in a Free Society," in E. S. Phelps, ed., *Economic Justice* (Baltimore: Penguin Books, 1973), pp. 363-67, and Tibor R. Machan, "Dissolving the Problem of Public Goods: Financing Government without Coercive

Block announces that "I shall attempt in the following a meticulous refutation of [Machan's views]" (p. 6). What we do get from Block is a lot of emotion-laden, colorful characterisation of my various points—"argument from authority," "fictitious entities," "fallacy," "giving the game away," "orgy of coercion," and so forth. But there is little discernible substance, let alone meticulous refutation, in his paper.

Actually, this is understandable since Block's central point is, as we have already noted, that what I call government isn't government at all because necessarily all governments are coercive (because they must tax and because they do not admit of competition within their jurisdictional boundaries). That all this is question-begging—that is to say, assumes the conclusion he seeks to prove in the premises with which he starts his argument—does not seem to bother Block.

At one point he does mention an issue that is of substance in the discussion of whether a market already requires laws for its operations, so that the establishment of law cannot be left solely to market processes. Making this point, which isn't original with me,[51] is to say that defense-insurance agencies that would operate so as to make laws already need laws—they need to have property rights in effect so as to operate their enterprise; they need to have contracts established and upheld between them and their clients; they need to have their articles of incorporation registered with some office that records such organisational arrangements, etc. A legal framework, even if only a very thin one, is presupposed by even the most minimal market processes, one reason why politics, which concerns law, cannot be reduced without remainder to economics.

In the course of touching on this matter, Block once again introduces language that is irrelevant—for example, where he says "If Machan was intent on bashing free market anarchism and elevating limited government" (p. 9).[52] Leaving that aside, my point about markets presupposing laws is that there are legitimate *political* concerns in human life, even if they be limited to the issue of effective and just defense of individual rights. (Block seems to equivocate between the concepts "political" and "criminal" or "coercive." But again he begs the question doing so.) The language deployed by anarchist libertarians suggests otherwise, although if one looks closer and translates the neologisms into normal English, it turns out that anarchist libertarians really do not believe that laws are produced in the market place. They must already be established, to some minimal degree, for markets to begin to operate.[53]

Measures," in T. R. Machan, *The Libertarian Reader* (Lanham, MD: Rowman & Littlefield, 1982), pp. 201-08. (Block's failure to mention this work is mysterious, given that he has a paper on free market roads in the same volume.)

51 See, David Kelley, "The Necessity of Government," *The Freeman 24* (April, 1974).

52 My practice in the course of these sorts of debates, even with persons whose views I find abhorrent because of what I believe they would produce if taken seriously and implemented, is not to engage in bashing or elevating but in assessing whether or not certain ideas are feasible and theories sound.

53 "Markets" are, of course, not some kind of entities but spheres of certain kinds of conduct, namely, commerce. It is people who engage in commerce and when and where they do this, when and where we find markets. Since commerce assumes the respect and protection of the right to private property—one cannot trade what one doesn't own—the organised institution of the law of property, especially in complex civilisations, must pre-date commerce

Block is eager to defend his anarchist position—which involves crisscrossing legal authorities—against my (once again not original) point that such legal operations would very easily produce chaos and indecision. For someone who chides me for committing the fallacy of "argument from authority," it is interesting that to answer my objections Block mainly mentions Murray N. Rothbard and David Friedman. He adds to this merely by noting that "there will be two kinds of courts in the free market: those who [sic] anticipate that their findings will sometimes conflict with others, and contractually obligated themselves to take their differences to an agreed upon different court as the final arbiter, and those who either do not make this forecast, and/or refuse to be bound by any third court" (p. 10). Only the latter pose a problem, according to Block.

The former, however, do not pose a problem only because they are unrealistically conceived. The supposed contract cannot work because there is no enforcement agency to uphold it. Block's reply reveals once again his question-begging policy as he argues his case: he assumes that there *will be* this benign agreement among various defense-insurance agencies. For someone who chides me for suggesting that government could be non-coercive, on grounds that they have rarely been that, Block accepts all too readily the possibility of such benign agreement between different defense-insurance agencies, including their clients (especially criminals). One need but look around the globe and notice how little agreement is extant among competing legal orders. One may wish that such agreement could be implemented but it is best not to *expect* this. In which case the alternative to the crisscrossing jurisdiction of whatever one wishes to call the legal authorities, namely, their operation in various pockets of homogenous regions, is a wiser, even rationally required, option.[54]

At one point Block makes a statement that is highly revealing of his methodology: He claims that the debate in which he and I are engaged—namely, whether libertarians adhere to some or no conception of government "is important because it helps us shed light on the bedrock essence of libertarianism. It demonstrates, *from my perspective*, that to be a truly consistent libertarian ... one must be an individualist anarchist and must, in the end, eschew minarchism" (p. 9, my emphasis). Of course, from his perspective he can demonstrate whatever he likes, given that his perspective already assumes everything he wants to establish. The crucial issue is whether he can defend *his perspective*!

Block states that "a government that acts 'purely defensively' is not a government at all" (p. 11), but this again is something true by stipulated definition for him, not established via argument. Once he has his undefended definition in tow, nothing else but this could be true.

In the end what we get from Professor Walter Block is no more than his oft-repeated reiteration of certain opinions about governments, coercion, taxation, markets, and

---

and, therefore, markets. (In primitive communities some of this can be carried out in simple, even unrecorded ways, but not for long.)

54 One might make the same point about governments: they could be non-coercive but aren't likely to turn out that way. But this very same point should be kept in mind about any kind of legal authority, including the allegedly different defense-insurance agencies Block likes.

competition in law enforcement. They do all square with his perspective, of course. But that perspective is in need of being defended as the best one concerning how justice is best upheld in human communities. Arguing in circles is not going to do any good for his case. And it is furthermore unfortunate that as he lays out this so called "argument," he manages to embark on endless self-certain polemics and hyperbole, as if zeal could substitute for the missing arguments.

PART 2
Anarchism

Chapter 6

Radical Freedom and Social Living

Aeon James Skoble

It might seem as though radical freedom and social living are incompatible concepts.[1] How can we maintain a maximal degree of individual freedom while also living in society, where we are answerable to others? The answer depends largely on how we understand the nature of freedom and the purpose of social living. The first thing we need to do prior to coming to an understanding of these is to note that talking about government is not the same thing as talking about society. One need not be an anarchist to recognise that society and state are not synonyms, but the position generally known as anarchism follows from some ways of parsing that distinction.

Why do we have society in the first place? One answer is that we just could not accomplish much by ourselves. Even before the classical economists of the eighteenth century formalised their theories about this, Plato observed that a division of labor among several people results in an improved standard of living for all. Rather than make my own clothes and grow my own food and so on, if each person specialises in one occupation, and then trades with the others, far more gets accomplished. Indeed, there are so many things that need to be done that it would be difficult to imagine doing everything oneself. Many of the tasks would involve knowledge not in one's possession. Even if one wanted to build a cabin in the woods and live in isolation, where would one get the nails? So there is a literal sense in which we need other people. But there are other senses as well. We seem to be, as Aristotle observes, social animals. It is not merely that we need social living in order to have productivity, but that we derive psychological or moral value from the company of others. A life without friendship would be a greatly impoverished one. Hence the need for social living, which thus seems to mean more than just the brute fact of living in proximity to others, but the great variety of interactions we have with the others. We have collaborative working relationships, we have commercial relationships, we have personal relationships ranging from close friends to nodding acquaintances.

But not all sorts of arrangements for social living are equally effective. A system of specialisation and trade is mutually beneficial, whereas a system in which one group enslaves another is not. Any society will have to have rules which govern people's interactions. Disputes may emerge, and there will need to be some mechanism for resolving these disputes. People may desire protection from predatory behavior on the part of others. Typically, people envision the state as the means by which society

---

1   I mean radically free in a political sense. As we shall see, this is not identical to a Stirnerite "freedom" to violate one's voluntary contractual obligations, or the rights of others.

regulates itself and ensures the provision of these mechanisms. But is that the only means by which these ends can be achieved? The state, after all, relies on coercion to accomplish its ends. Since coercion is not compatible with freedom, defenders of freedom may be skeptical as to whether the state is the best way to realise social living.

In what ways does the state involve coercion? Chiefly by asserting a monopoly on the provision of various services which are essential to social living, and often some which are not, and then using force or the threat of force to maintain (and fund) this monopoly. This characterisation sounds inflammatory, but defenders of the state would not so much disagree, but rather maintain that this coercion is necessary, and that is the real question: Can social order be achieved without a coercive state?

Tibor Machan has argued that "the justification and need of government arises from the objective value to all members of society of living with others without ... the general insecurity that goes with lawlessness. Individuals who recognize the value of social life readily acknowledge the value of establishing an agency to provide them with the protection and preservation of their rights in the context of a system of objective law."[2] Government activities could therefore, theoretically, be provided on a fee-for-service basis. Since the government, on his view, should only be in the business of adjudicating conflicts, protecting rights, and securing contracts, and since one could choose not to employ the government's services for most of these, funding for these activities could occur non-coercively, by having users of a service bear its costs. This state would still, according to Machan, have to bar others from offering the services the government offers, e.g., an alternative provider of rights protection. Is the protection of rights and the resolution of disputes – what we might recognise as a legal system – the sort of thing which *must* be the province of the state, or can it exist independently of the state?

In his three-volume *Law, Legislation, and Liberty*,[3] Friedrich Hayek distinguishes between what he calls *thesis*, the law of legislation, and *nomos*, the law of liberty. The former is imposed by the sovereign, in what he describes as a top-down, coercive, process; the latter is evolved, a spontaneously emerging (or bottom-up) process. While *thesis* reflects primarily the interests of the sovereign (or ruling class generally), *nomos* arises out of human interaction – the many iterations of people seeking to more effectively coordinate their actions and resolve disputes peaceably. This suggests that there can be social living without the state. The question becomes one of whether there is a real possibility of social cooperation sufficient not only for ordinary social and commercial interaction, but also for the establishment of adequate means of dispute-resolution.

The idea of a feasible system of alternative providers of rights protection is ultimately what will divide minimal-state libertarians from the anarchists. But assuming Machan's arguments about the "natural" monopoly of government on conflict resolution are valid, then the state he describes would be as non-coercive

---

2   Tibor Machan, "Dissolving the Problem of Public Goods," *The Libertarian Reader*, ed. by Machan (Totowa, NJ: Rowman and Littlefield, 1982), p. 204.

3   Friedrich A. Hayek, *Law, Legislation, and Liberty, Volume 1: Rules and Order*. (Chicago: University of Chicago Press, 1973).

as possible. This is not by itself a successful dismissal of the anarchist position. The anarchist argument is that although society is a good thing, coercion is a bad thing, and states as we know them essentially involve coercion. A state that employed no coercion, or as little as possible for society to exist, would not be the same state that anti-statists are against. Indeed, the whole point of contention turns out to be over this last qualifier, that since just a little coercion is required for society to exist, therefore the minimal state is justified.

The important point, however, is that minimal-state libertarians regard state power as a thing that needs to be justified *because* of its coercive features. This is a conception shared with anarchists. We have seen that both minimal-state libertarians and anarchist libertarians view the state as a political entity which essentially involves coercion, coercion is seen as detrimental to human freedom, and freedom is to receive the highest priority among political values when developing a theory. The anarchist criticism, then, is that *given* this view of coercion and state power, such a justification cannot be provided coherently. No state could possibly be legitimate on this view. The minimal-state response seems to be based on an implicit Hobbesian concern about the unfeasibility of a system of alternative providers of rights protection. Even libertarians who are supporters of the notion of private sanitation companies and private road ownership tend to remain skeptical about the idea of private courts. The anarchist must attempt to allay this skepticism not by showing how markets are more efficient providers of goods and services generally, but by demonstrating that rights enforcement is not an exception.

The intuitive appeal of the minimal-statist's concern rests on the common sense of the claim that society would be impossible if we were all attacking each other. One of the crucial assumptions here goes back to Hobbes himself, the claim that covenants cannot provide security in the absence of some sort of enforcement mechanism. It seems clear enough that recognisably civil society, one which permitted people to develop and pursue their ends and so on, would be impossible given the total war of all against all. What is problematic is the claim that the *state* is necessary in order to avoid this situation. If cooperation enforcement *can* be provided in the absence of political authority, then this Hobbesian worry is mistaken: political authority is not a necessary condition of society.

The primary consideration in Robert Nozick's account of the minimal state is efficiency. According to him, the services of protection and conflict resolution would be provided more efficiently with the minimal state than without it, and thus the state is inevitable. He defends the extension of the right to individual self-defense to one of collective self-defense in the sense that many might collectively engage the same means of exercising their right to self-protection, which means it would be morally legitimate to pay other people or companies to protect us. Then Nozick (famously) explains how, as a matter of economic efficiency, one of these protective agencies would come to dominate the others (at least in a particular geographic area) through a non-coercive process of mergers and acquisitions. This "dominant protective agency" would then fit the standard definitions of a state, as it provides protection for all and monopolises this service, but would also satisfy the "moral objections of the individualist anarchist"[4] because it arose in a way that did not violate anyone's rights. Competing services are not ruled out *a priori*; rather he thinks that stability and other market conditions will generate the dominant protective agency. Nozick argues that it would not be rights-violating for this "de facto monopoly" to coerce payment for the services. Presumably he arrives at this conclusion because each of the smaller protection agencies was voluntarily funded, so the new "parent company" is not violating rights to exact payment after the "merger." The question, then, is whether or not coercion is involved *after* the formation of the dominant protective agency. If someone who, despite having voluntarily subscribed to one of the smaller companies, disliked the operation of the new dominant protective agency wanted to "opt out," would this be permitted by the agency? Would he be entitled to secure this service from someone else? If the dominant protective agency must use coercion to bar market entry of competing services, and may force dissenters to continue paying them, then Nozick will be in error in claiming that no rights have been violated. (And if one *can* "opt out" of what is simply the largest provider of the service, then Nozick's vision will be indistinguishable from Rothbard's conception of a society without a state.)

The only remaining justification would be a concern that "permitting" entry into this market would mean that everyone's rights would be made less secure by the competition between protective agencies, and that therefore it is not wrong to prohibit this. Nozick develops this idea by arguing that these companies would be inclined to find their interests best served by preemptive attack, and that the known proclivity towards striking first when this seemed advantageous would, at the least, weaken everyone's ability to protect their rights, and at worst destroy society.

> A protective agency dominant in a territory does satisfy the two crucial necessary conditions for being a state. It is the only generally effective enforcer of a prohibition on others' using unreliable enforcement procedures [i.e., independent enforcement]. ... And the agency protects those nonclients in its territory whom it prohibits from using self-help enforcement ... even if such protection must be financed (in apparent redistributive fashion) by its clients. It is morally required to do this by the principle of compensation, which requires those who act in self-protection in order to increase their own security to compensate those they prohibit from doing risky acts which might have turned out to be harmless [i.e., seeking independent enforcement] for the disadvantages imposed on them.[5]

Of course it makes sense to argue that *if* the dominant protective agency may prohibit private enforcement on the grounds that its members feel that private enforcement is risky and makes them less secure, *then* the agency must compensate those so prohibited. But why should the dominant protective agency prohibit? Because, Nozick says, private enforcement entails not chaos, but the risk of chaos. "An independent might be prohibited from privately exacting justice because his procedure is known to be too risky and dangerous ... or because his procedure isn't

---

4 Robert Nozick, *Anarchy, State, and Utopia* (New York: Basic Books, 1974), p. 114.
5 Nozick 1974, pp. 113-14.

known not to be risky."[6] "Our rationale for this prohibition rests on the ignorance, uncertainty, and lack of knowledge of people. ... Disagreements about what is to be enforced ... provide yet another reason (in addition to lack of factual knowledge) for the apparatus of the state. ..."[7] This rationale is clearly based on a Hobbesian concern about the instability of a system of competing providers of rights protection.

Tibor Machan's arguments for the justification of state authority anticipate the aforementioned anarchist criticism, so they predominantly involve criticism of anarchist theories. In *Human Rights and Human Liberties*, Machan's argument for the legitimacy of the state specifically addresses Murray Rothbard's arguments for individualist anarchism. The key to Machan's criticism of Rothbard involves the idea that a "morally legitimate" state would satisfy the anarchist's objections. Rothbard and Machan agree on what "morally legitimate" entails here, that is, they both recognise the importance of individual liberty and the objections it poses to state coercion. "Governmental authority can be morally proper only when strictly limited to the protection and preservation of human rights."[8] Rothbard's point (this argument is also made by Randy Barnett) is that the services of conflict resolution and protection against violence can be provided more efficiently, and in greater concert with libertarian values, on an open market.

Rothbard has argued that there is no such thing as a morally legitimate state, since all states rely for their power on coercion.

> [If] no one may morally initiate physical force against the person or property of another, then [even] limited government has built within it ... impermissible aggression. ... All governments, however limited they may be otherwise, commit ... fundamental crimes against liberty and private property.[9]

Machan counters this by claiming that there is such a thing as a morally legitimate state, and that states of this sort are defensible on grounds that Rothbard should accept. "What I am saying against Rothbard is that it is in their interest and people are entitled to establish moral governments, ones that protect and preserve human rights (only)."[10]

Machan allows that, historically, states have contained the objectionable features Rothbard describes, although they ought not to be defined in this manner because they might conceivably be established without them.

> [W]e must acknowledge that Rothbard is here making something other than a historical claim about what governments have done. His contention is more general: there *could* not be a government that is not compulsory. ... His reason is that any government must serve some given geographical area, which already renders it compulsory because some

---

6 Nozick 1974, p. 88.
7 Nozick 1974, pp. 140-41.
8 Tibor Machan, *Human Rights and Human Liberties* (Chicago: Nelson-Hall, 1975), p. 146.
9 Murray Rothbard, "Will Free Market Justice Suffice-Yes," *Reason* (March 1972), p. 19.
10 Machan 1975, p. 152.

property owners who would prefer service from some other agency would not then be allowed to obtain it. But is this true? Would a government *have* to disallow secession?[11]

Machan's answer to this question is that the valid self-defense needs mentioned above might contractually rule out secession during specifically enumerated time periods, but that the government as legitimate hired agent of legitimate self-protection could be "fired" if it proved unsatisfactory. Thus the government must exist to protect human rights, but need not be coercive in the manner Rothbard objects to. Although "there must ... exist a court of last resort," Machan writes,

> [I]t follows from the principles of human rights that action ought to be taken to institute their systematic protection and defense. If "government" is the concept best suited to designate such agencies, then it is morally justified for people to establish (hire) a proper government. It may be that those administering the laws will do a bad job, in which case one is morally obligated to alter or abolish (fire) those involved, provided terms are met for such disassociation.[12]

Actually, Machan allows for the possible efficiency of market-generated protection and arbitration services and shows a considerable interest in the idea of non-coercive funding for government activities. If there were a free market in these services, and they were funded non-coercively, that would indeed satisfy both Machan's and Rothbard's conception of moral legitimacy, but it would fail to be a "state" by our (or indeed most people's) definition. Machan's claims about implicit consent to just government come so close to being anarchistic that the distinction is hard to ascertain. Machan says that the implicit consent to be governed need not imply consent to taxation, because the services traditionally provided by governments that make governments desirable in the first place can be provided non-coercively. But this is *precisely* Rothbard's point: that services traditionally provided by the state need not be (and that realising this helps de-legitimise the state). Despite this development with regard to most services normally associated with the state, Machan's primary worry seems to be the service of conflict resolution, the only one he cannot imagine emerging on the market. "Unless something on the order of a court of *final* authority exists, this [conflict resolution] is impossible in some cases, e.g., [when competing courts arrive at contrary decisions in a given case]."[13] This claim is certainly true. It is precisely this challenge that motivates recent work in anarchist thought, such as that of Randy Barnett and Bruce Benson.

The anarchists suggest hypothetical scenarios of how non-monopolistic and non-coercively financed legal systems would operate. Their claims about the feasibility of these systems depend on whether the state is *necessary* for social order. Is it possible for cooperative structures to emerge spontaneously, without political authority and coercion?

---

11 Machan 1975, p. 148.
12 Machan 1975, p. 151.
13 Tibor Machan, "Individualism and the Problem of Political Authority," *The Monist*, vol. 63, no. 4, October 1983, p. 523.

According to recent research in game theory, cooperation is the social strategy that produces the most favorable outcome in the long run, even if everyone is primarily concerned with self-interest. Libertarian minimal-statists argue that the state, although undesirable in general, is necessary to ensure that the minimal social cooperation necessary for society's existence is present. Libertarian anarchists argue that schemes of conflict resolution and security provision could arise without coercion because the minimal level of social cooperation postulated by the minimal-state theorists is the level that would arise spontaneously as a result of people pursuing their self-interest. What seems to be an insoluble hypothetical dispute about the necessity of the state for the provision of cooperation can be mediated, I think, by looking at what the game theory research suggests. If the minimal-state libertarians all have at their base something like the Hobbesian worry about the results of a lack of political authority, and this concern can be allayed, then the anarchist libertarians will have a much stronger position.

Many interpret the familiar "prisoner's dilemma" situation, a staple of decision theory, as an illustration of the necessity of political authority to ensure minimal social cooperation. Here is a prisoner's dilemma[14]:

	B cooperate	defect
A cooperate	A=3, B=3	A=0, B=5
A defect	A=5, B=0	A=1, B=1

From A's point of view, if B is going to cooperate, A ought to choose defection, because this secures a higher payoff. On the other hand, if B is going to defect, A minimises his (A's) penalty by choosing defection. In other words, it is rational for A to defect regardless of how B is expected to behave. However, B is in precisely the same situation relative to A. If both defect, the payoff to both is less than if both had cooperated. So both parties, acting quite rationally, end up in a worse situation than they might have, for mutual cooperation would result in a higher payoff for both. In a Hobbesian argument, the sovereign is necessary to foster cooperation; that is, to make sure that "players" (citizens) cooperate and therefore secure the more optimal "payoff" (mutual security). On this model, authorising state coercion is in one's best interest, and this *is* the justification.

The question, then, is whether cooperation can evolve spontaneously, i.e., without being imposed by a coercive entity such as a state. Hayek argues in *Law, Legislation, and Liberty* that the English common law is actually an example of this spontaneously evolved cooperative enterprise. The common law is essentially an enshrining of evolved practices which enable peaceable dispute resolution, and not the product of legislation, deliberate planning. Rules of law arise through repeated human interaction. Patterns, and expectations of adherence to patterns, emerge. Juries are asked to apply the commonly accepted rules for settling disputes which, in principle anyway, embody the general consensus about what is fair as revealed in actual practice. Judges are expected to follow precedent when applying principles in

---

14 R. D. Luce and Howard Raiffa, *Games and Decisions* (New York: Wiley, 1957).

their rulings. The common law is both stable and vital; that is, it contains elements that carry on across time, enabling people to have reasonable expectations about the future, and also elements that enable the procedures and policies to adapt to changing times. Without being the product of any intentional design, it nevertheless comes into being and produces order.

In his 1984 book *The Evolution of Cooperation*, Robert Axelrod describes computerised "tournaments" to test the long term success of different strategies for winning at the prisoner's dilemma (where "winning" is maximising payoff not once, but over a long period).[15] The outcome of several repetitions of the tournament was a clear victory for a strategy he calls "tit-for-tat." Tit-for-tat attempts to foster cooperation while retaining a capacity to "punish" when other "players" refuse to cooperate. The method is deceptively simple: Cooperate on the first round, and then on each subsequent round do whatever the other player did in the previous round. Thus, higher payoffs were secured overall. No other strategy did as well. For instance, purely selfish "players" who choose defection every round did not fare as well as "players" who attempted to foster cooperation.

Naturally the winning strategy in a one-shot prisoner's dilemma is to defect. The point is that most of the life situations that are thought to resemble a prisoner's dilemma are iterated (repeated) versions of the game, in which case the "winning strategy" turns out to be to develop the sort of responsive cooperation that Axelrod describes. Since Axelrod's influential work was first published, further experimentation has provided some interesting developments. Recently, Martin Nowak and Karl Sigmund have demonstrated greater success with a different strategy, one that outperforms tit-for-tat. It turns out that this new strategy, which they named Pavlov, also indicates that responsive cooperation of the sort described by Axelrod is indeed the most robust.

> The Prisoner's Dilemma is the leading metaphor for the evolution of cooperative behaviour in populations of selfish agents, especially since the well-known computer tournaments of Axelrod and their application to biological communities. In Axelrod's simulations, the simple strategy of tit-for-tat did outstandingly well and subsequently became the major paradigm for reciprocal altruism. ... Pavlov's success is based on two important advantages over tit-for-tat: it can correct occasional mistakes and exploit unconditional cooperators.[16]

The Pavlov strategy is "smarter" than tit-for-tat in that simple tit-for-tat cannot correct a "misunderstanding" between "players." Since tit-for-tat involves (simply) repeating the other player's previous move, tit-for-tat is reactive. It tries to foster cooperation by initiating it, but thereafter is stuck with responding. So if the other player is "dumb," that is, will not respond to tit-for-tat's attempt to cooperate, and defects, then tit-for-tat must defect. If both players are oriented towards tit-for-tat, but one makes a mistake, a cycle of mutual defection will result. Pavlov can adjust based on previous favorable or unfavorable outcomes by cooperating after securing higher payoffs and defecting after lower payoffs (Nowak and Sigmund call

---

15 Robert Axelrod, *The Evolution of Cooperation* (New York: Basic Books, 1984).
16 Martin Nowak and Karl Sigmund, "A strategy of win-stay, lose-shift that outperforms tit-for-tat in the Prisoner's Dilemma game," *Nature*, vol. 364, 1 July 1993, p. 56.

this "win-stay, lose-shift"). Thus errors are corrected quickly. Although Pavlov is more robust than tit-for-tat, we notice that Axelrod's main point is not challenged, but in fact supported, by these new findings, namely, that responsive cooperation is an effective strategy for maximising self-interest. If this is so, it is less clear that political authority is necessary to bring about cooperation. The social cooperation that is deemed necessary by minimal-statism is the sort of cooperation that would have to develop naturally if it is the sort of cooperation that is represented by the iterated dilemma.

Another way to interpret the game-theoretic justification for political authority might lead one to question the accuracy of what it portrays. There are other historical counter-examples to what the argument claims would be the result of a lack of political authority. First of all we might keep in mind the "international relations" objection to the claim. Upon reflection, one realises that individual nation-states *are* in the Hobbesian state of nature relative to each other, there being no world government, and yet the world is not in a perpetual state of war of all against all. Countries work out tit-for-tat-like or Pavlov-like cooperative strategies (more often than not). Michael Taylor makes this point in his 1987 book *The Possibility of Cooperation*. Although Hobbes did not apply to the international "state of nature" the analysis he made of the domestic one, Taylor argues, "there is no reason in principle why such an application should not be made. ... [So] the possibility of conditional cooperation amongst states in the absence of [a] supranational state has been taken more seriously in the last few years" regarding the possibility of cooperation generally.[17] Barnett also makes this observation: "The argument that we need court systems with geography-based jurisdictional monopolies does not stop at the border of a nation-state. Any such argument suggests the need for a single world court system. ... After all, the logic of the argument against a competitive legal order applies with equal force to autonomous nations."[18]

We have seen that Nozick argues that the dominant protective agency can prohibit private enforcement of justice because allowing it entails risks that threaten the security of its clients. Since one has a right, on Nozick's account, to prevent others from engaging in risky behavior that could decrease one's security, one has a right to authorise another to do this on one's behalf. But does it follow from this that one has a right to forbid others from joining other protective associations? Nozick himself brings up this question in order to respond to it in advance. His answer seems to undermine his own argument, however.

> We have found a distinction, which appears to be theoretically significant, that distinguishes a protective agency's forbidding others from using unreliable or unfair procedures to exact justice on its clients from other prohibitions – such as forbidding others to form another protective agency – which might be thought to be allowable if the first is. ... [But we] have rebutted the charge we imagined earlier that our argument fails

---

17 Michael Taylor, *The Possibility of Cooperation* (Cambridge, England: Cambridge University Press, 1987), p. 166.

18 Randy Barnett, "Pursuing Justice in a Free Society, Part II," *Criminal Justice Ethics*, Winter/Spring 1986, p. 42. Barnett discusses this at greater length in *The Structure of Liberty: Justice and the Rule of Law* (Oxford University Press, 2000).

because it "proves" too much, in that it provides a rationale not only for the permissible rise of a dominant protective association, but also for this association's forcing someone not to take his patronage elsewhere or for some person's forcing others not to join any association. *Our argument provides no rationale for the latter actions and cannot be used to defend them.*[19]

If the argument does not provide a justification for the dominant protective association forbidding individuals from opting out, then Nozick has no argument for the state beyond that one *could* arise without violating anyone's rights. However, he views this development as more than simply logical possibility. He argues that the minimal state is actually justified as a matter of collective decision making. As we have seen, Nozick argues that the dominant protective agency is justified in prohibiting people from seeking other means of settling disputes on the grounds that it would be too risky to permit such actions. Although he describes the fair (i.e., non-rights violating) procedures which would most likely be followed by the dominant protective agency, he must believe that no competitive set of such agencies could be fair and feasible. In fact, his dismissal of Rothbard's proposal for just such a system indicates this:

> Rothbard imagines that somehow, in a free society, "the decision of any two courts will be considered binding, i.e., will be the point at which the court will be able to take action against the party adjudged guilty."... Why is anyone who has not in advance agreed to such a two-court principle be bound by it? Does Rothbard mean anything other than that he expects agencies won't act until two independent courts (the second being an appeals court) have agreed?[20]

In fact, it is precisely Rothbard's point that the sensible thing to expect is that the agencies would only act after the adjudicating was complete, and that a likely arrangement would be one in which the various courts one might be a "client" of would have pre-arranged means for resolving *their* disputes. Do we have any reason to think the companies would seek this (cooperative) type of a solution, rather than resorting to violent conflict? According to Axelrod's research, we do have some reason for thinking this is plausible. Here we have a clear example of how the insights from game theory might support the position of an anarchist criticism of Nozick, specifically the one found in Randy Barnett's work.

Legal systems in our society involve monopolistic institutions, such as a court system and a police force. Unsurprisingly, these tend to be inefficient and susceptible to corruption, and, more to the point, they are coercive. Barnett thinks that a legal order need not involve any monopolistic institutions, and that doing without them better promotes justice, and without sacrificing individual liberty. According to Barnett, Nozick's "invisible-hand" justification for the state does not match his own values as well as it could, because his conception of a legal system, that is, a system providing for redress of grievances and torts, does not need to be monopolistic or coercive.

---

19 Nozick 1974, p. 129, emphasis added.
20 Nozick 1974, p. 343.

In his 1970 book *Power and Market*, one of Rothbard's arguments against a state-based conception of property rights is that the principles operative in a free society in the first place are ones that provide a theory of property rights already; namely, self-ownership and ownership of resources transformed by one's labor. This is (obviously) Lockean, and Rothbard thinks that this Lockean conception means that the state is not necessary to define or allocate property rights. In any case, it means that minimal-state libertarians should not be relying on the premise that the state is needed to define property rights.

Rothbard suggests we reexamine the Hobbesian concern present even in libertarians with irreverence.

> Suppose, for example, that we were all suddenly dropped down on the earth *de novo* and that we were all then confronted with the question of what societal arrangements to adopt. And suppose then that someone suggested: "We are all bound to suffer from those of us who wish to aggress against their fellow men. Let us then solve this problem of crime by handing all of our weapons to the Jones family, over there, by giving all of our ultimate power to settle disputes to that family. In that way, with their monopoly of coercion and of ultimate decision making, the Jones family will be able to protect us from each other." I submit that this proposal would get very short shrift, except perhaps from the Jones family themselves. And yet this is precisely the common argument for the existence of the state.[21]

Reading "the sovereign" for "the Jones family," we see Rothbard's parody of Hobbes' argument here. But then the question remains which societal arrangements to adopt. Rothbard suggests that we adopt not *a* system of conflict resolution, but several. We have already seen, for example in Machan, that any such suggestion will be challenged by the need to have a final arbiter of disputes if chaos is to be avoided. But Rothbard's response, that a spontaneously arising competitive legal system would be stable, is more plausible in light of Axelrod's conclusion that cooperation is the stronger social strategy, even for self-interested agents. This makes sense as long as there is sufficient social cooperation to allow the different enforcement agencies to develop strategies of coexistence that would not be chaotic. But according to Axelrod and the others, this condition can be met.

Barnett and Rothbard describe similar schemes whereby conflict resolution, conceived of as another service more efficiently provided on a market, is provided without a coercive authority, that is, by consent. The state, even when organised by majority rule, has free rein to violate the consent of the minority.

Barnett says that with regard to crime prevention, the problem of commons, i.e., the conception of parks and streets, etc. as being held in common, has an adverse effect on crime prevention for two main reasons: there is no right to exclude, since it "belongs to" everybody; and little incentive to commit resources to assist in crime prevention, since it is thought of as having already been paid for.[22] This is a necessary feature of any statist society.

---

21 Murray Rothbard, "Society without a State," *Nomos* 19 (1978), p. 195.
22 Barnett 1986, p. 32.

> When property rights are ill-defined, misallocations of resources will occur. If a particular resource is held in common ... then no person has the right to exclude others from using the resource. Without the right to exclude, it is unlikely that the benefits accruing to persons who privately invest in the care or improvement of a resource will exceed the costs of their efforts. ... For this reason, commonly held resources are typically overused and undermaintained.[23]

Barnett sees law-enforcement as, at least partly, a "commons" problem. He argues that this has adverse effects on the state's ability to prevent crime. A statist society that values freedom, for example, a libertarian minimal state, has to deny government police agencies the rights to regulate public property that private property owners enjoy. "Yet steps taken to protect society from the government also serve to make citizens more vulnerable to criminally inclined persons by providing such persons with a greater opportunity for a safe haven on the public streets ..."[24] Barnett argues that the only way to resolve this dilemma while preserving freedom is to adopt a robust approach to property rights and to permit competing agencies to provide adjudication and enforcement services.

The protective agencies, Barnett argues (with Rothbard), have market-generated incentives to respect the "rights of the accused" that monopoly police agents do not have; and also that competing "conflict resolution specialists" (judges) have market incentives to be fair in their decision making that monopoly judges do not have. According to Barnett, this will mean that violations of (compossible) rights will have an avenue for redress without a coercive state where such avenue would not in the process violate the rights of the innocent, particularly by not being coercively funded.

Bruce Benson makes a similar point when he argues that "The arguments for public provision of law and its enforcement are largely 'market failure' arguments, which imply that the private sector will not efficiently produce law and order. The implicit assumption underlying [this] ... is that when the market fails, government can do better."[25] Free riding is possible, he says, but "we can expect that contractual arrangements will evolve that exclude free riders from the benefits of reciprocally organized protection arrangements, as they did in [e.g.] Anglo-Saxon England."[26]

This is a crucial observation by Benson: that arguments for the justification of the state based on an economist's conception of market failure to provide conflict resolution or rights protection (or any other service, for that matter) assume that governments will provide the service flawlessly and without corruption. Rothbard has assailed this pattern of argumentation: "it is illegitimate to compare the merits of anarchism and statism by starting with the present system as the implicit given and then critically examining only the anarchist alternative".[27] Do governments in the real world provide services efficiently and uncorruptly, or are there moral and

---

23 Barnett 1986, p. 31.
24 Barnett 1986, p. 33.
25 Bruce Benson, *The Enterprise of Law* (San Francisco: Pacific Research Institute, 1990), p. 271.
26 Benson 1990, p. 276.
27 Rothbard 1978, p. 195.

pragmatic difficulties with the manner in which governments operate? One cannot use the necessity of the state as a premise and as a conclusion.

So what actually are the "checks and balances" that Rothbard, Barnett, and Benson think will make a non-monopolistic legal system work? Private courts would, on this model, depend for their success on a reputation for fairness and objectivity. What machinery ensures this? The normal operation of a system like this provides a finite number of scenarios. If Jones and Smith are in dispute, and both are clients of Adjudication Service A, or Court A, then both will have previously agreed to be bound by its decision. If Smith is a client of Court A, and Jones is a client of court B, then there are more possibilities (although still finite). In this case, if both Court A and Court B agree that Smith's case (or Jones') is the more meritorious, then both parties will have previously agreed to respect the result. The troubling scenario is the one in which Court A finds for Smith and Court B finds for Jones (or the other way around, I suppose). But as long as Court A and Court B have a prior arrangement to have *their* disputes resolved by some third adjudication service, the situation might not be so troubling after all. In this case, the decision of two of the three adjudicators makes the decision. There is still room for trouble. Suppose Smith, upon the decision of Courts B and C that he is in the wrong, decides to violate his prior agreement to abide by such a decision. What mechanisms could exist to respond to this? One possibility is that Smith would be dropped from the protection service that is part of agreeing to all this. The fear of losing his protective service would operate as an incentive on Smith to "behave." Being dropped from a protective service in this manner would have the same effect on his ability to engage other protective services as failure to make car payments has on obtaining credit from other lenders. Cooperation in this respect at least can be accounted for by self-interest, as Axelrod suggests. Repeatedly reneging on agreements such as these would be like defecting in an iterated prisoner's dilemma: an unsuccessful strategy. Indeed, Barnett makes a passing reference to Axelrod in the following passage, in which he (Barnett) offers his answer to the fear that the competing systems would war with each other:

> Extended conflict between competing court systems is quite unlikely. It is simply not in the interest of repeat players (and most of their clients) to attempt to obtain short-run gains at the cost of long-run conflict. Where they have the opportunity to cooperate, in even the most intense conflicts – warfare, for example – participants tend to evolve a "live and let live" philosophy [Barnett's footnote here is to Axelrod]. ... How much greater the incentive to cooperate would be if competing judicial services did not have access to a steady stream of coercively obtained revenue – that is, by taxation.[28]

This is Barnett's only mention of Axelrod, but clearly, the more one looks into Axelrod's work on cooperation, the more plausible Barnett's claims about cooperation become. When first reading Rothbard or Barnett on competing agencies of adjudication and enforcement, one's intuitions will either accept the claims as sensible or generate objections about whether such systems would break down. The game-theory material can help Barnett and Rothbard persuade readers of the latter disposition.

---

28 Barnett 1986, p. 41.

Nor is free riding a substantial worry, according to David Schmidtz:

> People would not be able to free ride on the general deterrent effect of other people's contributions for contract enforcement because the deterrent effect would be relevant only to those who have paid to become subject to it. If Jane's contract makes no arrangements for its own enforcement, the upshot is not that the level of enforcement suffers a light drop but rather that the *scope* of enforcement is not extended to protect Jane; Jane's contract is not enforced. ... The paradigmatically emergent justification for [the use of force involved in enforcement of mutually agreeable contracts] is based on actual consent.[29]

Supplementing (and lending credence to) the theoretical arguments of Rothbard and Barnett that mechanisms such as this would maintain social order, there is actually historical precedent for this sort of conflict resolution system. According to Terry Anderson and P. J. Hill,[30] during the settlement period in the American west, before federal power had extended into the territories, conflicts were resolved by exactly the sort of "private courts" Rothbard and Barnett envision: "[A]rbitration came from a 'private court' consisting of 'three disinterested men,' one chosen by each side and a third chosen by the two. ... Competition rather than coercion insured justice."[31] The wagon trains, mining camps, and frontier towns apparently maintained a considerable degree of social order and respect for persons and property prior to the arrival of federal power. Indeed, in each case Anderson and Hill cite, social order actually decreased after monopolistic justice arrived.

> [I]n five of the major cattle towns (Abilene, Ellsworth, Wichita, Dodge City, and Caldwell) for the years from 1870 to 1885, only 45 homicides were reported – an average of 1.5 per cattle-trading season. In Abilene, supposedly one of the wildest of the cow towns, "nobody was killed in 1869 or 1870."... Only two towns, Ellsworth in 1873 and Dodge City in 1876, ever had five killings in any one year.[32]

Surprising statistics like these suggest that the popular image of the "shoot-em-up" wild-west lifestyle is largely without basis in fact. In addition, the statistics are less surprising in light of what we learned from Axelrod about the stability of spontaneously evolved social cooperation when the disposition to respond reciprocally to "defection" is generally understood. Anderson and Hill's historical findings, like Benson's, fit Axelrod's theoretical framework neatly. Anderson and Hill suggest that social order was maintained in "anarchistic" ways partially because of certain points of "commonality that exist ... in the minds of the participants in some social situation."[33] Without making extravagant claims about human nature, it seems sensible that this sort of general agreement is what facilitates social cooperation in

---

29 David Schmidtz, *The Limits of Government* (Boulder: Westview, 1991), pp. 98-99.

30 Terry Anderson and P. J. Hill, "An American Experiment in Anarcho-capitalism," *Journal of Libertarian Studies*, vol. III, no. 1, 1979. Anderson and Hill have an expanded discussion of this matter in their *The Not So Wild, Wild West: Property Rights on the Frontier* (Stanford University Press, 2004).

31 Anderson and Hill 1979, p. 25.

32 Anderson and Hill 1979, p. 14.

33 Anderson and Hill 1979, p. 12.

the absence of a political enforcement mechanism. "Thus when a miner argued that a placer claim was his because he 'was there first,' that claim carried more weight than if he claimed it simply because he was most powerful."[34]

This conception of points of general agreement would account for many examples of non-monopolistic, consensual means of conflict resolution: the development of the English Common Law and Law Merchant prior to the consolidation of these by the crown, the Middle Eastern merchant associations, and the civil law in medieval Iceland and Ireland. The history of the development of law shows that socially emergent conceptions of legal principles, for example, that one is innocent until proven guilty, occur prior to their adoption by the political authority.

Benson explains why this is the case:

> The attributes of customary legal systems include an emphasis on individual rights because legal duty requires voluntary cooperation of individuals through reciprocal arrangements. Such laws and their accompanying enforcement facilitate cooperative interaction by creating strong incentives to avoid violent forms of dispute resolution. ... Thus, the law provides for restitution to victims arrived at through clearly designed participatory adjudication procedures, in order to both provide incentives to pursue prosecution and to quell victims' desires for revenge. Strong incentives for both offenders and victims to submit to adjudication as a consequence of social ostracism or boycott sanctions, and legal change occurs through spontaneous evolution of customs and norms.[35]

Benson's hypothesis explains both why the customary law, developed from the "bottom up" in just the way suggested by Hayek, is typically accepted by most people and why law imposed from the top down frequently is not. Benson arrives at this conclusion after noticing the extent to which Anglo-Saxon common law depended upon a conception of legal duty not rooted in imposed political power but in mutual benefit. Again, the insights we glean from Axelrod's findings make these arguments more plausible.

The conclusion one is directed towards by the theorising of Rothbard and Barnett and the examples cited by Anderson and Hill and Benson is that law ought to be construed as a natural consequence of the people's attempts to live and work together, in much the manner suggested by Hayek in *Law, Legislation, and Liberty*, and that it is something that, although necessary for society, does not presuppose a "coercive monopoly of power."[36] It would seem, then, that radical freedom is not incompatible with social living.

The fundamental dispute, then, appears to be centered around what form the final arbiter for conflict resolution takes, since all agree that some such mechanism is

---

34 Anderson and Hill 1979, p. 12.

35 Benson 1990, p. 36. On the history of the development of the common law, see also Arthur Hogue, *Origins of the Common Law* (Indianapolis: Liberty Fund, 1985), and Harold Berman, *Law and Revolution* (Harvard University Press, 1983).

36 I don't mean to imply that Hayek was an anarchist. My point is that a Hayekian understanding of the nature of law is more conducive to the anarchist position than it is to the minimal-statist position. I discuss Hayek's conception of law more fully in "Hayek the Philosopher of Law," in *The Cambridge Companion to Hayek*, edited by Edward Feser (Cambridge University Press, 2006).

necessary, and what sorts of social institutions will adequately provide the mechanisms for such conflict resolution, since all concerned agree that this, if not centralised political authority, is a necessary condition of society. The divide between minimal-state libertarians and anarchist libertarians is not due to serious disagreements about values, but rather to an intuition gap concerning practical matters. It remains a live controversy.[37]

---

[37] Portions of this chapter constitute a revised version of my "The Anarchism Controversy," in *Liberty for the 21st Century: Essays in Contemporary Libertarian Thought*, edited by Machan and Rasmussen (Totowa, NJ: Rowman and Littlefield, 1995). I explore these themes in greater detail in *Deleting the State: An Argument about Government* (Chicago: Open Court, 2008).

Chapter 7

The State: From Minarchy to Anarchy

Jan Narveson

The minarchist libertarian has a conceptual war on two fronts. In front, as it were, are the usual proponents of larger states. But nipping at his heels from the rear is the anarchist, who would abolish the state altogether. The purpose of this chapter is to see whether the minarchist can stand his ground against both. There are serious problems involved in doing so.

I have explored this question in an earlier article,[1] the main points of which I will begin by summarising.

To begin with, we are broadly assuming, for present purposes, the general view known as libertarianism. This could be – and certainly has been – questioned, of course. For present purposes, the immediately relevant concern is with anarchists who claim to be "communist" in some sense. I have argued elsewhere that the "socialist" version of anarchism is impossible.[2] If a social system inherently requires extensive redistribution, as in "from each according to his ability, to each according to his need," then it will require what amounts to a state to bring this about. By contrast, it appears that a completely decentralised social system is compatible with a free-market economy. Both of these might be (and certainly have been) denied. But as regards the first, I see no prospect of success for the would-be communist. As regards the second, extensive analysis is no doubt required, but on the face of it, anarchism of the capitalist type appears to be intrinsically possible, since it requires no redistribution, and indeed forbids compulsory redistribution. Since we will need to discuss certain aspects of this in detail, the above may be taken as programmatic for the present. But I will not linger with the communist versions of anarchy, since those appear to require wishful thinking and unreal assumptions.

Still, why libertarianism? Libertarianism is, roughly, the view that we *may* do *what we want*, subject to the constraint that we may *not* do what injures, harms, or more generally imposes *loss* on any other person. The qualifier "roughly" is important. First, the formula has to be qualified so as to make clear that people may lose their eligibility for treatment along libertarian lines, namely by infringing those lines themselves. Again roughly, it is the "innocent" who may not be treated in

---

1 *Minarchism* in the web journal Etica & Politica / Ethics & Politics, 2003, 2 http://www.units.it/etica/2003_2/NARVESON.htm

2 See Jan Narveson, *Respecting Persons in Theory and Practice* (Lanham, MD: Rowman & LIttlefield, 2002) chapter 10, "The Anarchist's Case," pp. 185-202; also in John T. Sanders and Jan Narveson, eds, *For and Against the State* (Lanham, MD: Rowman & Littlefield, 1996), ch. 10, pp. 195-216.

that way. But the relevantly guilty may: we may certainly defend ourselves against attackers, and more generally against those who employ force or fraud against us.

No point is more important concerning libertarianism than that its thesis is that we *may* do this, which is to say that it is *permissible* for us to do this – but it is *not obligatory* to do it – a point whose overlooking has given rise to an enormous amount of misunderstanding and misinterpretation of the libertarian view. If you hit me and I elect not to hit back, that's my option. But I may hit back, up to some point; moreover, I may enlist someone else to do the hitting for me, provided it is of the right amount. (And what is the "right amount"? That's a serious question, which could, as will be seen, affect the ensuing discussion. I therefore put that aside at this point, to be taken up later where pertinent.)

The libertarian principle attributes to everyone what are now generally known as "negative rights": that is to say, they impose on others the duty to *refrain* from certain activities; but they do not, on the face of it, impose on others any duty to *do* anything, just like that. Wrongdoers may be said to have a duty to repair the effects of their wrongdoing, where possible; but as regards our general relations with other non-wrongdoers, none of us may be *compelled* to do anything for them, in general. When such compulsion is ever in order, it has to be because we have authorised it, especially by voluntarily enlisting in some mode of association entailing duties which may be imposed on us if we do not perform up to the level enlisted for. (Again, just which activities constitute such enlistment requires some careful analysis. Making explicit contractual agreements does it. But does becoming someone's roommate do so? That's harder to say, and again, will be tabled for at least the time being.)

This feature of libertarianism is of the last importance for our topic. If we have no *duty* to help even ourselves, let alone others, enforce what libertarianism tells us are our rights, then there is a problem about a classic argument for the State. That classic view is that the State is necessary in order to enforce our rights. Of course it is important to ask whether the argument is correct for this claim. But whether or not it is so, there is a further issue. For the State is a paradigmatically *involuntary* organisation. It has power over *all* within its territory, whether they like it or not, whether they asked for its help or not, and regardless of why they happen to be *there*. And its "having power" is, specifically, its having the power to *compel* people to do what it tells them to do. Now, the only things it *may* tell us to "do" are *refrainings*: the State may *forbid*. But how can it *require*, seeing that we are not fundamentally required to do anything at all?

If we signed up for the State, of course, that would answer the last question. We are required because we said we would do it – so, *pay up!* Somebody can plausibly say the latter under that condition. But the condition doesn't obtain in all cases. *You* may *not* have "signed up." Now what? Apparently the State has no business compelling you, then, to do what it asks, except insofar as what it asks is to refrain from using force or fraud against others.

The "classic argument" now has to be strengthened by insisting that, somehow, even though we may deny it, we *did too* "sign up." That's what Socrates apparently thought. But he seems to have no argument for the view that we *did*. Perhaps he has an argument that we *should*. That's what Locke and others have. But, are they right?

That is to say: would it be right to hold that any rational person *would* authorise the State not only to intervene to prevent libertarianly wrongful activity, but also to collect something from me to help pay those who do the intervening? The idea is that it would be rational for me to accept, at t1, the duty to continue paying this at t2 ... tn – even if I don't, in my view, seem to be getting my money's worth!

The trouble is, that *doesn't* look rational. More precisely, it doesn't look so without some further premises. These include: it is not rational for me not to defend myself, and it is not rational for me to utilise any lesser agency than the State to do it, and that's because the State will do a *better job* than anybody else.

At this point the anarchist may well turn a bit sarcastic. The State, he may say, is an incompetent, bungling, and almost certainly *dishonest* organisation which does not deserve my support, voluntary or otherwise.

What does the defender of the State have to say to that? He may respond by discussing cases and producing what he supposes to be evidence. But it is unclear whether this kind of criticism is intended to be empirical or not. Certainly if it is empirical, the desired information is murky and hard to come by; moreover, there have been thousands of states over the centuries, and reputations have varied from extremely bad to very good. So do we turn to the good cases in support of the minarchist? Or to the bad cases in support of the anarchist?

But our issue is one of principle. And since it is, it won't be so easy to produce a case bad enough to support the anarchist, or good enough to support the minarchist. For everything will depend on the criteria employed. The libertarian's criterion is this: does government do evil to someone without compensating good *to that person*? If the question is whether they *ever* do that, it's hardly credible to reply in the negative.

Theorists with utilitarian sympathies may insist that this is the wrong criterion, and that we can compensate the bad done to A by good done to B, if it's great enough. Libertarians reject this. But they might not reject *this*: suppose that although sometimes governments visit evils on individuals not quickly compensated, yet in the longer run they are compensated.

Then the question becomes, firstly: how long is the "longer run"? And second, even if that works, might not a non-government supplier produce at least as good a result perhaps in a shorter term?

Suppose that supplier *might* indeed do that, but that governments, as typically will be the case, won't *let* the would-be supplier offer his services for sale. This will convict government of the claimed dishonesty. If it can do the job better, why not prove it in a fair match against those who claim that *they* can? This puts a rather strong burden of proof on government, and on the face of it a fair one.

Perhaps the supporter of government will claim that this is the kind of job that can only be done adequately by a single supplier: the claim will be that competition is the *problem*; monopoly the solution. Typically it would be added that control over the monopolist is nevertheless available: the voter decides – democracy fixes it.

Or does it? Democracy subjects everyone to majority rule. If the original complaint is valid, then democracy would seem not to be in much of a position to help. What's to keep a majority from extracting benefits from minorities at their expense?

Let's return again to the fundamental libertarian principle. It has rightly been interpreted as supporting private property. And it has rightly been interpreted as implying that what's right about owning something lies in *how you acquired it*, and not *how much it's worth*. Libertarians do not affirm that the earth belongs to us all in common. What, we ask, did "everybody" (including the unborn) *do* to acquire all that stuff? The answer, of course, is *nothing*. Particular people acquired this and that by stumbling upon it, using it, then staking claim to it.

A claimed case against libertarianism, or at least against its distinctiveness, is made by some, unfortunately apparently including Robert Nozick, who is almost universally taken to have the copyright on the entire libertarian idea, who surmise that the ownership of almost everything there is is called into question by past sins: My great-grandfather stole something from your great-grandfather, and therefore I owe you something. But that's a ground-floor mistake. If A stole x from B and sold it to unwitting C, then *A* owes B something – but it's not obvious that *C* does. On the contrary: A has falsely claimed that x belonged to A, and so A not only owes something to B, but he also owes it to C: C's money back, for instance. Saddling C with a debt that he had no reason to think he owed anyone is not on.

Moreover, these critics seem to think that we are all responsible for everyone's injustices. But we aren't. Suppose that A murders poor B, and nothing is done about this. That's bad, and it would be better if A were rounded up and put in jail, or hanged, or some such. However, if we ask, Who has to bell this particular cat? – the answer is, No one. We don't *owe* it to B that we avenge his death or rectify matters. In our own interest, yes, we may make efforts to apprehend the likes of A, so as to make the streets safer for ourselves. Or we may just take an interest in B, or we may take an interest in doing justice for its own sake. All legitimate, yes. But none of this obligates me or you or anybody. We just carry on – stupidly, as may be, but innocently, which is the point.

And for that reason it is not true that we all should be ready to submit to a tax to support a police force which will do all this for us. "For us"? Well, wait a minute. We'd be glad to have it done, perhaps: but maybe we don't think it's worth the price, thanks. We'll take our chances. Are we within our rights? Indeed we are.

This all comes back once again to the basic idea, the libertarian principle. This rather simple idea is that nobody gets to inflict uncompensated harm or damage on anybody else; and so, only those who have done that are eligible for treatment of the kind proscribed for all others. If our criterion of harmfulness is *what the individual in question accepts (or rejects)*, then the upshot is that police forces, and the like, purporting to do the individual a "service" stand before that individual as supplicants, begging his or her approval. When it comes to what is strictly *you,* so goes the principle, then the person with the last word on the subject is *you.* Nobody owns you; nobody has the authority to decide what is good or bad for you, at this End of the Line – nobody except *you yourself.*

So now we must ask the Minarchist: granted that you have the right general idea about what you are supposed to be doing, do you in fact have any *authority* to do it? Of course the answer is obvious: No! That is to say: maybe a *lot* of people want to be governed, but then there are others who do not, and they *count*. Not in the democratic sense, of course – one vote among n thousand – but in the contractarian sense, of, *do you buy this or don't you?* The point being that *if you don't, then the deal is off.* The customer is always right. The Consumer is King.

Of course the consumer has no authority over *anybody else*. That's not in question. What is in question is the eligibility of any centralised agency to claim the right to decide about *all matters*, domestic and foreign. Where would it get this right? Again, the answer seems clear enough on the libertarian view: it has it if and only if the individuals who participate in these "matters" give it to them.

****

In the celebrated argument by Robert Nozick, we begin in the customary anarchic condition. People note that there are bad guys around, and the question of what to do arises. The obvious answer is, Seek Help. In numbers there is strength, right? So: some form mutual-help agencies, while others purchase the services of protection entrepreneurs.

In the process, some questions arise. How does one trust the fellow helpers in the former? How can we rely on the contracts we make with the entrepreneurs in the latter? These are difficult questions, but still, we know from common experience that in practice they are answerable, pretty much. Protection entrepreneurs will be looked at with care by meta-protection entrepreneurs who will sell higher-level contracts to keep the ground-level protectors in line. It all works out. That's the idea.

But Nozick thinks it won't all work out. Nozick supposed that there is a "natural monopoly" in this area – unlike any other area we can think of. Customers would naturally move to the agency that can offer superior protection, and he supposed these would be the bigger ones. But is he right about that? There's room to doubt it.

The natural thought – in many minds, anyway – is, "Who Guards the Guardians?" In an anarchy, it's perhaps the higher-level agencies who keep tabs on the low-level agencies. And, of course, some against whom we have to be concerned to protect ourselves will be people from the other side of the mountain etc. Dealing with *them* may require a bigger association. In any case, there's the problem of the Neighbor Associations. You have yours, they have theirs, and the question is whether They have Your best interests at heart, the likely answer being in the negative. Anyway, Nozick's idea is that there is a natural advantage in Size: big guys beat up on little guys, big gangs beat up on little gangs, and bigger protection agencies will win in disputes with smaller protection agencies. So there is an increasing return to scale. And because there is, we can expect that in any given area (this being, notice, not defined), there will "emerge" a "dominant protection agency."

There's a lot more, but we should have our doubts about this. Consider all the commodities you know about. Do big guys eat little ones, just like that? I don't think so! In the world of consumer goods, we find companies of all kinds surviving, despite huge disparities in size: General Motors alongside Ferrari alongside Pescarola, and any number of others.

There's no real surprise in any of this. Those who are surprised, I think, are probably fixated on the "material production" aspect of production. Yes, a great big firm can make more widgets per hour of production-line worker than a little firm. But customers might prefer to deal with the little firm because the service is more personal, or because it can customise more efficiently, and so on. When we think about protection needs, surely they vary enormously. In many communities, there hardly is any need for it. People leave their doors unlocked, they make transactions on verbal promises alone, and so on. Where protection is needed, it might be very specific. And in any case, a small firm might be able to protect its customers much more effectively than a big one. People in threatened neighborhoods buy electronic devices, learn to shoot, join gun clubs, and perhaps register with small agencies that undertake to be on the job in an instant – in contrast to almost any police force anywhere. Generalising about this is not appropriate.

And Nozick supposed that the dominant protection agency would wind up with state-like duties in relation to its involuntary "clients." But the problem here is that real-world politically powerful organisations may well have no scruples of that kind. If they would, why would they? The reasons for this promise to be moral in kind. But if they are so, why wouldn't they also lead to the conclusion that what the State is trying to do is just wrong in the first place?

This takes us to what I believe to be the heart of the issue. A has some sort of dispute with B. Direct discussion between them doesn't solve it; each enlists his "protective service" to protect what he claims to be his rights. The thought now is that the stronger agency will make an offer that the weaker one can't refuse. So its success rate will be excellent, attracting more customers. – Or will it? Perhaps instead persons in the position of B will now form an association and create a stronger-yet protection agency.

But there is a third possibility: some entrepreneur C will come on the scene and offer to make an analysis of the situation with a convincing case why one party is in the right, or how the two can form an optimal compromise on some option they hadn't yet thought of.

There would be two reasons why people wouldn't quickly reach for their guns, or rather, why two people's agencies wouldn't reach quickly for *their* guns. One is that neither wants to get shot, and shooting at people has a way of resulting in that. If either A or B draws *his* gun, the other party's protective agency will be concerned to move in and prevent the gun-drawer from committing, and the other party from suffering, mayhem. But if the two agencies start gunning for each other, somebody is going to get hurt, and neither wants that. And if their clients are aware of their companies' bellicose tendencies, they'll look elsewhere for a safer, smarter firm to do business with.

A reputation for making good decisions is surely the best weapon anyone getting into this business could have. Reputation is what sells, and reputation comes from good service, or at least service perceived to be good. There having been two parties to the original dispute, input from both will be available. What could be more impressive than that the party who "lost" was nevertheless satisfied with the justice of the decision?

In contemporary times, of course, we can add that information of this sort can spread around very quickly indeed on the Internet. People making judgments on particular cases can quickly avail themselves of many past decisions on similar or comparable matters. The law libraries of the past fit comfortably on a few CDs; decisions everywhere can be consulted.

It is by now commonplace to point out that the law largely derives from common-law sources, not from legislation. Roger Scruton nicely describes it:

> Membership defined through place encourages people to see law as 'the law of the land.' This effect is amplified in the English and American case by the common law. Although common to the whole territory this law arose from local judgments and not from decrees issued by the sovereign ... The vast body of this law was, and remains, unwritten ... It is known as 'case law,' since it derives from the judgments delivered in individual cases. But it is not invented case-by-case ... Rather, it advances by a process of discovery, in which evils are identified and remedies proposed, guided by principles of judicial reasoning that have their root in natural justice.[3]

There are two points in this passage that may be thought to work in opposite directions. On the one hand, the system works because people identify with particular places and circumstances. On the other, the ultimate root is *natural* justice, which suggests general abstract principles. But in truth, these should be thought coordinate. The function of the law is to settle cases in a fair way, by reference to what the parties, and their cases, have in common. All disputes are particular, and so our data are all "case" in kind. Yet the point of a memory bank of cases is to see how they may be compared, how we can learn from one to the next. The fact that we can do this is itself ample evidence that the justice in question really is "natural." It is natural in that it arises from the nature of the case and of the circumstances. It is not a simple contest of wills, but of wills that claim to have a superior case – thus implying that "cases" are to be made and had.

This alters the situation drastically. We should not be conceiving the problems to be solved as ones essentially to be resolved by superior force of arms. We should instead be thinking of problems between people that can be solved by formulating and invoking common principles, deriving from common interests, even when the interests in the disputed cases do conflict.

The libertarian thesis is that there is no superior interest to peace, provided it be universal. Peace can extend everywhere and be enjoyed by everyone; war, if extended very much, results in misery for everyone. We all know that. And so those who would inflict misery for the sake of gain, or just for the thrill of it, are truly the enemies of mankind, and need dealing with as such. Now, this is not the sovereign laying down something; it is common sense. And the question is whether it can function in the absence of a "sovereign laying down something." But really, the question is why it wouldn't so function, especially since it actually *does* so function, ubiquitously. To say that power-hungry men will usurp the reasonably well-functioning relations of particular people is only to raise the question why they will be able to do so. Presumably they will depend on henchmen. Then there will be persons, their potential victims, who rise up to oppose them, and then what? Usually, one supposes, someone has "won." But what has won in recent times is, roughly, a system in which democracy and the rule of law figure prominently. Should not the fact that the democracy in question is flawed, the laws turn out to be the fiats

---

3   Roger Scruton, *The West and The Rest* (Wilmington, DE: ISI Press, 2002), pp. 49-50.

of tyrants rather than general principles to which all can appeal, without need of intermediaries in the form of legislators, matter?

These reflections take us back to our opening dilemma. Against the advocate of the Large State, such as we find almost everywhere today, the Minimalist complains that it is *too* large, that liberties are being unnecessarily or unjustly trampled. But that is the complaint that the anarchist levels against the minarchist, is it not? When we take up the slogan that "that government is best which governs least," then what is to prevent us going further and concluding, with Henry Thoreau, that the very best government is the one that doesn't govern *at all*?

Prospects for either, it must be confessed, are pretty dismal at present. The State is if anything expanding, and those who claim to be in favor of its diminution in fact have political programs that expand it. Unwary citizens buy the wares of politicians, unmindful of their costs. And then, threats from without and within arise to provide excuse, if not justification, for more action by the State.

This in turn raises the question of what the minarchist or the anarchist is to do? Forming a political party with a view to getting our program adopted by political means is, of course, playing into the hands of the enemy at one level – embracing the State to destroy it. But there is no attractive alternative to this. The figure of the terrorist is, to put it mildly, not an attractive one, not to mention that his methods are such as to guarantee failure. And in principle democracy is open to any sort of domestic program that can command a majority. Yet, as noted above, the trend is exactly the reverse to what we might expect. The generous half-, quarter- and null-truths of politicians continue to rule the day.

Some sort of an alternative, perhaps, is at hand in the form of evasion. And indeed, the State is considerably evaded in many areas of life, in one way or another. There is the "underground economy," in particular, and of course the Internet. So one thought would be that these very profitable activities will expand and fill the space of human relations. But I don't think anyone's betting on that, either.

The conclusion remains: if we are arguing on the plane of high moral theory, anarchism looks to rule the day. The minimal-stater can't urge realism against the anarchist, since his program is just as unrealistic; and it's hard to see how any genuinely principled case can be made for retaining a barely discernible government as against none at all. So the case rests.

Chapter 8

The Obviousness of Anarchy

John Hasnas[1]

"You see, but you do not observe."
Sherlock Holmes to Dr. John Watson in *A Scandal in Bohemia*

Introduction

In this chapter, I have been asked to present an argument for anarchy. This is an absurdly easy thing to do. In fact, it is a task that can be discharged in two words – look around. However, because most of us, like Dr. Watson, see without observing the significance of what we see, some commentary is required.

Anarchy refers to a society without a central political authority. But it is also used to refer to disorder or chaos. This constitutes a textbook example of Orwellian newspeak in which assigning the same name to two different concepts effectively narrows the range of thought. For if lack of government is identified with the lack of order, no one will ask whether lack of government actually results in a lack of order. And this uninquisitive mental attitude is absolutely essential to the case for the state. For if people were ever to seriously question whether government is really productive of order, popular support for government would almost instantly collapse.

The identification of anarchy with disorder is not a trivial matter. The power of our conceptions to blind us to the facts of the world around us cannot be gainsaid. I myself have had the experience of eating lunch just outside Temple University's law school in North Philadelphia with a brilliant law professor who was declaiming upon the absolute necessity of the state provision of police services. He did this just as one of Temple's uniformed private armed guards passed by escorting a female student to the Metro stop in this crime-ridden neighborhood that is vastly underserved by the Philadelphia police force.

A wise man once told me that the best way to prove that something is possible is to show that it exists. This is the strategy I shall adopt in this chapter. I intend to show that a stable, successful society without government can exist by showing that it has, and to a large extent, still does.

---

[1] Associate Professor, Georgetown University, J.D., Ph.D, LL.M. The author wishes to thank Ann C. Tunstall of SciLucent, LLC for her insightful comments and literary advice and Annette Hasnas of the Montessori School of Northern Virginia for a real world illustration of how rules evolve in the absence of centralised authority. The author also wishes to thank Ava Hasnas of Falls Church, Virginia for her invaluable help with his time management skills.

Defining Terms and Limitations

I am presenting an argument for anarchy in the true sense of the term; that is, a society without government, not a society without governance. There is no such thing as a society without governance. A society with no mechanism for bringing order to human existence is oxymoronic; it is not "society" at all.

One way to bring order to society is to invest some people with the exclusive power to create and coercively enforce rules which all members of society must follow; that is, to create a government. Another way to bring order to society is to allow people to follow rules that spontaneously evolve through human interaction with no guiding intelligence and may be enforced by diverse agencies. This chapter presents an argument for the latter approach; that is, for a spontaneously ordered rather than a centrally planned society.

In arguing for anarchy, I am arguing that a society without a central political authority is not only possible but desirable. That is all I am doing, however. I am not arguing for a society without coercion. I am not arguing for a society that abides by the libertarian non-aggression principle or any other principle of justice. I am not arguing for the morally ideal organisation of society. I am not arguing for utopia. What constitutes ideal justice and the perfectly just society is a fascinating philosophical question, but it is one that is irrelevant to the current pursuit. I am arguing only that human beings can live together successfully and prosper in the absence of a centralised coercive authority. To make the case for anarchy, that is all that is required.

An additional limitation on my argument is that I do not address the question of national defense. There are two reasons for this. One is the logical one that a society without government is a society without nations. In this context, "national" defense is a meaningless concept. If you wish, you may see this as an assertion that an argument for anarchy is necessarily an argument for global anarchy. I prefer to see it merely as the recognition that human beings, not nations, need defense. The more significant reason, however, is that I regard the problem of national defense as trivial for reasons I will expand upon subsequently.[2]

The Question

Whether government is necessary is not an abstract metaphysical question. It is an entirely practical question concerning the delivery of goods and services. The defenders of government argue that certain goods or services that are essential to human life in society can be supplied only by a government. Anarchists deny this. The question, then, is whether there are any essential goods or services that can be supplied only through the conscious actions of human beings invested with the power to enforce rules on all members of society.

Note that the question is *not* whether the "market" can supply all necessary goods and services, at least not the market as it is usually defined by economists. Some anarchists argue that the free market can supply all necessary goods and services. But

---

2 See *infra* p. 129.

the case for anarchy does not require that one assert this claim, and I do not. Anarchy requires, and I argue, only that no essential good or service must be supplied though the conscious actions of the agents of a coercively maintained monopoly. Properly understood, the question is whether there are some essential goods and services that must be provided politically or whether all such goods and services can be provided by non-political means.[3]

Many political theorists argue that there is a wide array of goods and services that must be provided by the state. In the present context, however, there is no need to consider whether the government must provide postal service, elementary schooling, or universal health insurance. The debate between anarchists and the supporters of a classical liberal, night watchman state concerns the core functions of government. The question thus resolves itself into whether these core functions can be supplied through non-political means.

The Answer

Rules of Law

CREATION

Supporters of government claim that government is necessary to provide the fundamental rules that bring order to human life in society. Without government to create rules of law, they contend, human beings are unable to banish violence and coordinate their actions sufficiently to produce a peaceful and prosperous society, and hence, are doomed to a Hobbesian existence that is "solitary, poor, nasty, brutish, and short."[4]

The proper response to this is: look around. Those of us residing in the United States or any of the British Commonwealth countries live under an extremely sophisticated and subtle scheme of rules, very few of which were created by government. Since almost none of the rules that bring peace and order to our existence were created by government, little argument should be required to establish that government is not necessary to create such rules. On the contrary, it is precisely the rules that *were* created by government that tend to undermine peace and order.

The Anglo-American legal system is often referred to as a common law legal system. This is unfortunate, given the anachronistic contemporary understanding of the term "common law." Currently, common law is associated with "judge-made" law. For most of the formative period of the common law, however, judges did not make the law, but merely presided over proceedings where disputes were resolved according to the accepted principles of customary law. Hence, describing the English common law as judge-made law is akin to describing the market as something created by economists.

English common law is, in fact, case-generated law; that is, law that spontaneously evolves from the settlement of actual disputes. Almost all of the law that provides the

---

3 In this chapter, the term "political" will be used to refer to the output of government, and "non-political" to the product of all other forms of action.

4 T. HOBBES, LEVIATHAN 107 (H. Schneider, ed., 1958) (1651).

infrastructure of our contemporary society was created in this way. Tort law, which provides protection against personal injury; property law, which demarcates property rights; contract law, which provides the grounding for exchange; commercial law, which facilitates complex business transactions; and even criminal law, which punishes harmful behavior, all arose through this evolutionary process. It is true that most of our current law exists in the form of statutes. This is because much of the common law has been codified through legislation. But the fact that politicians recognised the wisdom of the common law by enacting it into statutes, hardly proves that government is necessary to create rules of law. Indeed, it proves precisely the opposite.

English law provides a nice illustration of how law evolves when not preempted by government. When people live together in society, disputes inevitably arise. There are only two ways to resolve these disputes: violently or peacefully. Because violence has high costs and produces unpredictable results, human beings naturally seek peaceful alternatives. The most obvious such alternative is negotiation. Hence, in Anglo-Saxon times, the practice arose of holding violent self-redress in abeyance while attempts were made to reach a negotiated settlement. This was done by bringing the dispute before the communal public assembly, the *moot*, whose members, much like present-day mediators, attempted to facilitate an accommodation that the opposing parties found acceptable. When reached, such accommodations resolved the dispute in a way that preserved the peace of the community.

The virtue of settling disputes in this way was that the *moot* had an institutional memory. When parties brought a dispute before the *moot* that was similar to ones that had been resolved in the past, someone would remember the previous efforts at settlement. Accommodations that had failed in the past would not be repeated; those that had succeeded would be. Because the *moot* was a public forum, the repetition of successful methods of composing disputes gave rise to expectations in the community as to what the *moot* would recommend in the future, which in turn gave the members of the community advance notice of how they must behave. As the members of the community conformed their behavior to these expectations and took them into consideration in the process of negotiating subsequent accommodations, rules of behavior gradually evolved. This, in turn, allowed for the transformation of the dispute settlement procedure from one dominated by negotiation to one consisting primarily in the application of rules. The repetition of this process over time eventually produced an extensive body of customary law that forms the basis of English common law.[5]

It is true that, beginning in the late twelfth century, the common law developed in the royal courts, but this does not imply that either the king or his judges made the law. On the contrary, for most of its history, the common law was entirely procedural in nature. Almost all of the issues of concern to the lawyers and judges of the king's courts related to matters of jurisdiction or pleading; that is, whether the matter was

---

5 For a fuller account of this process, see John Hasnas, *Toward a Theory of Empirical Natural Rights*, 22 SOCIAL PHILOSOPHY AND POLICY 111 (2005) and John Hasnas, *Hayek, the Common Law, and Fluid Drive*, 1 NEW YORK UNIVERSITY JOURNAL OF LAW & LIBERTY 79 (2005). See also ARTHUR R. HOGUE, ORIGINS OF THE COMMON LAW, ch. 8 (1966).

properly before the court, and if it was, whether the issues to be submitted to the jury were properly specified. The rules that were applied were supplied by the customary law. As Harold Berman explains,

> [T]he common law of England is usually said to be itself a customary law. ... What is meant, no doubt, is that the royal enactments established procedures in the royal courts for the enforcement of rules and principles and standards and concepts that took their meaning from custom and usage. The rules and principles and standards and concepts to be enforced ... were derived from informal, unwritten, unenacted norms and patterns of behavior.[6]

Thus, as late as 1765, Blackstone identified the common law with "general customs; which are the universal rule of the whole kingdom, and form the common law, in its stricter and more usual signification."[7] Indeed, modern commercial law is derived almost entirely from the customary law merchant that Lord Mansfield engrafted onto the common law wholesale in the eighteenth century.[8]

The interesting thing about the common law process is that it creates law only where it is actually needed to allow human beings to live together peacefully. Consider the torts of assault and battery. Battery forbids one from intentionally making "harmful or offensive contact" with another. This prohibits not only direct blows, but snatching a plate out of someone's hand or blowing smoke in his or her face. Assault forbids one from intentionally causing another to fear he or she is about to be battered, but it does not prohibit attempts at battery of which the victim is unaware or threats to batter someone in the future. These torts protect individuals against not only physically harmful contact, but against all offensive physical contact as well as the fear that such contact will be immediately forthcoming.

When I teach Torts, I ask the students to account for these rules. Being products of the legislative age, they inevitably launch into some theory of justice or moral desert or human rights, which invariably fails to account for the contours of the law. After all, attempting to batter someone is morally blameworthy whether or not the intended victim is aware of it, and one hardly has the right not to be offended.

---

6   HAROLD BERMAN, LAW AND REVOLUTION 81 (1983).

7   1 WILLIAM BLACKSTONE, COMMENTARIES ON THE LAWS OF ENGLAND 67 (1765). *See also* FREDERICK POLLOCK, FIRST BOOK OF JURISPRUDENCE 254 (6th ed. 1929) ("[T]he common law is a customary law if, in the course of about six centuries, the undoubting belief and uniform language of everybody who had occasion to consider the matter were able to make it so.").

8   See LEON E. TRAKMAN, THE LAW MERCHANT: THE EVOLUTION OF COMMERCIAL LAW 27 (1983). The story of the evolution of modern commercial law from the customary law merchant is an often told tale. In addition to Trakman's account, see also HAROLD BERMAN, LAW AND REVOLUTION ch. 11 (1983); BRUCE BENSON, THE ENTERPRISE OF LAW 30-35 (1990); and John Hasnas, *Toward a Theory of Empirical Natural Rights*, 22 SOCIAL PHILOSOPHY AND POLICY 111, 130-31 (2005).

For a useful account of the customary nature of the English common law see, Todd Zywicki, *The Rise and Fall of Efficiency in the Common Law: A Supply-Side Analysis*, 97 Nw. U. L. REV. 1551 (2003). See also J. H. BAKER, AN INTRODUCTION TO ENGLISH LEGAL HISTORY 72-74 (4th ed. 2002) and John Hasnas, *Hayek, Common Law, and Fluid Drive*, 1 NEW YORK UNIVERSITY JOURNAL OF LAW & LIBERTY 79 (2005).

The students fail because they think of the law as created by conscious human agency to serve an intended end. Thus, they miss the simpler evolutionary explanation. In earlier centuries, one of the most urgent social needs was to reduce the level of violence in society. This meant discouraging people from taking the kind of actions that were likely to provoke an immediate violent response. Quite naturally, then, when disputes arising out of violent clashes were settled, the resolutions tended to penalise those who had taken such actions. But what type of actions are these? Direct physical attacks on one's person are obviously included. But affronts to one's dignity or other attacks on one's honor are equally if not more likely to provoke violence. Hence, the law of battery evolved to forbid not merely harmful contacts, but offensive ones as well. Furthermore, an attack that failed was just as likely to provoke violence as one that succeeded, and thus gave rise to liability. But if the intended victim was not aware of the attack, it could not provoke a violent response, and if the threat was not immediate, the threatened party had time to escape, enlist the aid of others, or otherwise respond in a nonviolent manner. Hence, the law of assault evolved to forbid only threats of immediate battery of which the target was aware.

This example shows how the common law creates the rules necessary for a peaceful society with minimal infringement upon individual freedom. Law that arises from the settlement of actual conflicts, settles conflicts. It does not create a mechanism for social control. Common law is law that is created by non-political forces. As such, it can give us rules that establish property rights, ground the power to make contracts, and create the duty to exercise reasonable care not to injure our fellows, but not those that impose a state religion, segregate races, prohibit consensual sexual activity, or force people to sell their homes to developers. Only government legislation, which is law that is consciously created by whomever constitutes the politically dominant interest, can give us rules that restrict the freedom of some to advance the interests or personal beliefs of others.

The unenacted common law provides us with rules that facilitate peace and cooperative activities. Government legislation provides us with rules that facilitate the exploitation of the politically powerless by the politically dominant. The former bring order to society; the latter tend to produce strife. Hence, not only is government not necessary to create the basic rules of social order, it is precisely the rules that the government does create that tend to undermine that order.

U*NIFORMITY*

Supporters of government claim that government is necessary to ensure that there is one law for all and that the law applies equally to all citizens. If the government does not make the law, they contend, there would be no uniform code of laws. People in different locations or with different cultural backgrounds or levels of wealth would be subject to different rules of law.

The proper response to this is probably the one Woody Allen made to Diane Keaton in *Annie Hall* when she complained that her apartment had bad plumbing and bugs, which was: "You say that as though it is a negative thing." How persuasive is the following argument? Government is necessary to ensure that there is one style of dress for all and that all citizens are equally clothed. If the government does not provide clothes, there would be no uniform mode of dress. People in different locations or with different cultural backgrounds or levels of wealth would be clothed in garments of different styles and quality.

Why would anyone think that uniformity in law is any more desirable than uniformity in dress? The quest for uniformity leads us to treat the loving husband who kills his terminally ill wife to relieve her suffering the same way we treat Charles Manson, to apply the same rules of contracting to sophisticated business executives purchasing corporations and semi-literate consumers entering into installment contracts, and to act as though the slum lord in the Bronx and the family letting their spare room in Utica should be governed by the same rules of property law.

There are, of course, certain rules that must apply to all people; those that provide the basic conditions that make cooperative behavior possible. Thus, rules prohibiting murder, assault, theft, and other forms of coercion must be equally binding on all members of a society. But we hardly need government to ensure that this is the case. These rules always evolve first in any community; you would not even have a community if this were not the case.

The idea that we need government to ensure a uniform rule of law is especially crazy in the United States, in which the federal structure of the state and national governments is designed to permit legal diversity. To the extent that the law of the United States can claim any superiority to that produced by other nations, it is at least partially due the fact that it was generated by the common law process in the "laboratory of the states."[9] Allowing the development of different rules in different states teaches us which rules most effectively resolve disputes. To the extent that the conditions that give rise to disputes are the same across the country, the successful rules tend to be copied by other jurisdictions and spread. This creates a fairly uniform body of law.[10] To the extent that the conditions that give rise to disputes are peculiar to a particular location or milieu, they do not spread. This creates a patchwork of rules that are useful where applied, but would be irrelevant or disruptive if applied in other settings.

One of the beauties of the common law process is that it creates a body of law that is uniform where uniformity is useful and diverse where it is not. This is the optimal outcome.

Government legislation, in contrast, creates uniformity by imposing ill-fitting, one-size-fits-all rules upon a geographically and ethnically diverse population. Once again, not only is government not necessary to the creation of a well-functioning body of law, it is a significant impediment to it. Please consider this the next time you find yourself wondering why all businesses must be closed on Sunday in the Orthodox Jewish sections of Brooklyn.

---

9 See New State Ice Co. v. Liebmann, 285 U.S. 262, 311 (1932) (Brandeis, J., dissenting).

10 Fairly, but not fetishistically. The law against homicide functions quite effectively despite the fact that the definitions of first and second degree murder and voluntary and involuntary manslaughter differ from state to state.

ACCESSIBILITY

Supporters of government claim that government must make the law in order for it to be accessible to the citizens to be governed by it. The government promulgates its legislation in statute books that are available to all citizens. The unenacted rules of common law, they claim, are unintelligible to the lay person. Consisting of rules abstracted from cases over long periods of time, the common law is known only to the judges and lawyers who deal with it as part of their profession. A system of law that requires citizens to hire attorneys merely to find out what the law is is obviously unacceptable.

The proper response to this is: Are you serious? Look around. Please! Can any human being possibly be aware of the myriad arcane government regulations to which he or she is subject? Have you ever seen the Code of Federal Regulations? When was the last time you tried to prepare your income tax return? Critics of the common law contend that lay people would need professionals to tell them what the law is. Yet, year after year, studies demonstrate that even most professional tax preparers *and IRS employees* cannot understand what the United States tax code requires. The common law rule that protects citizens against unintentional injury is the requirement to exercise the degree of care a reasonable person would employ to avoid causing harm to others. This is hardly inaccessible. Does anyone know what all the rules are that the Federal Trade Commission, the Consumer Product Safety Commission, and the National Highway Traffic Safety Administration have issued to accomplish the same end?

The common law consists of rules that have proven over time to be successful in resolving disputes. Only rules that are both intelligible to the ordinary person and correspond to the ordinary person's sense of fairness can achieve this status. Rules which are inaccessible to those to be governed by them cannot be effective. This is why, for example, the common law rules of contract and commercial law specifically incorporate references to customary business practice and the duty to act in good faith. It is also why no legal expertise is required to know that the law of self-defense permits one to use deadly force to repel a life-threatening attack, but not to shoot the aggressor after the immediate danger has passed. Understanding the traditional rules of common law requires only that one be a member of the relevant community to which the rules apply, not that one be an attorney.

Government legislation, in contrast, need have no relationship to either the understanding or the moral sensibility of the ordinary person. Legislation is law created through the political process. As such, it is inherently responsive to political considerations. Such considerations can, and frequently do, produce rules that are not intelligible to the ordinary person. This is not merely because special interests can skew the legislative process. Even if legislators were selflessly devoted to the common good, they would still need some principle of justice or moral ideal to guide their law-making. But there is no guarantee that the measures necessary to effectuate such principles or ideals will correspond to the understanding of the ordinary person. The Civil Rights Act of 1964 may have been the noblest legislative effort of our age, but the ordinary person is unlikely to understand why requiring pizza delivery men to be clean shaven constitutes illegal racial discrimination[11] or how a company with a work force consisting of almost all minorities can nevertheless be guilty of discrimination.[12]

Fraud, as it evolved at common law, consists of intentionally misrepresenting a material fact that another relies upon in parting with his or her property. It is not difficult for the ordinary person to appreciate that such action may be against the law. Fraud, as defined by federal legislation, consists of any scheme or artifice to defraud. It does not require a misrepresentation of fact. Any misleading statement or non-disclosure will do. It does not require that anyone actually be misled or rely on the statement or non-disclosure. It does not require that anyone suffer any loss.[13] Martha Stewart was recently put on trial for securities fraud for the act of publicly declaring her innocence of insider trading.[14] It is probably fair to say that the ordinary person would not know that Stewart's comments to the media constituted a federal crime.

I understand the argument that if we had a night watchman state whose legislation was limited to simple, clear rules that are designed to secure individual rights, the law would be perfectly accessible. There are only two problems with this argument. The first is that in such a case, the legislation would merely reproduce the basic rules of common law. There is no need to create a government merely to publicise such rules. This can be, and is, done privately. The "restatements" of the common law are currently privately produced, easily accessible, and widely cited. The second is that it is impossible. The idea that there is a concise set of simple, clear rules that can preserve a peaceful, free society is a fantasy.[15] This becomes apparent even with regard to the fundamental rules barring aggression as soon as one attempts to specify the conditions under which force may be used in self-defense or for the defense of others, or is excused by mistaken belief or insanity. And that is without considering that these fundamental rules must be supplemented by the rules of contract, property, and tort law that are necessary for people to coordinate their behavior well enough to engage in peaceful cooperation.

Legislation, even libertarian legislation, will either reproduce the common law or depart from it to gratify a political interest or realise some conception of justice. In the former case, it is precisely as accessible or inaccessible as the common law. In the latter, it will diverge from the common-sense morality of the ordinary person, producing rules that are less accessible than the common law. Not only is government not necessary to ensure that the rules of law are accessible, it inevitably renders them less so.

---

11 See Bradley v. Pizzaco of Nebraska, Inc., 7 F.3d 795 (8th Cir. 1993).

12 See Connecticut v. Teal, 457 U.S. 440 (1982).

13 For a fuller account of the federal fraud statutes, see John Hasnas, *Ethics and the Problem of White Collar Crime*, 54 AMERICAN UNIVERSITY LAW REVIEW 579 (2005).

14 See Indictment, United States v. Stewart 37 (S.D.N.Y. 2003) (No. 03 Cr. 717).

15 For more on this, see John Hasnas, *The Myth of the Rule of Law*, 1995 WISCONSIN LAW REVIEW 199 (1995).

Courts

Now that we have eliminated the legislature, what about the judiciary? Supporters of government claim that government is necessary to provide a system of courts for settling disputes. In the absence of the government provision of "a known and indifferent judge,"[16] human beings would have no way to peacefully resolve interpersonal disputes. For "men being partial to themselves,"[17] adverse parties would inevitably seek to employ judges who would favor their interests; and judges, who would receive their fees from the litigants, would naturally favor those who could pay the most. Hence, they would not be impartial. Because parties would be unable to agree on a neutral arbiter, they would be forced to resort to violence to resolve their disputes. Thus, without government courts, peaceful coexistence is impossible.

I know this is getting boring, but the proper response to this is: look around. This is the age of globalisation. Business is contracted around the world among parties from virtually all countries. Although there is neither a world government nor world court, businesses do not go to war with each other over contract disputes. News is almost always the news of violent conflict. The very lack of reporting on international business disputes is evidence that international commercial disputes are effectively resolved without the government provision of courts. How can this be?

The answer is simplicity itself. The parties to international transactions select, usually in advance, the dispute settlement mechanism they prefer from among the many options available to them. Few choose trial by combat. It is too expensive and unpredictable. Many elect to submit their disputes to the London Commercial Court, a British court known for the commercial expertise of its judges and its speedy resolution of cases that non-British parties may use for a fee.[18] Others subscribe to companies such as JAMS/Endispute or the American Arbitration Association that provide mediation and arbitration services. Most do whatever they can to avoid becoming enmeshed in the coils of the courts provided by the federal and state governments of the United States, which move at a glacial pace and provide relatively unpredictable results. The evidence suggests that international commercial law not only functions quite well without government courts, it functions better because of their absence.

But there is no need to focus on the international scene to observe that human beings do not need government courts to settle disputes peacefully. Labor contracts not only specify wage rates and working conditions; they create their own workplace judiciary, complete with due process guarantees and appellate procedures. Universities regularly provide their own judicial processes, as do homeowner associations.

---

16 JOHN LOCKE, SECOND TREATISE OF GOVERNMENT 66 (C.B. Macpherson, ed. 1980) (1690).

17 *Id.*

18 See Mary Heaney, *Where Business is King: London's Commercial Court Hears International Clashes*, NAT'L L.J., June 5, 1995, at C1; Campbell McLachlan, *London Court Reigns as an International Forum: Parties in Cross-Border Disputes Welcome the Commercial Court's Expertise, Neutrality, and Speed*, NAT'L L.J., June 5, 1995 at C4.

Stockbrokers agree to submit employment disputes to binding arbitration as a condition of employment.[19] Religious groups regularly settle disputes among congregants by appeal to priest or rabbi. Disfavored groups, for whom prejudice makes trial in government courts a mockery, readily devise alternative mechanisms for settling disputes without violence.[20] Insurance companies provide not only compensation for personal injury and property damage, but liability insurance, by which they assume the responsibility for resolving conflicts between their clients and those of other insurance companies according to antecedently specified agreements that allow them to avoid the morass of the government judicial system. And empirical evidence demonstrates that when potential litigants in the government court system are directed into mediation, a significant portion of the lawsuits are resolved without trial.[21]

But don't just look around. Look back. Tax supported courts of general jurisdiction are an entirely modern phenomenon. Anglo-American law evolved in the context of a richly diverse set of competing jurisdictions. The royal courts, once they developed, existed in parallel with the antecedently extant hundred, shire, manorial, urban, ecclesiastical, and mercantile courts.[22] These court systems had fluid jurisdictional boundaries, and because the courts collected their fees from the litigants, they competed with each other for business. Indeed, the law of contracts and trusts, which evolved in the ecclesiastical courts, and commercial law, which evolved in the mercantile courts, entered the common law as a result of this competition. Further, the royal courts themselves consisted of four different and competing courts: king's bench, common pleas, exchequer, and chancery. These courts, like the others, collected their fees from the litigants, and hence, competed among themselves for clients. It was only with the Judicature Act of 1873 and the Appellate Jurisdiction Act of 1876 that the British government assembled its courts into its present monolithic, hierarchical structure, with American courts following suit at varying intervals thereafter.

Further, focusing on the competition among the common law courts misleadingly underestimates the diversity of the dispute settlement mechanisms that were actually employed. Because the cost of utilising the common law courts was too great for the typical working man, those courts were virtually irrelevant to the majority of the population. Most citizens resolved their disputes according to informal, customary procedures that varied with the location (urban or rural) and class of those employing them.[23]

Since our present relatively non-violent, capitalistic society evolved in the context of a diverse and competitive system of courts and dispute settlement mechanisms,

---

19 Of course, this is mainly a measure designed to allow financial firms to escape from the quagmire of United States employment litigation.

20 See Yaffa Eliach, *Social Protest in the Synagogue: the Delaying of the Torah Reading*, in THERE ONCE WAS A WORLD 84-86.

21 See Joshua D. Rosenberg and H. Jay Folberg, *Alternative Dispute Resolution: An Empirical Analysis*, 46 STAN. L. REV. 1487 (1994).

22 See HAROLD BERMAN, LAW AND REVOLUTION (1983).

23 See E. P. THOMPSON, CUSTOMS IN COMMON: STUDIES IN TRADITIONAL POPULAR CULTURE (1993).

it cannot be the case that government provision of courts is necessary for peaceful settlement of disputes. In fact, a comparison of the amount of rancorous dissatisfaction produced by the contemporary government-supplied judiciary (consider the tort reform movement) with that associated with the more variegated traditional system of resolving disputes suggests that the government provision of courts reduces rather than augments social peace.

Police

Regardless of whether a state is needed to supply law and courts, supporters of government are adamant that police must be supplied exclusively by government. It may be true that the market can adequately supply most goods and services, but police services are unique in that they inherently involve the use of coercion. Obviously, no civilised society can permit competition in the use of violence. Civil society is formed precisely to escape from that situation. Unless government brings the use of violence under its monopolistic control, peaceful coexistence is impossible, and life is indeed as "nasty, brutish, and short"[24] as Hobbes contended.

Before I respond to this by suggesting that you look around, reflect for a moment on the silliness of this argument. For if civil society cannot exist without a government monopoly over the use of coercion, then civil society does not exist. Societies do not spring into existence complete with government police forces. Once a group of people has figured out how to reduce the level of interpersonal violence sufficiently to allow them to live together, entities that are recognisable as governments often develop and take over the policing function. Even a marauding band that imposes government on others through conquest must have first reduced internal strife sufficiently to allow it to organise itself for effective military operations. Both historically and logically, it is always peaceful coexistence first, government services second. If civil society is impossible without government police, then there are no civil societies.

In the 1960s Broadway musical *Oliver*, there is a song called "Be Back Soon" in which Fagin's boys sing the line "We know the Bow Street Runners." The Bow Street Runners were famous because they were London's first government sponsored police force, organised in the latter half of the eighteenth century by the magistrates of the Bow Street court, Henry and John Fielding. I think it is fair to say that the formation of the Bow Street Runners does not represent the moment that London was transformed from a Hobbesian state of nature to a civil society.

Note also the conflation of police services with coercion. Coercion may be employed aggressively for purposes of predation or defensively to repel attempts at predation. Police services involve the use of coercion for defensive purposes only. Competition among aggressors is, indeed, a bad thing that is antithetical to the existence of civil society. But it is not competition for the provision of police services. If competition among those offering the defensive use of coercion inevitably resulted in the equivalent of aggressive gang warfare, then we would want to eschew such competition. But whether this occurs is the very question under consideration. Identifying competition among providers of police services with competition among

---

24 T. Hobbes, Leviathan 107 (H. Schneider, ed., 1958) (1651).

aggressors is entirely question-begging. It is avoiding, rather than making, an argument.

But I digress. The proper response to the claim that government must provide police services is: look around. I work at a University that supplies its own campus police force. On my drive in, I pass a privately operated armored car that transports currency and other valuable items for banks and businesses. When I go downtown, I enter buildings that are serviced by private security companies that require me to sign in before entering. I shop at malls and department stores patrolled by their own private guards. While in the mall, I occasionally browse in the Security Zone store that sells personal and home protection equipment. I converse with attorneys and, once in a while with a disgruntled spouse or worried parent, who employ private detective agencies to perform investigations for them. I write books about how the United States Federal government coerces private corporations into performing criminal investigations for it.[25] When I was younger, I frequented nightclubs and bars that employed "bouncers." Although it has never happened to me personally, I know people who have been contacted by private debt collection agencies or have been visited by repo men. Once in a while, I meet people who are almost as important as rock stars and travel with their own bodyguards. At the end of the day, I return home to my community that has its own neighborhood watch. I may be missing something, but I haven't noticed any of these agencies engaging in acts of violent aggression to eliminate their competitors.

Ah, but that is because the government police force is in the background making sure that none of these private agencies step out of line, the supporters of government contend. Really? How does that explain London before the Bow Street Runners? The New York City police force was not created until 1845. The Boston Police Department, which describes itself as "the first paid, professional public safety department in the country"[26] traces its history back only to 1838. What kept the non-political police services in line before these dates?

Regardless of Hobbes' and Locke's philosophical musings, for most of English history, there was little government provision of police services.[27] It is true that as the kings of England learned how to collect revenue by declaring all violence and sinful activity a breach of the King's peace for which they were owed payment, they began to develop an administrative machinery to facilitate the collection of fines for "criminal" activity. Thus, the local representative of the Crown, the shire reeve (later sheriff), became tasked with reporting and eventually apprehending offenders. But since the sheriffs were only interested in pursuing offenders with the means to pay the amercement, this never represented a significant portion of the police activity within the realm. The customary, non-political methods of policing provided security for most of the population of England until quite recently.

My father's oldest brother, who was born in 1902, often told me about the tontine insurance arrangement my grandfather participated in through his fraternal

---

25 See JOHN HASNAS, TRAPPED: WHEN ACTING ETHICALLY IS AGAINST THE LAW (2006).

26 See Boston Police Department web site at: http://www.cityofboston.gov/police/glance.asp.

27 See BRUCE BENSON, THE ENTERPRISE OF LAW 73-74 (1990).

organisation that provided both term life insurance and an old age annuity. Since the advent of the federal social security program, you don't hear much about tontine insurance. Most residents of New York City, who assume that only the government can provide and maintain the city's subway system, are puzzled as to why part of the system is named the BMT and part the IRT. They have no idea that in 1940, the City of New York purchased the privately built and operated Brooklyn-Manhattan Transit Corporation and the Interborough Rapid Transit Company to create the city-run Metropolitan Transportation Authority. When government begins providing services formerly provided non-politically, people soon forget that the services were ever provided non-politically and assume that only government can provide them. But just as this is not true for old age annuities and subway service, it is not true for police services. Traditionally, police services were not provided by government and, to a large extent, they still are not. Therefore, government is not necessary to provide police services.

Advocates of government can still argue that because of the special nature of police services, a government monopoly can provide such services more efficiently than non-political entities can. I must concede that there is nothing *a priori* wrong with this argument. It is certainly possible that when it comes to police services, a miracle occurs and investing a single politically directed agency with the power to supply the desired services by exacting involuntary payment from all members of society actually produces a better result than allowing the services to be supplied by non-political means. I can, however, find no evidence for this in the real world. To all outward appearances, when police services are supplied by a politically controlled monopoly, the public receives police services driven by political, rather than efficiency, considerations. Thus, disfavored, politically powerless groups are typically underserved, police resources are frequently directed toward politically favored ends (e.g., suppression of victimless crimes) rather than their most productive use (e.g., suppression of violence), and the nature of the service is determined by political budgetary concerns rather than actual need (e.g., SWAT teams in Wisconsin). Further, because government police are not dependant on voluntary contributions for their revenue, they are less likely to be responsive to the concerns of the public (e.g., police brutality) and more susceptible to corruption (see e.g., the Knapp Commission Report[28] or just watch the movie *Serpico*).

Supporters of government often point to the high inner-city crime rate, the profusion of violent gangs, and the persistence of organised crime and drug cartels to argue that we dare not abandon the government monopoly on police services. I confess to being perplexed by this argument. How can highlighting the utter failure of the government system of policing possibly be an argument for its necessity?

It is worth noting that the contemporary crime problem is most severe where non-political methods of policing have been most completely displaced by government. The inner cities are the areas most dependant on government policing. Arguing that the high rate of inner-city crime and the presence of gangs implies that we must maintain a government monopoly on police services is a bit like arguing that the

---

28 See KNAPP COMMISSION, THE KNAPP COMMISSION REPORT ON POLICE CORRUPTION (1973).

abysmal quality of inner-city public schools implies that we should not permit parents to use their tax money to send their children to private schools. And it can hardly be surprising that it is difficult to suppress the violent organisations that exist to exploit the black markets created by government prohibitions on the legal marketing of drugs, prostitution, gambling, and other "vices." But how any of this demonstrates the necessity of government provision of police is beyond me.

If a visitor from Mars were asked to identify the least effective method for securing individuals' persons and property, he might well respond that it would be to select one group of people, give them guns, require all members of society to pay them regardless of the quality of service they render, and invest them with the discretion to employ resources and determine law enforcement priorities however they see fit subject only to the whims of their political paymasters. If asked why he thought that, he might simply point to the Los Angeles or the New Orleans or any other big city police department. Are government police really necessary for a peaceful, secure society? Look around. Could a non-political, non-monopolistic system of supplying police services really do worse than its government-supplied counterpart?

Internalising Externalities

Supporters of government often argue that government is essential to provide needed regulation of market activities. Individuals contracting with each other in a market often act in ways that impose harm or unconsented to costs on others. Manufacturers make and consumers purchase products whose use imposes an unacceptable risk of injury on third parties. For example, automobile companies can produce and drivers will purchase cars that can move at speeds or have handling properties that create an unreasonable risk of injury to pedestrians. Oil companies can ship oil to consumers in ways that create an unreasonable risk of spills that would pollute the land or body of water over which the oil is transported. More generally, because people do not bear the costs their activities impose on others, they will often act in ways that impose greater costs on society than are justified by the personal benefits they realise. These unconsidered costs to others are the social costs of market activity; what economists call negative externalities. Supporters of government contend that only government can regulate market activity to ensure that private contractors consider the social costs of their transactions. Thus, even if rules of law, courts, and police services could be supplied non-politically, government would nevertheless be essential to internalise externalities.

I must confess that I am at a loss as to how to respond to this argument. Look around is not enough. That this argument has any plausibility at all is a testament to how completely oblivious people can be to the world around them. In a world in which one of the dominant political issues is tort reform; in which businesses are continually complaining to Congress that they are over-regulated by the common law of tort and begging government to protect them from this non-political method of internalising externalities, how can anyone seriously assert that government regulation is needed to deal with the problem of social costs?

It is true that economists posit a fictitious realm in which human beings engage in voluntary transactions free from all forms of regulation. But they do so because such an idealised conception of the market is useful to their exploration of the science of human interaction in much the same way that the concept of a perfect vacuum is useful to physicists exploring the laws of nature; not because they think it corresponds to anything in reality. In the real world, human interaction is always subject to regulation; by custom, by people's ethical and religious beliefs, and, in our legal system, by the common law. Tort law is precisely that portion of the law that evolved to protect individuals' persons and property from the ill-considered actions of their fellows; that is, to internalise externalities. It is only by ignoring the existence of these forms of non-political regulation; that is, only by believing that the economists' model of the market is a description of reality, that one could possibly believe that government is necessary to address the problem of social costs. Of course, one should never underestimate the power of a conceptual model to blind intellectuals to what is going on in the real world.

But, supporters of government claim, common law can never be an adequate regulatory mechanism because it is necessarily retroactive in operation. Lawsuits arise only after harm is done. Therefore, civil liability could never provide the type of proactive regulation necessary to prevent serious harm from occurring. Really? The basic rules of tort law prohibit individuals from intentionally harming others and require them to act with reasonable care to avoid causing harm inadvertently. There is nothing retroactive about this. It is true that precisely what constitutes reasonable care may have to be determined on a case by case basis, but in this respect, the common law is no different than government legislation that announces a general rule and then leaves it up to the courts to determine how it applies in particular cases. Furthermore, the common law can act prospectively in appropriate cases. The injunction, an order not to engage in a specified activity, evolved precisely to handle those cases in which one party's conduct poses a high risk of irreparable harm to others.[29] And by the way, government legislation is almost always retroactive as well. Limitations on human knowledge (not to mention public choice considerations) mean that legislators are rarely able to accurately anticipate future harm. Megan's law required public notification when a known sex offender moves into a community. It is called Megan's law because it was enacted after Megan was killed by a repeat sex offender who lived in her community. If I remember correctly, Sarbanes-Oxley was passed after Enron collapsed. And when was the USA Patriot Act passed? Oh, yes, after 9/11.

Until 1992, fast food restaurants served coffee at between 180 and 190 °F, a temperature at which the coffee can cause third degree burns in two to seven seconds if brought into contact with human skin. This posed a considerable risk of serious injury, given how often coffee served in styrofoam cups is spilled. I did not notice any proactive legislative regulation designed to internalise this externality. In 1992,

---

29 Note that to obtain an injunction at common law and thereby curtail another citizen's freedom, one must meet a very high evidentiary threshold by establishing a *high likelihod* of *irreparable* harm. This is in contrast to government legislation that can curtail citizens' freedom whenever the politically dominant faction of the legislature deems it necessary, even if only to effectuate the "precautionary principle." I leave it to the reader to decide which is the superior standard for addressing potential future harm.

Stella Liebeck won a judgment against McDonald's for injuries received when she spilled coffee on herself equal to her medical expenses plus the amount of profit McDonald's earned in two days from knowingly selling coffee at a dangerously high temperature.[30] The next day every fast food restaurant in the United States served its coffee at 158 °F, a temperature at which it takes 60 seconds to cause third degree burns; a sufficient amount of time for customers to brush the coffee off their clothes or skin. There may be many things wrong with contemporary tort law,[31] but being ineffective at internalising externalities is most assuredly not among them. The only way to believe that government is necessary to resolve the problem of social costs is to be studiously blind to the nature of both common law and government legislation.

Public Goods

Supporters of government claim that government is necessary to produce "public goods;" goods that are important for human well-being but either cannot be produced or will be under-produced by the market. Public goods are goods that are both non-rivalrous in consumption; that is, its use by one person does not interfere with its use by others, and nonexclusive; that is, if the good is available to one person, it is available to all whether they help produce it or not. Supporters of government argue that such goods cannot be produced without government because, due to the free rider and assurance problems, individuals will not voluntarily contribute the capital necessary for their production. The free rider problem refers to the fact that because people can enjoy public goods without paying for them, many will withhold their contribution to the goods' production and attempt to free ride on the contribution of others. The assurance problem refers to the fact that in the absence of some assurance that others will contribute enough to produce the good, people are more likely to regard their own contribution as a waste of money and withhold it. Therefore, government is necessary to ensure the production of important public goods.

The proper response to the argument that government is necessary to produce public goods is: Like what? Like lighthouses? The light they provide is available to all ships and its use by one does not impair its value to others. But wait, lighthouses can be and have been supplied privately.[32] Like radio and television? A wag I know likes to say that he does something impossible every night by watching commercial television. After all, television signals are non-rivalrous in consumption and

---

30 The judgment was reduced by 20 per cent to take account of Ms. Liebeck's contributory negligence with regard to how she opened the cup. This amount was further reduced on appeal.

31 Almost all of which are attributable not the way it evolved at common law, but to twentieth-century efforts to improve upon the outcome of this evolution. See John Hasnas, *What's Wrong with a Little Tort Reform?* 32 IDAHO LAW REVIEW 557 (1996).

32 See Ronald H. Coase, *The Lighthouse in Economics*, 17 JOURNAL OF LAW AND ECONOMICS 357 (1974).

nonexclusive. Therefore, they cannot be produced by the market. Like the internet? But wait, that is privately funded also.

Perhaps like police and courts? Theorists frequently argue that police services and courts are public goods that must be supplied by government. With regard to police services, for example, the argument is made that:

> Security of person is to a large degree a collective good. ... [A]n important part of the service provided by public police and systems of criminal justice generally is to *deter* potential violators from harming people. And this deterrence is an indivisible nonexcludable good to neighbors and visitors. ... In addition to deterrence, there may be the benefits that follow from incarceration of the thief – namely, incapacitation – benefits that are also indivisible and nonexcludable.
>
> Social order, at least security of persons and possessions, then, is to a considerable degree a collective good. Accordingly, to the degree that this is the case, social order may not be efficiently provided in the absence of a state.[33]

Similarly, with regard to courts, it is argued that because the existence of definite and widely known rules of behavior provides a nonexcludable benefit to all, private courts lack an incentive to establish the clear precedents that give rise to rules. Indeed, because clear precedents "would confer an external, an uncompensated benefit, not only on future parties, but also on competing judges, ... judges might deliberately avoid explaining their results because the demand for their services would be reduced by rules that, by clarifying the meaning of the law, reduce the incidence of disputes."[34] Hence, government courts are necessary for the development of rules of law.

These are perfectly logical theoretical arguments belied only by the facts of reality. The evidence that police services and courts are not public goods is that, like lighthouses, television, and the internet, they have been supplied non-politically for most of human history. It is true, of course, that if government exists and creates areas of unowned, politically controlled property that no private party has an interest in maintaining, police services are likely to be under-produced in these locations. Policing of this "public" property may indeed have to be supplied by the government. However, this is not because police services are a public good that cannot be supplied by the market, but because police services will not be supplied when the market has been suppressed by the government. And although it is certainly true that private police services produce an uncompensated positive externality in that their deterrent effects make even those who have not paid for them more secure, this can hardly be a reason for believing that such services will not be produced. It is actually quite difficult to think of any useful activity that does not produce some uncompensated positive externality. My using deodorant and going about clothed certainly do, but government is not required to pay me to induce me to bathe and dress. Further, it is at least odd to argue that a system of competitive courts will not produce rules of

---

33 CHRISTOPHER W. MORRIS, AN ESSAY ON THE MODERN STATE 60-61 (1998).

34 See William M. Landes and Richard A. Posner, *Adjudication as a Private Good*, 6 JOURNAL OF LEGAL STUDIES 235 (1979).

law when the rules on which our civilisation rests actually arose out of just such a system.³⁵

Like national defense? National defense is perhaps the archetypical public good. The security it provides is both non-rivalrous in consumption and benefits all members of society whether they pay for it or not. Can national defense be adequately supplied without government?

If "national defense" refers to the type of military expenditures associated with contemporary national governments, the answer is an obvious "no." Once a state becomes invested with the power to expropriate the wealth of its citizenry to provide for national defense, almost any desired expenditure begins to look like a requirement of national defense. Before long propping up Southeast Asian dictators and overthrowing Middle Eastern ones are being characterised as urgent national defense concerns. The fact that there is no non-governmental way to raise sufficient capital to realise this conception of national defense proves nothing about the viability of anarchy, and, in fact, serves as one more argument in favor of markets.

However, if "national defense" refers to only what is strictly necessary to protect the citizens of a nation against outside aggression, I am willing to admit that I do not know the answer to this question. I am not discomforted by this admission, however, because as I said at the outset, the question of national defense is, as a practical matter, a trivial one. No one believes that we can transition from a world of states to anarchy instantaneously. No reasonable anarchist advocates the total dissolution of government tomorrow. Once we turn our attention to the question of how to move incrementally from government to anarchy, it becomes apparent that national defense would be one of the last governmental functions to be de-politicised. If my argument for anarchy is flawed and anarchy is not a viable method of social organisation, this will undoubtedly be revealed long before doing away with national defense becomes an issue. On the other hand, to the extent that the gradual transition from government to anarchy is successful, the need for national defense continually lessens.

Consider what it would mean for a nation to seriously undertake a process of de-politicisation. Every reduction in the size and scope of government releases more of the creative energy of the population. The economic effects of this are well known and are currently being demonstrated in China. As economists point out, revolutionary change can be wrought by marginal effects. Even a slow process of liberalisation *that is sustained over time* will produce massively accelerated economic and technological growth. And the increase in freedom and prosperity in the liberalizing nation would have profound external effects as well. Many of the bravest and most industrious residents of more repressive nations would attempt to immigrate to the liberalising one, and some other nations would learn by the liberalising nation's example and begin to copy its policies.

---

35 For the true intellectuals among my readers who simply cannot accept that facts should be allowed to undermine a perfectly good theoretical model, I refer you to DAVID SCHMIDTZ, THE LIMITS OF GOVERNMENT: AN ESSAY ON THE PUBLIC GOODS ARGUMENT (1991). Schmidtz explains how the assurance problem can be handled by the assurance contract or money back guarantee and how the free rider problem can be cabined to a relatively small number of cases in which using coercion to produce the public good is ethically questionable.

As the economic and technological gap between the liberalising nation and the rest of world widens, as the rest of the world becomes more dependent upon the goods and services manufactured and supplied by that nation, and as a greater number of other nations are moved to adopt liberalising policies themselves, the threat the rest of the world poses to the liberalising nation decreases. Evidence of this is supplied by the demise of the Soviet Union. Radical regimes and terrorist organisations may constitute a serious and continuing threat, but consider it in historical context. Such a threat is considerably less serious and less expensive to address than the threat of thermonuclear war.

Recall that we are considering the cost only of protecting citizens against aggression, not the cost of foreign adventures or "pre-emptive" warfare. How significant a threat of foreign invasion does the United States currently face? How much of its "national defense" spending is actually devoted to preventing such invasion? After years or decades of continual and sustained reduction in the size of government, how much wider will the economic and technological gap between the prenatal anarchy and the more repressive nations be? How much more sophisticated its defensive technology? How much more dependent will the repressive nations be on its goods and services? Let a nation begin to tread the path toward anarchy and by the time the question of whether national defense is a public good that must be supplied by government becomes relevant, it is very likely to be moot.

Conclusion

Aristotle called man the rational animal, identifying human beings' ability to reason as their essential defining characteristic. I think this is a mistake. I think man is the imaginative animal. Human beings undoubtedly have the ability to reason, but they also have the ability to imagine that the world is different than it is, and the latter is a far more powerful force. People root for the Chicago Cubs because they can imagine the Cubs winning the World Series, despite all evidence to the contrary. People regularly get married because they can imagine that they will change their obviously incompatible partner into the ideal husband or wife. People devote their time, effort, and money to political campaigns because they can imagine that if only Bill Clinton or Bob Dole or George W. Bush or John Kerry were elected, Washington, DC would be transformed into Camelot. And more significantly, people volunteer to fight wars because they can imagine themselves running through a field of machine-gun fire unscathed. Only the ability to imagine an afterlife for which they have absolutely no evidence can explain why human beings would strap explosives to themselves and blow themselves up in an effort to kill as many innocent people as possible.

Do you ever wonder why people believed in the divine right of kings, despite the fact that the monarchs of their time were patently not the type of individuals an all-knowing, all-good god would choose to reign over them? They believed in it because they were taught to believe in it and because they could imagine that it was so, regardless of all evidence to the contrary. We no longer believe in such silly things as the divine right of kings. We believe that government is necessary for an orderly peaceful society and that it can be made to function according to the rule of law. We believe this because we have been taught to believe it from infancy and because we can imagine that it is so, regardless of all evidence to the contrary.

One should never underestimate the power of abstract concepts to shape how human beings see the world. Once one accepts the idea that government is necessary for peace and order and that it can function objectively, one's imagination will allow one to see the hand of government wherever there is law, police, and courts, and render the non-political provision of these services invisible. But if you lay aside this conceptual framework long enough to ask where these services originated and where, to a large extent, they still come from, the world assumes a different aspect. If you want the strongest argument for anarchy, simply remove your self-imposed blinders and look around.

Chapter 9
Market Anarchism as Constitutionalism

Roderick T. Long

A *legal system* is any institution or set of institutions in a given society that provides *dispute resolution* in a systematic and reasonably predictable way. It does so through the exercise of three functions: the judicial, the legislative, and the executive. The judicial function, the adjudication of disputes, is the core of any legal system; the other two are ancillary to this. The legislative function is to determine the rules that will govern the process of adjudication (this function may be merged with the judicial function, as when case law arises through precedents, or it may be exercised separately), while the executive function is to secure submission (through a variety of means, which may or may not include violence) to the adjudicative process and compliance with its verdicts. A *government* or *state* (for present purposes I shall use these terms interchangeably) is any organisation that claims, and in large part achieves, a forcibly maintained monopoly, within a given geographical territory, of these legal functions, and in particular of the use of force in the executive function.

Now the market anarchist objection to government is simply a logical extension of the standard libertarian objection to coercive monopolies in general.[1] First, from a moral point of view, among people regarded as equals[2] it cannot be legitimate for some to claim a certain line of work as their own privileged preserve from which others are to be forcibly excluded; we no longer believe in the divine right of kings, and on no other basis could such inequality of rights be justified. Second, from an economic point of view, because monopolies are insulated from market competition and hold their customers by force, they lack both the *information* and the *incentive* to provide consumers with fair, efficient, and inexpensive service. The anarchist accepts these arguments, and merely asks why they should apply with any less force to the provision of legal services.

---

1 It's sometimes suggested that government is not really a coercive institution, because its subjects have implicitly consented to its authority, either by voting or else by simply remaining within its borders. (The latter argument goes back to Plato's *Crito*.) For a compelling refutation of the claim that voting constitutes consent, I refer the reader to Spencer 1851 and Spooner 1870. As for remaining within the state's borders, the very question at issue is whether the state's claim of authority within those borders is *legitimate*. If I suddenly claim that your house lies within my sphere of authority, your remaining in your house does not constitute consent to my rule.

2 For the essentially egalitarian insight underlying libertarianism see Long 2001 and Long 2005.

Locke *versus* Locke

The minarchist has answers to this question, of course.[3] The great ancestor of all minarchist critiques is John Locke, who famously lists three defects or "inconveniences" of the state of nature, or anarchy.[4] In fact, however, each of Locke's points presents a far more serious problem for *government* than for anarchy. Let's consider them in turn.[5]

> First, there wants an established, settled, known law, received and allowed by common consent to be the standard of right and wrong, and the common measure to decide all controversies between them. For though the Law of Nature be plain and intelligible to all rational creatures, yet men, being biased by their interest, as well as ignorant for want of study of it, are not apt to allow of it as a law binding them in the application of it to their particular cases.[6]

Locke's claim is that under anarchy there will be no generally known and agreed-upon body of law. But he offers no reason for thinking this; the inseparability of *law* and *monopoly government* seems to be an unargued, unquestioned, and probably unnoticed assumption on his part.

Minarchists raise the similar worry that competing providers of legal services in an anarchic order will have conflicting interpretations of justice. No doubt they will. But how is this different from the system that minarchists favor? The whole

---

　　3　Perhaps the most popular argument for the state nowadays is the so-called "public goods" or "market failure" problem. I shall have little to say about this issue, beyond pointing to the growing literature on how markets can, and historically have, successfully solved such problems. (See, e.g. Anderson and Hill 2004; Axelrod 1984; Bell 1992; Benson 1990; Ellickson 2005; Loan 1992; Schmidtz 1991; Stringham 2006; and Wooldridge 1970.) But one brief point is worth making. Let it be granted that markets can generate perverse incentives. This by itself can hardly be an argument for government intervention, since governments, too, generate perverse incentives; the *public choice* (or "rent-seeking") problem is the governmental analogue of the market's public goods problem. Markets, however, contain a built-in mechanism for *correcting* their perverse incentives: any entrepreneur who can figure out how to solve a public goods problem stands to make a profit (and historically has). It's unclear that governments contain any analogous mechanism for correcting their own deficiencies; on the contrary, the poorer a governmental institution's performance, the more revenue it tends to receive.

　　The specific topic of an anarchist region's military defense against neighboring states lies beyond my present topic; but see Hoppe 2003 and Long 1995b.

　　4　Strictly speaking, for Locke the state of nature is not identical with anarchy; it signifies not the absence of a government but the absence of a contractually established civil society – neither of which, in his system, entails the other, just as possession and rightful ownership do not entail one another. (For example, when a government establishes itself by unjust conquest rather than by consent, we still have a state of nature, but not anarchy; when a legitimate, contractually established government is unjustly overthrown, we have anarchy, but not a state of nature.) But in these passages Locke is clearly thinking of an *anarchic* state of nature.

　　5　It's worth noting that Locke's three "inconveniences" correspond to the three functions of any legal system: the legislative, the judicial, and the executive.

　　6　*Two Treatises of Government* II.ix.124.

point of having a constitutionally limited government, with checks and balances, is that the agents who administer the system will have conflicting interpretations of justice. There'd be no point in having distinct branches of government limiting each other, or having the people limit the government through the franchise, if unanimity on questions of justice could be expected. In *both* market anarchism and limited government, then, the working of the system will involve different parties trying to enact their several conceptions of justice. The best system is not one that eliminates such conflict – no system can eliminate it – but one that does the best job of providing its constituent agents with an incentive to resolve their disputes a) peacefully, and b) in a manner favorable to individual liberty. The question is: which does a better job of this – markets or governments?

But under market anarchism, aren't there are a variety of competing legal standards and legal enforcers, with none having final say? Yes, absolutely. But *how does this differ from a minarchist legal system*? Or indeed from *any* legal system? Polycentricity is not an all-or-nothing characteristic, but rather one direction on a continuum; just about every legal system in human history has comprised a variety of competing legal standards and legal enforcers – and the *more* polycentric ones have generally been the more successful. (Not all historical cases of highly polycentric legal systems are particularly appealing by libertarian standards; but the more monocentric systems are almost always *worse*.)

As for the desideratum of an "established, settled, known law," markets seem likelier than government to converge on a relatively uniform set of laws for the same reason that they tend to converge on a single currency: consumer demand. Consider: why are there no triangular credit cards? Government regulation is not the reason; rather, if someone started offering cards that wouldn't fit in the standard machines, nobody would accept them (unless forced to do so by law). Similar reasons explain why the market no longer carries both VHS and Betamax video cartridges, but only VHS;[7] the market creates uniformity when customers need it, and diversity when they need that instead. Diversity in movie titles available is a benefit to consumers; diversity in shape and size of video cassettes is not. Hence the market tends to provide the former and suppress the latter.

The history of the body of commercial law known as the Law Merchant (*lex mercatoria*) illustrates this dynamic. The Law Merchant arose because existing, government-provided mercantile law was *not* sufficiently uniform; each country had its own regulations governing contracts, for example, and the courts of one country often would not uphold contracts made under the laws of another country. Such an obvious impediment to international trade was immensely frustrating to the mercantile community; but the courts, as government monopolies unaccountable to consumer interests, had little incentive to correct the situation. So the merchants of

---

7   Here I am relying on the assumption that the dominance of VHS is the result of market forces. Strictly speaking, of course, in a regulated market it is often very difficult to determine which particular phenomena are primarily the results of market forces and which are primarily the results of state intervention.

various countries joined together and set up their own uniform body of mercantile law and their own private courts (with no power of enforcement but the boycott).[8]

The minarchist may counter that once market providers converge on a uniform set of legal standards, the system is now a monopoly state rather than an anarchy. But first, such legal uniformity need not be imposed *by force*; it may come about simply because agencies whose policies are incompatible with the majority system will lose customers, going the way of Betamax. Second, even if legal uniformity *is* imposed by force, what's required is a set of *standards*, not a set of specific organisations. If there are no barriers to entry – if a new security agency can start up any time – how is the system not competitive?[9]

Contrary to Locke's assumption, the lack of a known and agreed-upon body of law is a much more serious problem for government than for anarchy. Governments typically generate ever-increasing mountains of bureaucratic regulations that no one has time to read; such a situation is the effective *equivalent* of having no known law. Under a private legal system where changes in law occur as a response to customer demand, such problems are much less likely; it is precisely government's *insulation* from customer demand that creates the problem in the first place.

Let's turn to Locke's second objection.

> Secondly, in the State of Nature there wants a known and indifferent judge, with authority to determine all differences according to the established law. For every one in that state being both judge and executioner of the Law of Nature, men being partial to themselves, passion and revenge is very apt to carry them too far, and with too much heat in their own cases, as well as negligence and unconcernedness, make them too remiss in other men's.[10]

Locke's worry here is that, in the absence of a monopoly government, each individual will have to act as a judge in his or her own case, a situation that inevitably raises the specter of partiality and bias. Now I think Locke is quite right in judging that, emergencies aside, submitting one's disputes to a neutral arbiter is preferable to judging them oneself; the offices of prosecutor and judge are better separated than combined. But how does an argument for neutral arbiters suddenly become an argument for monopoly government? The historical record shows that stateless legal orders tend to generate quite effective incentives for people to submit their disputes to arbitration.[11]

Locke appears to be drawing an erroneous inference from the premise "Each person should delegate retaliation to an impartial third party" to "There should be an impartial third party to whom each person delegates retaliation." This is simply a fallacy of composition, analogous to the inference from "Everyone likes at least one television show" to "There's at least one television show that everyone likes."

---

8 On the Law Merchant see Wooldridge 1970 and Benson 1990.

9 For the crucial ways in which a cooperative network of security agencies differs from a state, see Caplan and Stringham 2003.

10 Locke, *op. cit.*, II.ix.125.

11 See Anderson and Hill 2004; Axelrod 1984; Bell 1992; Benson 1990; Ellickson 2005; Loan 1992; and Wooldridge 1970.

It is actually government, not anarchy, that suffers from the problem of judicial bias. Under anarchy, *any* dispute can be submitted to third-party arbitration; but under a governmental system, in disputes between a citizen and the state, the state – which as a monopoly of course recognises no judicial authority but its own – *necessarily* acts as a judge in its own case. Division of governmental powers alleviates the situation somewhat, but even so, those with a grievance against one branch of an organisation are unlikely to receive unbiased justice from another branch of the same organisation. (Would you feel secure in having your complaint against the marketing division of IBM adjudicated by the legal division of IBM?)

Market anarchists reject the concept of monopoly government, insisting that every legal institution must be subject to correction from without. It follows, of course, that any agency doing the correcting must also be subject to correction, and so on. This doesn't lead to an infinite regress, however, because while any legal institution is subject to correction from other legal institutions, those in turn are subject to correction from the first one; legal institutions check and balance *each other*.

It might be objected that the *entire group* of competing institutions is not subject to correction from without, and so constitutes a monopoly. But this would be a mistaken view. On the dynamic Austrian view of monopoly (as opposed to the static neoclassical focus on "market share"), a field counts as non-monopolistic so long as new firms are *allowed* to enter the field at any time; they need not actually exist *now*.

What of Locke's third objection?

> Thirdly, in the State of Nature there often wants power to back and support the sentence when right, and to give it due execution. They who by any injustice offended will seldom fail where they are able by force to make good their injustice. Such resistance many times makes the punishment dangerous, and frequently destructive to those who attempt it.[12]

Locke is concerned that without a government, individuals will lack the power to enforce respect for rights. But why should this be so? Locke neglects the possibility of forms of *organised defence* that fall short of coercive monopoly. This is rather ironic, given that Locke was writing in the days before England had introduced the institution of *police*. When such governmental institutions are ineffective or absent, it is common for private, non-governmental organisations for the enforcement of rights to emerge; instances include the thief-takers' associations of pre-Peel England and the vigilance committees of the old American frontier. (The Hollywood stereotype of the latter as lawless lynch mobs has been thoroughly debunked by the work of libertarian historians.)[13] The alternative to having government provide all the shoes is not to have each person make his or her own shoes.

Here once again it is government, not anarchy, that is truly vulnerable to Locke's objection. When the forcible defense of rights is monopolised by a single organisation, it becomes much more difficult for individuals to defend their rights against *it*.

---

12 Locke, *op. cit.*, II.ix.126.
13 See Anderson and Hill 2004; Benson 1990; and Wooldridge 1970.

The Specter of Plutocracy

Another commonly expressed worry is that under market anarchism justice would go to the highest bidder, thus generating a plutocratic rather than a libertarian order. Now I certainly agree that the power of the wealthy might pose a danger to liberty in a market anarchist society.[14] But the notion that the danger of plutocracy is *less* under government is hard to believe. On the contrary, government *magnifies* the power of the rich. Government officials control the spending of money that is not theirs; hence wealthy special interests only need to spend a few *thousands* to persuade some politician or bureaucrat to divert *millions* toward their goals. By contrast, when people control only their own property, their costs are internalised; hence a thousand-dollar bribe yields only a thousand dollars' worth of results.[15]

The minarchist's worries about the fate of the poor and marginalised under anarchy sound oddly like the typical state socialist's complaints that because *he*, the state socialist, cannot imagine how markets could help such people, the market must be rejected. Such failure to recognise the ingenuity of the market is not surprising in the state socialist, but it is more so in the minarchist.

For example: only the government can protect the poor from crime, the minarchist insists, because the poor cannot afford justice on a for-profit basis. But have minarchists never heard of the American Civil Liberties Union, or the Institute for Justice, or all the many other non-profit providers of legal services? Aren't non-profit organisations part of the market? And wouldn't they have even more resources to work with under a market system? (Nor are specifically profit-oriented solutions to be dismissed either. Under the medieval Icelandic system, poor people who were the victims of aggression could sell, to a richer and more powerful neighbor, their right to compensation.[16] In any case, if libertarian economic theory is correct, a libertarian society would see the virtual elimination of poverty.)

Minarchists like Ludwig von Mises have long compared the free market to a voting system that specifically empowers the ordinary consumer:

> In the capitalistic society, men become rich ... by serving consumers in large numbers. ... The capitalistic market economy is a democracy in which every penny constitutes a vote. The wealth of the successful businessman is the result of a consumer plebiscite. Wealth, once acquired, can be preserved only by those who keep on earning it anew by satisfying the wishes of consumers. The capitalistic social order, therefore, is an economic democracy

---

14 See my discussion of this problem, and possible solutions to it, in Long 1998.

15 For some of the ways in which governments, even allegedly "left-wing" or "progressive" ones, systematically benefit the rich at the expense of the poor, see Beito 2000; Carson 2004; Childs 1971; Grinder and Hagel 1977; Kolko 1963; Kolko 1977; Long 1994; Long 1998; Martin 1975; Radosh and Rothbard 1972; Ruwart 1993; Shaffer 1997; Siddeley 1992; Stromberg 2001; and Weaver 1988.

16 A simple extension of this approach could also solve the problem of murder victims who leave no heirs: courts can simply treat these victims' right to compensation as a *homesteadable claim*; see Long 1999.

in the strictest sense of the word. In the last analysis, all decisions are dependent on the will of the people as consumers.[17]

Anarchists simply draw the logical conclusion – as David Friedman does in the following passage:

> You can compare 1968 Fords, Chryslers, and Volkswagens, but nobody will ever be able to compare the Nixon administration of 1968 with the Humphrey and Wallace administrations of the same year. It is as if we had only Fords from 1920 to 1928, Chryslers from 1928 to 1936, and then had to decide what firm would make a better car for the next four years. … Imagine buying cars the way we buy governments. Ten thousand people would get together and agree to vote, each for the car he preferred. Whichever car won, each of the ten thousand would have to buy it. It would not pay any of us to make any serious effort to find out which car was best; whatever I decide, my car is being picked for me by the other members of the group.[18]

Hence, Friedman concludes, the provision of "governmental" services should be transferred from the political plebiscite to the economic.[19]

It's sometimes objected that under such "market democracy" a rich person has more votes than a poor person, while under political democracy each person has one vote. This objection rests on an equivocation. If by having more votes one means having more ability to bring about the outcomes one votes for, then under even an ideal political democracy, 49 per cent of the population have, *in that sense*, no votes at all. (Under actually existing political democracies, of course, the rich have many more votes than they would have under market democracy, for the reasons explained above.)

Anarchism is a Constitutionalism

Minarchists often insist, as an objection to anarchism, that the use of force needs to be subjected to constitutional restraints. But here I suspect that the minarchist is being misled by a metaphysically illusive picture of what constitutional restraints are and how they work.

First of all, when we speak of constitutional restraints we are presumably not talking merely of restrictions written into a legal document. Such paper prohibitions are neither necessary (look at Britain) nor sufficient (look at Soviet Russia) for

---

17 Mises 1978, p. 178. Mises, like many libertarians, uses the term "capitalistic" to mean free-market or *laissez-faire*. Some libertarians, however, prefer to use the term for the economic system prevailing in industrialised countries, which they identify as an *unfree* market characterised by pro-corporate governmental regulation. For the ambiguity of "capitalism" see Johnson 2007; I make a case for abandoning the term entirely in Long 2006a.

18 Friedman 1989, pp. 131-32.

19 For present purposes I use the term "political" in its narrowly governmental sense – the sense in which Karl Hess (1969) called for "The Death of Politics." For a defense of a broader notion of the political, see Lavoie 1993 and Long and Johnson 2005.

actually operative restraints. What matters is a nation's "constitution" in the original sense of the actual institutions, practices, and incentive structures that are in place.

But a constitution in that sense has no existence independent of the actual behavior and interactions of actual human beings. The metaphysical illusion I referred to is the habit of thinking of constitutional restraints (checks and balances, separation of powers, etc.) as though these structures existed *in their own right*, as external limitations on society as a whole. But in fact those structures exist only insofar as they are continually *maintained* in existence by human agents acting in certain systematic ways. A constitution is not some impersonal, miraculously self-enforcing robot. It's an ongoing pattern of behavior, and it persists only so long as human agents continue to conform to that pattern in their actions.[20] In Gustav Landauer's words: "The state is a relationship between human beings, a way by which people relate to one another; and one destroys it by entering into other relationships, by behaving differently to one another."[21]

The confused assumption that a legal framework must (or even can) be external to what it constrains tends to make political structure *invisible* except insofar as it is realised in familiar state-monopoly institutions. And this in turn helps to explain what anarchists often find puzzling: namely, the tendency among non-anarchists to treat a single unsuccessful or undesirable instance of a stateless society as a refutation of anarchism *per se* – whereas nobody regards a single unsuccessful or undesirable instance of a state as a decisive objection to the state as such. The reason for this puzzling double standard is that while people generally recognise that states can come in a variety of different political structures, so that the failure of one type proves nothing against another, it is implicitly assumed that *anarchies are all alike* in structural terms – that is, that they are all *structureless* – and so the failure of one counts against all. But in fact mere statelessness is compatible with a variety of different institutional and cultural arrangements, and one would expect differences in such arrangements to have a significant impact on a stateless society's viability.

Since human beings have free will, no social pattern of behavior can be *automatically* self-perpetuating; nothing whose survival depends on the choices of free agents can be *guaranteed* to survive. But such social patterns can be more or less *likely* to survive. A way of interacting that tends, by and large, to give most of the people participating in it an *incentive* to keep interacting in that way is more likely to survive than one that does not. And some anarchies will do a better job at this than others, just as some states do a better job at this than others.

It is sometimes objected that legal services cannot be supplied on the market because a functioning market *presupposes* a functioning legal order. Now it is true that a functioning market requires a functioning legal order; but it is equally true that a functioning legal order requires a functioning market. This is obviously true

---

20 I argue in Long (2006b) that the minarchist's implicit assumption that a society's legal system must be something *external* to society that *makes* it orderly is akin to the error, diagnosed by Wittgenstein, that there must be some mental item that all by itself guarantees its own meaning regardless of how one goes about applying it in practice.

21 Gustav Landauer, "Weak Statesmen, Weaker People," *Der Sozialist*, 1910; quoted in Graham 2005, p. 165.

if the legal order is market anarchism; but *it is no less true when the legal order is a government*. As Anthony de Jasay points out,[22] states can arise only in societies wealthy and orderly enough to maintain them. Hence a state cannot exist unless there is a functioning economy of some sort. (Anarchists take this to show that the state is a *parasite* on productive activity; the most the minarchist can claim is that it is a *luxury good*.) In any case, a functioning market and a functioning legal order arise *together*; it's not as though one shows up on the scene first and then paves the way for the other. To think otherwise is to fall once more into the metaphysical illusion that economic activity takes place against the background of a legal framework whose existence is somehow *independent* of the activity it constrains.

The "constitution" of a free society, then, needs to be a pattern of interaction in which people act – and in so doing give themselves, and one another, an incentive to keep acting – in ways that tend to maintain freedom. Market anarchists and proponents of limited government *both* claim to be offering such a pattern. The choice between government and anarchy, then, is not a choice between having a constitution and not having one; it is a choice between two different constitutions. Far from eschewing checks and balances, market anarchists take *market competition*, with its associated incentives, to *instantiate* a checks-and-balances system, and to do so far more reliably than could a governmental system.

Despite the best intentions of those who framed the U.S. Constitution's checks-and-balances system, there has been sufficient convergence of interests among the three branches that, occasional squabbles over details notwithstanding, each branch has been complicit with the others in expanding the power of the central government. Separation of powers, like federalism and elective democracy, merely *simulates* market competition, within a fundamentally monopolistic context.

Anarchy thus represents the *extension*, not the negation, of constitutionalism. Instead of thinking of anarchy as a situation in which government has been squeezed down to nothingness, it might be more helpful – at least for minarchists – to think of anarchy as a situation in which government has been extended to include everybody. This is what Gustave de Molinari, the founder of market anarchism, meant when he wrote, in 1884: "The future thus belongs neither to the absorption of society by the State, as the communists and collectivists suppose, nor to the suppression of the State, as the [non-market] anarchists and nihilists dream, but to the diffusion of the State within society."[23]

A "diffused" legal system is preferable on pragmatic grounds because anarchy *multiplies* checks and balances; handing all power over to a single monopoly agency is too risky. It is also preferable on moral grounds, because it recognises the equal right of all persons to practice any legitimate profession, and because the alternative – a monopoly government – would necessarily run afoul of the Lockean prohibition on being a judge in one's own case. A monopoly government, i.e. an agency that refuses to submit its use of force to external adjudication, is by definition *lawless*; thus anarchy is the *completion*, not the negation, of the rule of law. Anarchy "comes not to destroy but to fulfil the law."

---

22 De Jasay 2002.
23 Molinari 1888, pp. 393-94; translation mine.

The Final Legal Frontier

In case of disagreement among protection agencies, the minarchist asks, must there not be some force in society that *makes* the agencies first submit their disputes to, and then abide by the results of, arbitration? Certainly. But the assumption that securing compliance with the results of arbitration is the function of some *one* agency, rather than of the entire system of interacting agencies, is precisely what market anarchism challenges.

Indeed, the minarchist position appears, once more, to run into an infinite regress. If people cannot cooperate peacefully unless they are subjected to some organisation serving as final arbiter, then the members of that organisation likewise cannot cooperate peacefully unless there is some further "final" arbiter over them, and so on *ad infinitum*. And as we have seen, even invoking a Hobbesian dictatorship would not be enough to terminate the regress, since no individual possesses the might – *without cooperation from her subjects* – to compel acquiescence.

We can in any case turn the question back on the minarchist: how are disputes among different branches of the minarchic government resolved, and *who* makes the disputing parties abide by the result? The answer, of course, is that under the sort of constitutional regime that the minarchist generally favours, there is no *one* branch, let alone one individual officer, who makes such judgments stick. (This is precisely why seventeenth-century theorists of royal absolutism, like Thomas Hobbes and Robert Filmer, thought that one-man dictatorship was the only stable form of government.) Nor are government officials characterised by *unanimity*. Yet most of the time government officials are not waging war against one another. What leads them to resolve their disputes peacefully? *Constitutional restraints.*

But once again, it is not as mere *paper guarantees* that constitutional restraints are effective. What matters is *institutional structure*, with *checks and balances* and other incentival and informational mechanisms. Securing cooperation among the branches of government is the function of such checks and balances between one branch and another, not the function of some unchecked superordinate branch. Anarchy is simply a *generalisation* of this principle; that's why I've been describing market anarchism as a species of, rather than as an alternative to, constitutionalism. When minarchists ask what anarchists can rely on to maintain order in an anarchist society, the answer is: the same thing minarchists rely on to maintain order within a minarchic government. What's sauce for the goose is sauce for the gander. The only difference is that anarchists rely on the natural incentive system of the market rather than trying to construct an artificial incentive system in the social-engineering mode.

Minarchists sometimes charge market anarchy with lacking "legal finality" or a "final arbiter."[24] Let's consider what such "finality" means. This concept could be

---

24 See, e.g. Bidinotto 1994 and my subsequent online debate with Bidinotto (Long 2003a; Bidinotto 2003a; Long 2003b; Bidinotto 2003b; Bidinotto 2004a; Bidinotto 2004b; Long 2004a). Portions of the present chapter are drawn from my side of that debate.

interpreted either Platonically or realistically.[25] Platonically, legal finality would mean an absolute guarantee that disputes are settled beyond any possibility whatsoever of being revived. Realistically, legal finality would mean that in practice disputes do fairly reliably get brought to an end.

Platonic legal finality is of course impossible. Neither anarchy nor minarchy can provide it; nor can any other conceivable legal system. What person or institution is the final legal arbiter, for example, under the current U.S. system? Is it Congress? No, the Supreme Court can declare its laws unconstitutional. The Supreme Court? No, Congress can initiate the process of amending the Constitution to get around the Supreme Court. The only system that allows for a final arbiter would be a Hobbesian dictatorship, with all power vested in a single person (for even a small ruling council might have internal disputes, and who then would have the final say in resolving them?). But as La Boétie (2003) and Hume[26] pointed out centuries ago, no individual ruler (unless she hails from Krypton) possesses in her own right sufficient power to compel obedience from everybody else; hence any dictator's power depends on the concurrence of those she rules. Thus a final arbiter in the sense after which the minarchist hankers is an illusion, a Platonic ideal – it cannot be realised *on this earth*.[27]

The original U.S. Constitution notoriously had *nothing* to say about how disputes between different branches of the Federal government, or between the Federal government and the States, were to be resolved. (Incredibly, it didn't even say whether the member states had a right to secede.)[28] It made clear that the Constitution was the "supreme law of the land," but it was utterly silent on the question of what should be done if a given branch of government overstepped its constitutional authority. When the U.S. Supreme Court declared President Andrew Jackson's "Trail of Tears" policy unconstitutional, Jackson proceeded with the policy anyway, quipping "[Chief Justice] Marshall has made his decision; now let him enforce it!" Customs governing cooperation among the branches of government evolved only gradually;[29] the current system, under which the Supreme Court is recognised as having the power to declare the actions of other branches unconstitutional, *has never been codified in law*; it emerged instead through precedent and informal acquiescence.

Even where the rules for resolving disputes within the state apparatus *are* legally codified, such "paper guarantees" are meaningless except insofar as they are honored in actual practice. In the early years of the Roman Empire, the popular fiction that Augustus had "restored the Republic" was officially maintained; *on paper*, all political authority was still vested in "the Senate and the People," while the Emperor had *no legal existence*, i.e. there was initially *no such office* as "Emperor." But of

---

25 I choose the adjective "Platonic" by analogy with Reisman 2005's "Platonic Competition."

26 David Hume, "Of the First Principles of Government," in Hume 1985, pp. 32-36.

27 See Cuzán 1979.

28 This omission enabled each side in the 1861-65 U.S. Civil War to claim constitutional support, with some color of plausibility.

29 See, e.g. Axelrod 1984. When cooperation finally did evolve, it did so in a malignant way, with each branch of government concurring in the expansion of the power of the others.

course the Emperor's *de facto* authority, resting on the support of the army, far exceeded the authority of Rome's *de jure* rulers. Similar remarks apply to the *de facto* constitutional role of the military in the Turkish Republic in recent decades; *in practice*, the Turkish army's chief function has been to check the rise of Islamism and Communism in the civilian government by staging a coup whenever Islamists or Communists gain too much power; after each coup the army, rather than holding on to the power it has seized, steps back and holds democratic elections. This has happened so regularly and predictably over the course of the Turkish Republic's history that it must be described as part of Turkey's *de facto* constitution, though of course nothing *on paper* authorises the army to seize power – or guarantees that it will relinquish it afterward.

The point is that what gets disputes resolved within a legal system is not the rules *per se*, but rather an *incentive structure* that makes the system's administrators likely to act in accordance with such rules. Hence minarchy, no less than anarchy, must rely on such an incentive structure. Under market anarchism, it is economic competition that provides that incentive structure. (And if the objection is that such incentive structures presuppose a functioning legal system, the answer, once again, is that these structures are precisely what *constitutes* a functioning legal system, and so cannot "presuppose" it in the sense that the minarchist requires.)

Minarchists sometimes ask: under market anarchism, *who decides* what counts as a rights-violation? But this question is ambiguous. If it means "whose authority *makes* an action count as a rights-violation?" the answer is that nobody under any system has or could have any such power.[30] If it means "whose sole decision brings about legal finality in cases of disputes over rights?" the answer, once again, is that no *person* has the power to bring this about unaided, whether under minarchy or under anarchy (and if anyone did possess such monopolistic power it would be unjust for her to exercise it). Or if it means only "how does legal finality get achieved?," then the answer is that in a market system, legal service providers will tend to gain more profits to the extent that they succeed in cooperating with other providers in such a way as to secure (realistic) legal finality. But whether a *particular* adjudicator's decision ends up bringing a dispute to an end in any *particular* case always depends not on the adjudicator's sole say-so but always on the overall pattern of interaction among legal service providers and their clients; and again, this is as true under minarchy as under anarchy.

Consider: under the limited constitutional government favored by the minarchist, if a court rules against a disputant, she can appeal to a higher court. If the highest court rules against her, she and her friends can petition Congress to pass a law reversing the Court's decision. If the Court declares the new law unconstitutional, she can petition the President to fill upcoming vacancies on the Court with judges friendlier to her point of view – or she can work to have the Constitution amended. Failing that, she can try to foment a revolution. *All of these options are in principle open to her*. No agency or institution in a governmental system can truly issue a *final verdict* in such a way as to *guarantee* beyond all possible doubt that the case really is closed. Hence legal finality in the Platonic sense is something that *a governmental*

---

30 See Rand 1990, pp. 17-22, and Sharvy (f2007).

system is no better able to provide than an anarchist one, because legal finality in the Platonic sense is something that has no reference to reality.

In any case, no legal system *needs* Platonic legal finality; for any legal system intended for use *on this earth*, realistic legal finality is perfectly adequate. Thus the fact that a market anarchist system lacks a "final arbiter" does not by itself show that it lacks realistic legal finality, unless one assumes what the minarchist needs to prove, namely that a social system cannot perform a function unless some one specific agency is authorised to perform that function. ("Under capitalism, who will be in charge of making the shoes?")

Given that "final say" is impossible, one might wonder why this doesn't show that government itself is impossible – in which case we should stop clamoring for anarchy and instead recognise that we already have it. The answer is that a government is not an agency that genuinely *possesses* "final say" – for indeed no such agency exists. Rather, a government is an agency that *claims* to possess "final say," and that gets enough people to support its claim that it ends up being empowered to violate many people's rights and to inflict a great deal of damage in the course of attempting to enforce its nonexistent authority. (Likewise state socialism does not really succeed in destroying the market – and if it did succeed, universal starvation would quickly follow[31] – but it does succeed in imposing massive *distortions* and *inefficiencies* on the functioning of market forces.)

Voiding the Warranty

Brian Barry (1975), in his infamous "review" of Robert Nozick's *Anarchy, State, and Utopia*, accused the libertarian Nozick of "proposing to starve or humiliate ten percent or so of his fellow citizens (if he recognizes the word) by eliminating all transfer payments through the state, leaving the sick, the old, the disabled, the mothers with young children and no breadwinner, and so on, to the tender mercies of private charity, given at the whim and pleasure of the donors and on any terms that they choose to propose" (p. 332).

Note that Barry evidently felt no need to explain why it should be thought preferable to leave these needy individuals to the "tender mercies" of *state welfare*, likewise "given at the whim and pleasure of the donors and on any terms that they choose to propose." Here we have two modes of social interaction – the peaceful and the violent (or as the nineteenth-century libertarians called them, the "industrial" and the "militant") – *neither* of which functions *automatically*. To cite the teaching of La Boétie and Hume once again: violent institutions *no less than peaceful ones* depend for their continued operation on the ongoing voluntary activities of free agents – in particular, in this case, on the cooperation of the coerced with the coercers (given that ordinarily the coerced vastly outnumber the coercers, such cooperation cannot be achieved by brute force alone) *and* on the cooperation of the coercers with one another. The question is: which pattern of interaction – the peaceful or the violent, the

---

31 See Mises 1990.

egalitarian or the hegemonic – is most likely, given its incentival and informational constraints, to generate desirable outcomes?

Now once the question of welfare is put in terms of comparative institutions, libertarians can readily show – indeed, have pretty thoroughly shown – that peaceful, egalitarian, market-based methods of poor relief are more efficient and reliable than violent, hegemonic, governmental methods.[32] But Barry's magical picture of the state forestalls so much as the idea of comparative institutional analysis: in his eyes the state – magically, somehow – *guarantees* what a market system leaves *un*guaranteed.

Libertarians generally avoid making Barry's mistake. Indeed, one might go so far as to say that rejecting this magical picture of the state just is one of the defining features distinguishing libertarianism from its ideological rivals. But minarchist libertarians, I suggest, have not disentangled themselves from the magical picture so thoroughly as anarchist libertarians have. Instead, they often write (*when discussing anarchism*, though seldom when discussing any other topic) as though a government's *decreeing* some desired result is equivalent to its *achieving* it – and then contrast this idealised picture of government with the muddling reality of anarchy, to the latter's detriment.[33]

This magical picture of government appears to underlie the minarchist's demand to know what *guarantees* that private entrepreneurs under market anarchism will not behave in tyrannical and abusive ways? The answer, of course, is that *nothing* "guarantees" it, just as nothing "guarantees" that governmental politicians will not behave likewise. But once we leave aside the magical approach for a comparative-institutions approach, we can ask a more useful question: under which system is such behavior most *likely* to be restrained? The superiority of anarchy over government here lies in the fact that under government the tie between the *decision* to commit aggression and the *cost* of that aggression is far weaker than under market anarchism. Under a governmental system, the cost of state policies leading to war is borne by taxpayers and conscripts, not by the politicians who crafted those policies. Under market anarchism, by contrast, agencies who resolve disputes through violence rather than arbitration will have to charge higher premiums and will thus lose customers.[34] A government *can't* lose "customers" (taxpayers) unless they take the drastic step of moving to a new country; by contrast, switching protection agencies would be as easy as switching long distance service. This is also the reason that governments are so warlike: they can buy war at *less* than the market price by shifting the costs to their subjects.

Similar reasoning applies to some minarchists' worry that each special interest group might hire its own protection agency. Well, so they might. But of course the phenomenon of interest-group politics will be a problem under minarchy as well.

---

32 See, e.g. Andreoni 1993; Beito 2000; Edwards 2007; Gosden 1973; Green 1993; Long 1994; Siddeley 1992; Tanner 1996; and Woodson 1989.

33 I discuss the implicit view of government decrees as *incantations*, bringing about their results as though requiring no intermediate process, in Long 2001.

34 Or donors, or co-op members, depending on whether the protection agency is organised as a cash-for-profit, cash-charity, or labour-charity enterprise; see Jacobson 1995.

The question is which system will do a *better* job of handling this problem. Now under minarchy, the government will presumably lack the constitutional authority to give these various interest groups the favors they want; but constitutions can be amended, or creatively reinterpreted, or indeed simply ignored. (Look at the case of the United States.) Even under minarchy, then, interest groups will vie – through voting blocs, propaganda, campaign contributions, and bribes legal or illegal – to transform the One Big Protection Agency into one that promotes their own agenda. The difference is that under anarchy, the costs of such codification are *internalised*; interest groups must *themselves* foot the bill for the regulations they favor.

Moreover, if agency A seeks to resolve its disputes with agency B by resorting to warfare, the costs to agency A's clients will skyrocket. This will not deter A's more fanatical clients, but more will surely be deterred than would be the case under a monopoly government, where such costs can be externalised by spreading them across all the government's "clients." Under the present governmental system, special interest groups don't have to pay the full costs of their policies; they get politicians to fund their schemes out of the general tax base. It's relatively costless for special interests to demand that government impose their particular values on society. But suppose that, under market anarchism, when you get your monthly bill from Acme Security Company, you see that you're paying 100 hayeks for "basic service" (protection against force and fraud) and 800 hayeks for "premium service" (snooping on your neighbors to make sure that they're not taking drugs or having abortions or playing violent video games). The number of bigots who would be willing to *pay* to have their own values forcibly imposed is bound to be smaller than the number of bigots who merely *advocate* such imposition; talk is cheap. (And the few fanatics who *are* willing to put their money where their mouth is would be easier to deal with under anarchy; you can't arrest people who *lobby* for government-imposed aggression, but you can arrest people who actually aggress.) The threat of clashing interest groups is thus an argument *for*, not against, market anarchism.

It's true, as opponents of market anarchism charge, that people living under anarchy might disagree about the definition of aggression. But if two security agencies disagree about how exactly to define property rights in some particular case, they can fight it out – thus sending their costs through the roof and their customers to the nearest competitor – or they can resolve their dispute through peaceful arbitration, thus keeping their costs low and their customers happy. Governments resort to force far more often, since they don't have to worry so much about losing customers – though it's worth noting that even governments interact peacefully most of the time, *despite* facing an artificially low cost of war. Private security agencies, which would have to buy at the market price, would choose war even less often.

Indeed, the problems that minarchists raise for market anarchy often seem as good, or bad, arguments for world government as for a geographically delimited nation-state. What happens, for example, when Switzerland and Austria have a disagreement – about customs duties, or rivers flowing from one country into the other, etc.? Must Switzerland either coercively enforce its preferences on Austria, or else resign itself to impotence? Obviously these are not the only options. Most disputes between countries are resolved through peaceful negotiation, rather than through either warfare or total surrender. The same would naturally apply to disputes between rival protection agencies – except that, as noted above, such agencies would be *more* likely than states to choose negotiation, because their costs of going to war would be internalised – whereas states can pass the costs of war on to their captive customer base. Few customers will care to pay the high fees of warfare-prone agencies; and surrender-prone agencies will obviously not be a big winner with customers either; thus negotiation would be the dominant strategy.

So disputes under anarchy are likely to be resolved *peacefully*. But how likely are they to be resolved *correctly*? Admittedly nothing "guarantees" this. But a) a competitive court system is more likely to be information-generating than a top-down legislative system, for familiar Hayekian reasons; and b) since aggression is costlier than non-aggression, the dispute-resolution will tend to favor laws with a broadly libertarian content.

The case for anarchy over minarchy thus lies, above all, in the following two facts: first, a system of freely competing protection agencies *could* exist without aggression, while government by definition must aggress by prohibiting non-aggressive competitors; second, a competitive system will *in practice* involve less aggression than will a minarchic system, because anarchy involves a more extended system of checks and balances (the number of protection agencies makes collusion among them more difficult than collusion among branches of a single government), a more effective incentive system (because the market internalises externalities), and greater accountability (the familiar superiority of market democracy over political democracy).

No Truce With Kings

Nor would anarchist objections be met if, as has sometimes been suggested,[35] the minarchist state were to confine itself to acting as a sort of licensing agency, granting licenses to protection agencies that operate in accordance with a certain set of legal rules, and coercively putting protection agencies out of business or overriding their decisions if they either operate unlicensed or violate the conditions of license. Let's see why not.

To begin with, we must consider whether such a licensing agency is to be envisioned as imposing a full legal code in all its detailed specificity, or only a set of general legal principles.

Suppose it's the former. How could the licensing agency be justified in doing this? It seems implausible to assume that there's only one possible correct legal code; while presumably there is just one correct set of legal *principles*, there will always be many different specific ways of applying such principles. Sometimes those different ways will be equally legitimate; in those cases requiring agencies to employ specification A in lieu of equally legitimate specification B constitutes aggression (a moral objection to the licensing agency). At other times one specification will have some superiority over another[36] – but, for familiar Hayekian reasons, the best

---

35 See Hasnas 2003; Bidinotto 2004a.

36 In some cases, one specification that has no *inherent* superiority over another may acquire such superiority from context; for example, there are different, equally legitimate,

way to *discover* which specification is best is ordinarily going to be through market competition (a practical objection to the licensing agency).[37] In either case, pure anarchy is preferable to the licensing agency.

Perhaps what's supposed to justify the licensing agency in imposing a single specification is not that there's only one correct specification but rather that a legal system can't function properly unless all parties accept the *same* specification. (For example, driving on the left and driving on the right are equally good systems, but it matters that everyone driving on the same road accept the *same* system.) Well, it depends. Sometimes uniformity matters and sometimes it doesn't. (England and Scotland are part of the same legal system, but have different laws on many matters; ditto for Nevada and Utah. Yet residents of those states manage to do business successfully with one another.) In any case, private legal systems have a history of providing legal uniformity when it's needed; the Law Merchant, let's recall, succeeded precisely because it provided *more* legal uniformity than the government courts.

Neither a moral case nor a practical case has been made for coercively imposing a single legal specification on all protection agencies. Where uniformity is needed, the market will provide it, and coercive imposition is superfluous; where uniformity is not needed, coercive imposition is disastrous.

Suppose instead that the licensing agency confines itself to imposing only those general principles that are required by justice. Surely imposing *those* principles is justified; so why wouldn't the licensing agency then be permissible?

Well, let's see what we're supposed to be imagining. Here we have a variety of competing protection agencies, and *one* of them takes upon itself the job of forcing all the other ones to conform to the general principles of justice. Is it the *only* organisation doing this? Does it forbid new entrants into *this* field, thus functioning as a *second-order* monopoly – permitting competition in protecting rights, but not in the *certification* of protectors of rights, even when other certifiers would be certifying in accordance with the right principles? If so, it is an unjust aggressor; for if *ex hypothesi* the coercive imposition of these general principles of justice is permissible, then it is permissible for anybody, not just for this one agency. Such a monopoly would also be dangerous on incentive grounds; it would in effect be in

---

"default" construal of unstated terms in a contract, but the fact that a certain construal has become common practice and was known to be so by the contracting parties can be legitimate grounds for imposing that construal when enforcing a contract.

37 One source of minarchist confusion about market anarchism may be a conflation of two different sorts of "monopoly." A market anarchist can certainly think that some rights-claims are correct and others are mistaken, and that agencies acting on correct views have the moral right to defend their clients, by force if necessary, against agencies acting on mistaken views. In that sense, market anarchists have no objection to the idea that *actions based on correct views of justice have a right to a "monopoly" against actions based on a mistaken view of justice*. What market anarchists deny is the further inference that this "monopoly" is best achieved through a monopoly *agency* or *institution*. On the contrary,

charge of licensing its competitors, a system unlikely to work better for protection agencies than it does for other businesses.[38]

On the other hand, if the licensing agency does allow other agencies to compete with it in forcing protection agencies to use the right principles, how does it maintain sufficient power to impose its will on the *entire* network of competing agencies? After all, it will then be just one of many competitors in the same field, with no guarantee of a dominant market share. In other words, it'll just be one more protection agency, with no unique status at all.

There is simply no way to have a government unless it claims some sort of monopoly for itself. Either the activity it monopolises is an inherently permissible activity or it is not. If it is permissible, then in forbidding competitors in this activity the government is behaving as an aggressor. And if it is impermissible, then the government shouldn't be engaging in it. The licensing-agency version of minarchy is trying to have its cake and eat it too.

Bibliography

Anderson, Terry L., and Hill, Peter J. 2004. *The Not So Wild, Wild West: Property Rights on the Frontier* (Stanford: Stanford University Press).

Andreoni, James. 1993. "An Experimental Test of the Public Goods Crowding Out Hypothesis." *American Economic Review* 83, no. 5 (December).

Axelrod, Robert. 1984. *The Evolution Of Cooperation* (New York, NY: Basic Books).

Barry, Brian. 1975. Review of Robert Nozick's *Anarchy, State, and Utopia*. *Political Theory* 3, no. 3 (August), pp. 331-36.

Beito, David T. 2000. *From Mutual Aid to the Welfare State: Fraternal Societies and Social Services* (Chapel Hill: UNC Press).

Bell, Tom W. 1992. "Polycentric Law," *Humane Studies Review* 7, no. 1 (Winter); also online at: osf1.gmu.edu/~ihs/w91issues.html

Benson, Bruce L. 1990. *The Enterprise of Law: Justice Without the State* (San Francisco: Pacific Research Institute).

---

38 The suggestion, by Rand 1964 (pp. 125-34) among others, that a monopoly government might be legitimate if it charged only user fees rather than taxes, must likewise be rejected. Even if there should emerge a minarchic regime that did not technically rely on taxation, such a state would still have to engage in activities that are the moral and economic equivalent of taxation. The U. S. Postal Service, for example, likes to brag that it is not funded by taxes. This is true. But it remains a coercive monopoly, since competition in the field of first-class mail delivery is illegal in the United States. Because of the knowledge and incentive problems notoriously associated with monopolies, the Postal Service inevitably costs its customers more – both in actual fees and in quality-related opportunity costs – than would a free market in mail delivery. This differential cost may not technically be a tax, but the respects in which it differs from a tax seem neither morally nor economically significant. We may call it a *de facto* tax. A monopolistic legal system will necessarily be engaged in *de facto* taxation for precisely the same reasons.

Bidinotto, Robert J. 1994. "The Contradiction in Anarchism." Published online at: rous.redbarn.org/objectivism/Writing/RobertBidinotto/ContradictionInAnarchism.html

Bidinotto, Robert J. 2003a. "Contra Anarchism." Blog entry for 21 December 2003; online at: bidinotto.journalspace.com/?entryid=55

Bidinotto, Robert J. 2003b. "Contra Anarchism, Part II." Blog entry for 29 December 2003; online at: bidinotto.journalspace.com/?entryid=56

Bidinotto, Robert J. 2004a. "Contra Anarchism, Part III." Blog entry for 20 January 2004; online at bidinotto.journalspace.com/?entryid=67

Bidinotto, Robert J. 2004b. "The Goal of Law: Justice or 'Utility'?" Blog entry for 10 January 2004; online at: bidinotto.journalspace.com/?entryid=59

Caplan, Bryan, and Stringham, Edward. 2003. "Networks, Laws, and the Paradox of Coperation." *Review of Austrian Ecnomics* 16, no. 4, pp. 309-26; also online at: www2.sjsu.edu/depts/economics/faculty/stringham/docs/Caplan-Stringham-Networks.pdf

Carson, Kevin A. 2004. "Austrian and Marxist Theories of State-Monopoly Capital." Online at: www.libertarian.co.uk/lapubs/econn/econn102.pdf

Childs, Roy A. 1971. "Big Business and the Rise of American Statism." *Reason* (Feb. & Mar.); also online at: praxeology.net/RC-BRS.htm

Cowen, Tyler. 1992. *Public Goods and Market Failures: A Critical Examination* (New Brunswick NJ: Transaction).

Cuzán, Alfred G. 1979. "Do We Ever Really Get Out of Anarchy?" *Journal of Libertarian Studies* 3, no. 2 (Summer), pp. 151-58; also online at: www.mises.org/journals/jls/3_2/3_2_3.pdf

De Jasay, Anthony. 2002. *Justice and Its Surroundings* (Indianapolis: Liberty Fund).

Edwards, James Rolph. 2007. "The Costs of Public Income Redistribution and Private Charity." *Journal of Libertarian Studies* 21, no. 2 (Summer), pp. 51-68

Ellickson, Robert C. 2005. *Order Without Law: How Neighbors Settle Disputes* (Cambridge, MA: Harvard University Press).

Friedman, David. 1989. *The Machinery of Freedom: Guide to a Radical Capitalism*, 2nd ed. (LaSalle: Open Court).

Gosden, P. 1973. *Self-Help: Voluntary Associations in the 19th Century* (London: Batsford Press).

Graham, Robert, ed. 2005. *Anarchism: A Documentary History of Libertarian Ideas. Volume One: From Anarchy to Anarchism (300 CE to 1939)* (Montreal: Black Rose Books).

Green, David. 1993. *Reinventing Civil Society: The Rediscovery of Welfare Without Politics* (London: IEA).

Grinder, Walter E., and Hagel III, John. 1977. "Toward a Theory of State Capitalism." *Journal of Libertarian Studies* 1, no. 1; also online at: mises.org/journals/jls/1_1/1_1_7.pdf

Hasnas, John. 2003. "Reflections on the Minimal State, *Politics, Philosophy, and Economics* 2, no. 1, pp. 115-28; also online at: mason.gmu.edu/~jhasnas/06_Hasnas.pdf

Hess, Karl. 1969. "The Death of Politics." *Playboy* (March); also online at: fare.tunes.org/books/Hess/dop.html

Hoppe, Hans-Hermann. 1999. "The Private Production of Defense." *Journal of Libertarian Studies* 14, no. 1 (Winter), pp. 27-52; also online at: www.mises.org/journals/jls/14_1/14_1_2.pdf

Hoppe, Hans-Hermann, ed. 2003. *The Myth of National Defense: Essays on the Theory and History of Security Production* (Auburn, AL: Ludwig von Mises Institue); also online at: www.mises.org/etexts/defensemyth.pdf

Hume, David. 1985. *Essays: Moral, Political, and Literary* (Indianapolis: LibertyFund).

Jacobson, Philip E. 1995. "Three Voluntary Economies." *Formulations* 2, no. 4 (Summer); also online at: libertariannation.org/a/f24j1.html

Johnson, Charles. 2007. "Liberty, Equality, Solidarity: Toward a Dialectical Anarchism," this volume.

Kolko, Gabriel. 1977. *Railroads and Regulation, 1877-1916* (Westport: Greenwood).

Kolko, Gabriel. 1963. *The Triumph of Conservatism: A Reinterpretation of American History, 1900-1916* (New York: Free Press).

La Boétie, Étienne de. 2003. *The Politics of Obedience: The Discourse of Voluntary Servitude*, trans. Harry Kurz (Montreal: Black Rose).

Lavoie, Don. 1993. "Democracy, Markets, and the Legal Order: Notes on the Nature of Politics in a Radically Liberal Society." *Social Philosophy & Policy* 10, no. 2 (Summer), pp. 103-20.

Loan, Albert. 1992. "Institutional Bases of the Spontaneous Order: Surety and Assurance." *Humane Studies Review* 7, no. 1 (Winter); also online at: osf1.gmu.edu/~ihs/w91essay.html

Long, Roderick T. 1994. "Who's the Scrooge?: Libertarians and Compassion." *Formulations* 1, no. 2 (Winter); also online at: www.libertariannation.org/a/f12l1.html

Long, Roderick T. 1995a. "Funding Public Goods: Six Solutions." *Formulations* 2, no. 1 (Autumn); also online at: libertariannation.org/a/f2114.html

Long, Roderick T. 1995b. "Defending a Free Nation." *Formulations* 2, no. 2 (Winter); also online at: libertariannation.org/a/f22l3.html

Long, Roderick T. 1996. "The Athenian Constitution: Government by Jury and Referendum." *Formulations* 4, no. 1 (Autumn); also online at: www.libertariannation.org/a/f4111.html

Long, Roderick T. 1998. "Toward a Libertarian Theory of Class." *Social Philosophy and Policy* 15, no. 2 (Summer), pp. 303-49.

Long, Roderick T. 1999. "The Irrelevance of Responsibility." *Social Philosophy and Policy* 16, no. 2 (Summer), pp. 118-45.

Long, Roderick T. 2001. "Equality: The Unknown Ideal." Mises Daily Article (16 October); also online at: www.mises.org/story/804

Long, Roderick T. 2003a. "Anarchism as Constitutionalism: A Reply to Bidinotto." Blog entry for 7 December; online at: praxeology.net/unblog12-03.htm#02

Long, Roderick T. 2003b. "Anarchism as Constitutionalism, Part 2." Blog entry for 26 December; online at: praxeology.net/unblog12-03.htm#14

Long, Roderick T. 2004a. "Anarchism as Constitutionalism, Part 3." Blog entry for 16 February; online at: praxeology.net/unblog02-04.htm#14

Long, Roderick T. 2004b. "Civil Society in Ancient Greece: The Case of Athens." Online at: praxeology.net/civsoc.htm

Long, Roderick T. 2005. "Liberty: The Other Equality." *Freeman* (October), pp. 17-19. Also online at: www.fee.org/pdf/the-freeman/0510Long.pdf

Long, Roderick T. 2006a. "Rothbard's 'Left and Right': Forty Years Later." Mises Daily Article, 8 April; online at: mises.org/story/2099

Long, Roderick T. 2006b. "Rule-Following, Praxeology, and Anarchy." *New Perspectives on Political Economy* 2, no. 1, pp. 36-46. Also online at: pcpe.libinst.cz/nppe/2_1/nppe2_1_3.pdf

Long, Roderick T., and Johnson, Charles W. 2005. "Libertarian Feminism: Can This Marriage Be Saved?" Online at: charleswjohnson.name/essays/libertarian-feminism

Martin, James J. 1975. "Business and the New Deal." *Reason* (December); also online at: tmh.floonet.net/articles/bigbiznewdeal.html

Mises, Ludwig von. 1978. *On the Manipulation of Money and Credit* (Dobbs Ferry, NY: Free Market Books).

Mises, Ludwig von. 1990. *Economic Calculation in the Socialist Commonwealth*, trans. S. Adler (Auburn, AL: Ludwig von Mises Institute); also online at: mises.org/econcalc.asp

Molinari, Gustave de. 1888. *L'Évolution Politique et la Révolution* (Paris: Reinwald/Guillaumin).

Radosh, Ronald, and Rothbard, Murray N., eds. 1972. *A New History of Leviathan: Essays on the Rise of the American Corporate State* (New York: Dutton).

Rand, Ayn. 1964. *The Virtue of Selfishness: A New Concept of Egoism* (New York, NY: New American Library).

Rand, Ayn. 1990. *The Voice of Reason: Essays in Objectivist Thought* (New York: Penguin).

Reisman, George. 2005. "Platonic Competition." Mises Daily Article, 20 December, online at: www.mises.org/story/1988

Ruwart, Mary J. 1993. *Healing Our World: The Other Piece of the Puzzle* (Kalamazoo: Sunstar); also online at: www.ruwart.com/Healing/rutoc.html

Schmidtz, David. 1991. *The Limits of Government: An Essay on the Public Goods Argument* (Boulder, CO: Westview Press).

Shaffer, Butler. 1997. *In Restraint of Trade: The Business Campaign Against Competition, 1918-1938* (Lewisburg: Bucknell U. Press).

Sharvy, Richard. 2007. "Who's to Say What's Right or Wrong? People With Ph.D.s in Philosophy, That's Who." *Journal of Libertarian Studies* 21, no. 3 (Fall), pp. 3-24.

Siddeley, Leslie. 1992. "The Rise and Fall of Fraternal Insurance Organizations." *Humane Studies Review* 7, no. 2 (Spring); also online at: mason.gmu.edu/~ihs/s92essay.html

Spencer, Herbert. 1851. "The Right to Ignore the State." Chapter 19 of Spencer, *Social Statics: or, The Conditions essential to Happiness specified, and the First of them Developed* (London: John Chapman, 1851); also online at: www.panarchy. org/spencer/ignore.state.1851.html

Spooner, Lysander. 1870. *No Treason No. VI: The Constitution of No Authority* (Boston: Lysander Spooner); also online at: praxeology.net/LS-NT-6.htm

Stringham, Edward, ed. 2006. *Anarchy, State, and Public Choice* (Cheltenham, UK: Edward Elgar).

Stromberg, Joseph. 2001. "The Role of State Monopoly Capitalism in the American Empire." *Journal of Libertarian Studies* 15, no. 3 (Summer); also online at: mises.org/journals/jls/15_3/15_3_3.pdf

Tanner, Michael. 1996. *The End of Welfare* (Washington, DC: Cato Institute).

Weaver, Paul H. 1988. *The Suicidal Corporation: How Big Business Fails America* (New York: Touchstone).

Woodson, Robert L. 1989. *Breaking the Poverty Cycle: Private Sector Alternatives to the Welfare State* (Harrisburg, PA: Commonwealth Foundation).

Wooldridge, William C. 1970. *Uncle Sam, The Monopoly Man* (New Rochelle, NY: Arlington House).

Chapter 10

Liberty, Equality, Solidarity
Toward a Dialectical Anarchism

Charles Johnson

The purpose of this essay is political revolution. And I don't mean a "revolution" in libertarian political theory, or a revolutionary new political strategy, or the kind of "revolution" that consists in electing a cadre of new and better politicians to the existing seats of power. When I say a "revolution," I mean the real thing: I hope that this essay will contribute to the overthrow of the United States government, and indeed all governments everywhere in the world. You might think that the argument of an academic essay is a pretty slender reed to lean on; but then, every revolution has to start *somewhere*, and in any case what I have in mind may be somewhat different from what you imagine. For now, it will be enough to say that I intend to give you some reasons to become an individualist anarchist,[1] and undermine some of the arguments for preferring minimalist government to anarchy. In the process, I will argue that the form of anarchism I defend is best understood from what Chris

---

1 For the purposes of this chapter, I will mostly be using the term "anarchism" as shorthand for "individualist anarchism"; since the defense of anarchism I will offer rests on individualist principles, it will not provide a cogent basis for communist, primitivist, or other non-individualist forms of anarchism. And I will use the term "individualist anarchism" in a broad sense, to describe any position that (1) denies the legitimacy of any form of (monopoly) government authority, (2) on individualist ethical grounds. As I will use it, the term picks out a family of similar *doctrines*, not a particular self-description or historical tradition. Thus it includes, but is not limited to, the specific nineteenth and early twentieth-century socialist movement known as "individualist anarchism," whose members included Benjamin Tucker, Victor Yarros, and Voltairine de Cleyre. It also includes the views of twentieth and twenty-first-century "anarcho-capitalists" such as Murray Rothbard and David Friedman; contemporary self-described "individualist anarchists" and "mutualists" such as Wendy McElroy, Joe Peacott, and Kevin Carson; and of others, such as Gustave de Molinari, Lysander Spooner, or Robert LeFevre, who rejected the State on individualist grounds but declined (for whatever reasons) to refer to themselves as "anarchists." Many self-described "socialist" anarchists deny that "anarcho-capitalism" should be counted as a form of anarchism at all, or associated with individualist anarchism in particular; many self-described "anarcho-capitalists" deny that "socialist" anarchism should be counted as a form of genuine individualism, or genuine anarchism. With all due respect to my comrades on the Left and on the Right, I will use the term in an ecumenical sense, for reasons of style, and also because the relationship between anarchism, "capitalism," and "socialism" is one of the substantive issues to be discussed in the course of this chapter.

Sciabarra has described as a *dialectical* orientation in social theory,[2] as part of a larger effort to understand and to challenge interlocking, mutually reinforcing systems of oppression, of which statism is an integral part—but only one part among others. Not only is libertarianism part of a radical politics of human liberation, it is in fact the natural companion of revolutionary Leftism and radical feminism.

My argument will take a whole theory of justice—libertarian rights theory[3]— more or less for granted: that is, some version of the "non-aggression principle" and the conception of "negative" rights that it entails. Also that a particular method for moral inquiry—ethical individualism—is the correct method, and that common claims of collective obligations or collective entitlements are therefore unfounded. Although I will discuss some of the intuitive grounds for these views, I don't intend to give a comprehensive justification for them, and those who object to the views may just as easily object to the grounds I offer for them. If you have a fundamentally different conception of rights, or of ethical relations, this chapter will probably not convince you to become an anarchist. On the other hand, it may help explain how principled commitment to a libertarian theory of rights—including a robust defense of private property rights—is *compatible* with struggles for equality, mutual aid, and social justice. It may also help show that libertarian individualism does not depend on an atomised picture of human social life, does not require indifference to oppression or exploitation other than government coercion, and invites neither nostalgia for big business nor conservatism towards social change. Thus, while my argument may not *directly* convince those who are not already libertarians of some sort, it may help to remove some of the obstacles that stop well-meaning Leftists from accepting libertarian principles. In any case, it should show non-libertarians that they need another line of argument: libertarianism has no necessary connection with the "vulgar political economy" or "bourgeois liberalism" that their criticism targets.

The threefold structure of my argument draws from the three demands made by the original revolutionary Left in France: *Liberty*, *Equality*, and *Solidarity*.[4] I

---

2 See Chris Matthew Sciabarra (2000), *Total Freedom: Toward a Dialectical Libertarianism*. See also Sciabarra 1995a and 1995b.

3 "Libertarianism" as discussed in this chapter is a theory of political justice, not a position on the Nolan Chart. "Small government" types who speak kindly of economic freedom or civil liberties may or may not qualify as "libertarians" for the purpose of my discussion. Those who treat liberty as one political good that must be balanced against other goods such as social stability, economic prosperity, democratic rule, or socioeconomic equality, and should sometimes be sacrificed for their sake, are unlikely to count. Since they are not committed to the ideal of liberty as a principled constraint on *all* political power, they are no more likely to be directly convinced by my arguments than progressives, traditionalists, communists, etc.

4 Of course, the male Left of the day actually demanded *fraternité*, "brotherhood." I'll speak of "solidarity" instead of "brotherhood" for the obvious anti-sexist reasons, and also for its association with the history of the labor movement. There are few causes in America that most twentieth-century libertarians were less sympathetic to than organised labor, but I have chosen to speak of "the value of solidarity," in spite of all that, for the same reasons that Ayn Rand chose to speak of "the virtue of selfishness:" in order to prove a point. The

will argue that, *rightly understood,* these demands are more intertwined than many contemporary libertarians realise: each contributes an essential element to a radical challenge to any form of coercive authority. Taken together, they undermine the legitimacy of *any* form of government authority, *including* the "limited government" imagined by minarchists. Minarchism eventually requires abandoning your commitment to liberty; but the dilemma is obscured when minarchists fracture the revolutionary triad, and seek "liberty" abstracted from equality and solidarity, the intertwined values that give the demand for freedom its life, its meaning, and its radicalism. Liberty, understood in light of equality and solidarity, is a revolutionary doctrine *demanding* anarchy, with no room for authoritarian mysticism and no excuse for arbitrary dominion, no matter how "limited" or benign.

Liberty

Individual liberty is essential to political justice for both minarchist and anarchist libertarians. Both understand political liberty as freedom from organised coercion: force, under libertarian theory, can *only* be legitimate in *defense* of an individual person's liberty, never when *initiated* against those who have not trespassed against any identifiable victim. Libertarians often draw boundaries between liberty and invasion through the principle of *self-ownership:* you are rightly your own master, and nobody else, individually or collectively, is entitled to claim you as their property.[5] That includes governments: self-ownership is held to be unconditional and "prepolitical," in that it does not depend on the guarantees of political constitutions or legislation, but rather logically precedes them and *constrains* the constitutions and legislation that can legitimately be established. Thus anarchists and minarchists agree that political power should be subordinated to the principle of self-ownership, and everyone left alone to do as she pleases with her own person and property provided she respects the same freedom for others. But they disagree over what these principles entail. Minarchists argue that the rights of liberty and self-defense, delegated and institutionalised, establish the *legitimacy* of a "night-watchman" State,[6] limited by a written constitution and devoted to the rule of law. For anarchists, the rights of liberty and self-defense expose even the "night-watchman" State as professionalised

---

common criticisms of organised labor from the twentieth-century libertarian movement, and the relationship between liberty and organised labor, are one of the topics I will discuss below.

5   Thus the libertarian emphasis on both personal freedom and private property rights. One way to treat someone as if she were your slave is to force her to serve your ends rather than her own: bby forcing her to apply her own labor and property to some end that she would not have freely agreed to support, or by forcing her to withhold her own labor and property from some end that she would have freely agreed to support. Another way to treat someone as if she were your slave is to force her to labor for your profit. Even if you do not force her to work on one job rather than another, you are still effectively enslaving her by taking the fruits of her labor for your own purposes.

6   Thus Jefferson 1776a: "… That to secure these rights, Governments are instituted among Men [*sic*], deriving their just powers from the consent of the governed" (¶ 2).

usurpation, and reveal all government laws and written constitutions as mere paper without authority. Such a conflict demands explanation, and clarification of the terms of the dispute.

I won't hazard a *definition* of either "government" or "state" here, but some essential features can be described. States have governments, and governments, as such, claim *authority* over a defined range of territory and citizens. Governments claim the right to issue *legitimate orders* to anyone subject to them, and to use *force* to compel obedience.[7] But governments claim more than that: after all, *I* have the right to order you out of my house, and to shove you out if you won't go quietly. Governments claim *supreme* authority over *legally enforceable claims* within their territory; while I have a right to order you off my property, a government claims the right to make and enforce decisive, final, and exclusive orders on questions of *legal right*[8]—for example, whether it *is* my property, if there is a dispute, or whether you have a right to stay there. That means the right to review, and possibly to overturn or punish, my demands on you—to decisively settle the dispute, to *enforce* the settlement over anyone's objections, and deny to anyone *outside* the government the right to *supersede* their final say on it. Some governments—the totalitarian ones—assert supreme authority over *every* aspect of life within their borders; but a "limited government" asserts authority only over *a defined range of issues,* often enumerated in a written constitution. Minarchists argue not only that governments should be limited in their authority, but specifically that the supreme authority of governments should be limited to the adjudication of disputes over individual rights, and the organised enforcement of those rights. But even the most minimal minarchy, at *some*

---

7 It should be clear that this is a necessary but not a sufficient condition for counting as the government of a given State. Anybody might claim the right to issue enforceable legal orders, but only some of the claimants are part of the government. (I gather that there are still Bourbon pretenders who *claim* the right to rule France; but whatever their aspirations, they are not currently the government of France.) But for any institution to count as the government, it must at least make the claim, or act in a way that manifests the claim: an institution that did not even claim the right to make enforceable legal orders might very well issue political position papers; it might give advice on how to live; but it would not be making *laws*.

8 This is a deliberate revision to the Weberian conception of the State as a monopoly on the use of legally accepted force. While most *modern* governments claim such sweeping authority over enforcement, it is sheer anachronism to try to build a claim of territorial monopoly into the *definition* of the State. Historically many constitutions have taken it for granted that certain forms of force (e.g. by parents against children, by husbands against wives, by masters against slaves) are simply outside of the purview of the law. It's true that under most States throughout history, parents have been able to beat their children without legal repercussions. But it would be a serious mistake to infer from this that the government (as sole arbiter of legal enforcement in the territory within which the family lives) has *authorised* or *deputised* parents to beat their children. Rather, the enforceable authority of parents over children was thought simply to be a "private" matter, beyond the "public" realm of questions that the State claims to address. The enforceability of parental authority is quite arguably treated as a political given that the State recognises, more akin to one State's *recognition* of the sovereignty of other States than to the State's *authorisation* of the use of force by deputies, posses, or militias. Some implications of this idea are teased out below in the discussion of "application thickness."

point, must claim its citizens' *exclusive allegiance*—they must love, honor and obey, forsaking all others, or else they deny the government the prerogative of *sovereignty*. And a "government" without sovereign legal authority is no government at all.

Authority, in the political sense, is correlative with *deference*. Insofar as Twain is subject to Norton's authority, Twain is obliged to defer to Norton's decisions, and Norton can compel him to obey. But the *sort* of deference must be carefully distinguished. Robert Paul Wolff notes that

> An authoritative command must ... be distinguished from a persuasive argument. When I am commanded to do something, I may choose to comply even though I am not being threatened, because I am brought to believe that it is something which I ought to do. If that is the case, then I am not, strictly speaking, obeying a command, but rather acknowledging the force or rightness of a prescription. ... But the person himself [sic] has no authority—or, to be more precise, my complying with his command does not constitute an acknowledgment on my part of any such authority. (1970, 6)

Reason is no respecter of persons, but authority is *personal*: if Norton has *legitimate authority* over Twain, then Twain's obligation to defer doesn't come from the nature of *what* Norton decided, but from the fact that *Norton* decided it.[9] Wolff's point could be sharpened by further distinguishing *epistemic* authority from *imperative* authority. There are cases where you should defer to an authority because she possesses some special *expertise* on the issue at hand.[10] But this is more scientific authority than political authority, and not really what Wolff seems to have in mind. The reason that lawyers bring their cases before the Supreme Court is not just that the Nine have some special expertise on the requirements of the law. Maybe they do, but the *reason* that others are supposed to defer to their judgment has to do with the offices they personally hold; their *status* is *constitutive* of the binding force of the judgment. However *expert* a mere lawyer may be, her opinion still amounts only to a *brief*, not a *ruling,* unless and until the judge personally authorises it. It's not that

---

9 By using "legitimate" as a modifier on "authority," I've illustrated an important point, but also run a serious risk. If I speak of "legitimate authority," that might seem to suggest that I'm not distinguishing *authority* from *mere power*, but rather distinguishing two different kinds of authority—the legitimate kind and the illegitimate kind. Then it would seem that the issue between minarchists and anarchists is not whether governments have the authority they claim, but rather whether the authority they have is legitimate authority or illegitimate authority. But this is a serious mistake, which I think leads to other mistakes. For now, it will be enough to note that, as I am using the terms "legitimacy" and "authority," all *genuine* authority is *legitimate* authority. "Illegitimate authority" is not a special kind of authority which is illegitimate, any more than "counterfeit money" is a special kind of money which is counterfeit. Illegitimate authority is, rather, mere power, fraudulently portrayed as rightful authority.

10 Suppose, for example, that Norton is an avid birder, and Twain cannot tell a jackdaw from a magpie. Then when Norton points out a bird and says, "That is a jackdaw," Twain ought to consider it a jackdaw, because *Norton* said so—even if Twain has no other reason for considering it a jackdaw besides Norton's say-so. Why? Because Norton said so, and Norton knows something about jackdaws whereas Twain knows nothing about them, so Twain ought to defer to Norton's judgment.

the issue lies within the court's *expertise,* but that it (supposedly) lies within their *prerogative.*

It is not enough, then, for a minarchist just to postulate an ideal government that makes some rulings worth enforcing on their own merits. *If* a judgment is worth enforcing on its own merits, then it surely is perfectly legitimate to enforce it, but then the legitimacy comes from the *content* of the judgment, not from its *source.*[11] That justifies enforcing the judge's ruling, but it does *not* establish that the judge's *authorisation* confers any special legitimacy on the enforcement, above or beyond what *private citizens* could confer, either individually or cooperatively in private "defense associations," given enough wisdom, study, and application. Minarchists need a theory that legitimates exclusive government authority through the *special positions* that government agents occupy, and the *sovereign status* of the government they represent. Without one, they have no justification for the special prerogatives claimed by even the most scrupulously limited of governments.

I claim that minarchists *cannot* consistently offer the kind of theory that they need to offer, because no possible theory can connect *sovereign authority* to *legitimacy,* without breaking the connection between *legal right* and *individual liberty.* My case for this claim consists of three challenges, each developed in the anarchist literature, which demonstrate a conflict between individual liberty and one of the forms of special authority that minarchists have traditionally wanted governments to exercise.[12] Since the clearest expression of the first, and most basic, challenge is in Roy Childs's "Open Letter to Ayn Rand," we might call it the Childs challenge. Rand argues that a government must be strictly limited to the defensive use of force in order to be morally distinguishable from a robber gang.[13] She holds that even the legitimate functions of a properly limited government must be funded *voluntarily* by the governed, condemning taxation in any form.[14] However, she insists on the legitimacy of *sovereignty* and explicitly rejects individualist anarchism.[15] Childs, accepting Rand's description of a government as "an institution that holds the *exclusive* power to *enforce* certain rules of social conduct in a given geographical

---

11 Similarly, it is not enough for a minarchist to show that if you organise government officials into such-and-such a constitutional order, the institution you've organised will systematically tend towards making correct rulings on matters of legal right. While the source of the ruling may justify a (defeasible) presumption that it can legitimately be enforced, the *way* that it justifies has nothing to do with government authority.

12 Taken *severally,* each challenge poses a problem for one of the forms of special authority that minarchists have traditionally wanted governments to exercise. I think the import of each individual challenge is actually *less* than anarchists have historically thought: minarchists could respond to any individual challenge by revising their theory, and promoting an even more minimalist government that abdicates the function that each challenge called into question. But taken *together,* the three challenges jointly whittle a "properly limited government" down to no government at all: any institution that minarchists could make consistent with liberty, in light of *all three* challenges, would have abandoned all claims of sovereign authority, and thus abdicated the throne.

13 See, for example, "The Nature of Government," in Rand 1964, 113.

14 See "Government Financing in a Free Society," in Rand 1964, 116-20.

15 "The Nature of Government," in Rand 1964, 112-13.

area,"[16] argues that no institution can claim that authority and remain limited to the defensive use of force at the same time:

> Suppose that I were distraught with the service of a government in an Objectivist society. Suppose that I judged, being as rational as I possibly could, that I could secure the protection of my contracts and the retrieval of stolen goods at a cheaper price and with more efficiency. Suppose I either decide to set up an institution to attain these ends, or patronize one which a friend or a business colleague has established. Now, if he [sic] succeeds in setting up the agency, which provides all the services of the Objectivist government, and restricts his *more efficient* activities to the use of retaliation against aggressors, there are only two alternatives as far as the "government" is concerned: (a) It can use force or the threat of it against the new institution, in order to keep its monopoly status in the given territory, *thus initiating the use or threat of physical force against one who has not himself initiated force*. Obviously, then, if it should choose this alternative, it would have initiated force. Q.E.D. Or: (b) It can refrain from initiating force, and allow the new institution to carry on its activities without interference. If it did this, then the Objectivist "government" would become a truly marketplace institution, and not a "government" at all. There would be competing agencies of protection, defense and retaliation—in short, free market anarchism. (Childs 1969, ¶ 8)

Rand's theory of limited government posits an institution with sovereign authority over the use of force, but her theory of individual rights only allows for the use of force in defense against *invasions* of rights. As long as private defense agencies limit themselves to the defense of their clients' rights, Rand cannot justify using force to suppress them. But if citizens are free to cut their ties to the "government" and turn to private agencies for the protection of their rights, then the so-called "government" no longer holds sovereign authority to enforce its citizens' rights; it becomes only one defense agency among many.[17] Childs formulated his argument as an internal critique of Ayn Rand's political theory, but his dilemma challenges *any* theory combining libertarian rights with government sovereignty. Any "limited government" must either be ready to forcibly suppress private defense agencies—in which case it ceases to be limited, by initiating violence against peaceful people— or else it must be ready to coexist with them—abdicating its claim to sovereignty and ceasing to be a government. Since maintaining sovereignty *requires* an act of aggression, any government, in order to remain a government, must be ready to trample the liberty of its citizens, in order to establish and enforce a coercive monopoly over the protection of rights.[18]

---

16 *Ibid.*, 107; emphasis on "exclusive" added.

17 It could go on *calling* itself a "government," of course—just as Emperor Norton went on calling himself Emperor of North America even though he had no subjects except those who voluntarily played along with his game. But it would no longer be a "government" in any sense that's incompatible with individualist anarchism. (Specifically, whatever it fancied itself, it would no longer be claiming the sovereign authority of the State; see the section on Equality below.)

18 Classical liberals and minarchist libertarians have sometimes tried to sidestep anarchist objections by appealing to the consent of the governed. Even if government sovereignty entails limitations on private citizens' freedom to defend themselves directly, not all limitations on

At this point, some minarchists—most famously Robert Nozick—*accept* that a properly limited government cannot simply *suppress* competition from rights-respecting defense agencies (without ceasing to be properly limited), but reply that it *can* rightfully *constrain* competing defense agencies to obey certain norms, and in particular to respect certain procedural immunities for the accused. A lynch mob has no right to demand that they be allowed to "compete" with courts; a properly limited government has the right to prohibit procedures that impose unacceptable risks of punishment on the innocent.[19] If it can prohibit unreliable procedures, then it can force defense associations either to adopt permitted procedures or disband. But then government sovereignty reasserts itself, as the government becomes "the only generally effective enforcer of a prohibition on others' using unreliable enforcement procedures ... and ... oversees these procedures" (Nozick 1974, 113-14). If a properly limited government reserves the right to authorise enforcement by approved defense agencies, and prohibit enforcement by rogue defense agencies, then it remains the sovereign *authoriser* of enforcement, even if it becomes one of many *direct providers*.

Governments probably are entitled to forbid enforcement procedures that violate the procedural immunities due to the accused. But unless the minarchist introduces some further reason to *reserve* this prerogative for the government, the Childs challenge applies as much to the protection of procedural immunities as to the ordinary protection of rights. If the government has a right to suppress rogue agencies, then so does *anyone*, as a matter of individual self-defense.[20] The *universality* of the right

---

liberty violate libertarian principles: free people can bind themselves to new obligations by agreeing to contracts. Liberal theorists draw up the analogy of a "social contract," and claim that private citizens can be bound to recognise the government's sovereignty by explicit, or tacit, or hypothetical consent to the terms of the political system. This sort of reply could be made to any of the three challenges that I pose, and so deserves a response. Unfortunately, constraints of space prevent me from giving an adequate response. Fortunately, excellent systematic critiques of the claim already exist in Spooner 1867-1870 and the first chapter of Barnett 2004. In any case minarchists should be very hesitant to draw on appeals to tacit consent: exactly the same argument could just as easily be used to justify all forms of taxation (on the theory that citizens consented to pay for government expenses when they consented to the contract), many forms of invasive laws (on the theory that citizens consented to abide by the government's standards of conduct or hygiene), etc. Most serious defenders of minarchism in the twentieth century have seen this difficulty and have tried to develop theories which provide for the legitimacy of government without the need for unanimous consent, whether tacit or explicit.

19 Cf. Nozick 1974, 105-08.

20 Nozick, unlike some who advance the procedural argument, takes *this* point in stride: his argument is not that the government enjoys a *special right* over and above what private citizens enjoy, but rather that a locally dominant defense association, in the course of carrying out its daily business, will be put in the *special position* of either permitting or forbidding any efforts at private enforcement within its sphere of influence, due to its special position as the local hegemon. Nozick argues that this gives the agency a *de facto* monopoly on the authorisation of force, without the exercise of special prerogatives and without treading on the liberty of the defense associations and private citizens constrained by the procedural protections. If this argument worked, then Nozick would have established a legitimate path

draws out a second point. Nozick makes the transition from dominant protective agency to minimal State by using language that suggests *deputising* private citizens: the government makes a list of who can be trusted to enforce the law, and if you're not on the list, then the government will stop you from taking the law into your own hands. What matters is whether or not the government has *given you permission* to act as a law-enforcer. The picture depends on a blurring of the distinction amongst argument, authoritative testimony, and prerogative. Defense associations may have the right to stop other enforcers from using unreliable procedures, but whether a procedure is unacceptably risky or not is a matter of fact, which can be characterised and discovered *independently* of the say-so of the government. The government's seal of approval plays no *constitutive* role in the right of an agency to use procedures that are demonstrably legitimate, and the government's *own* procedures must be subject to objective criticism as much as any private enforcer's. A right to suppress unacceptably risky efforts at enforcement establishes no right to demand direct oversight of agencies' procedures,[21] or to suppress "unauthorised" enforcers simply for not having the official approval of the government.

The language of "permission," "prohibition," and "oversight" obscures the distinction; but in fact the protection of procedural immunities is not properly understood in terms of *giving permission* at all, but rather *respecting* a general *right*.[22] The more generally and impersonally a defense agency specifies its procedural protections, the less they will resemble anything that could intelligibly be described as "oversight," "giving permission," or, broadly, the exercise of political authority. The more they resemble interventionist "oversight," "giving permission," or political authority, the more they will tread on the freedom of innocent people to enforce their own rights using reliable but unofficial procedures. The government in Nozick's "minimal state" must either adopt general policies allowing for free competition

---

for a locally dominant defense agency to assert sovereignty, without treading on the liberty of others. He also would have made the argument in precisely the way that I suggested a minarchist would need to: his argument would have demonstrated the connection between sovereignty and the special position of the government within society—specifically the special position conferred by being the sole dominant protective agency in a given locality. But as I shall argue presently, Nozick's transition from procedural protection to *ex ante* procedural "oversight" will not bear scrutiny.

21 A defense association (A) may very well be entitled to suppress a would-be enforcer (B) who *refuses to disclose* the procedures that she used to determine guilt. If A cannot discover whether a procedure is reliable or completely arbitrary, then they may be entitled to treat the claim as arbitrary pending further investigation. But it is up to A to do the leg-work of finding out what B's procedures are before they declare that they cannot discover them. A can try to find out about B's procedures by directly asking B, or by sending someone to sit in on B's proceedings, or by asking former participants in B's proceedings, or by finding out whether B has informed anyone else of her procedures, or in any number of other ways. A *cannot* simply sit back and demand that B submit to "oversight" as defined by A, or suppress B simply for failing to fill out the right forms. If A fails to make serious efforts at discovery, then it is *they, not B, who are* guilty of arbitrary and unreliable enforcement procedures.

22 Suppose I announce, "I will stop anyone who tries to stab me with a knife. But I will not stop anyone who is only using a knife to slice a loaf of bread." Have I claimed the right to *oversee* the use of knives? Have I *permitted you* to slice bread with a knife?

without requiring grants of official permission—and once again cease to exercise sovereignty—or else it must enforce its demands of oversight and official approval, even on agencies that are following reliable procedures—and once again cease to be limited to defensive uses of force.

There is another possible reply I find more promising—indeed, convincing. Strictly speaking, Childs's dilemma applies to only one *branch* of the government: he demonstrates that governments cannot claim a monopoly on *enforcing* the rights of citizens, i.e., on the *executive* functions of government. It establishes that anyone, not just the government and its official deputies, can enforce citizens' rightful claims to person and property. But how is it determined *which* claims are rightful, and *which* claims are baseless? Robert Bidinotto has objected that anarchism demands not only "'competition' in the protection of rights," but also "'competition' in defining what 'rights' are" (1994, ¶ 20); without a government established as the "final arbiter on the use of force in society" (1994, ¶ 25), there is no way to fix objective rules for the assertion of rights, and no possibility of meaningful settlement of disputes over rights-claims. So even if a minimal government cannot claim a monopoly on the executive functions, perhaps a "microscopic" government could claim a monopoly on *legislation*.[23]

Provided that the government legislature and government courts do not try to interfere with protection of rights by private citizens or defense associations, I cannot see how the Childs challenge could undermine sovereignty over legislation. But a second challenge, vigorously expressed in the later works of Lysander Spooner, can.

---

23 Although this reply would indeed preserve a form of sovereignty against the Childs challenge, it is worth noting how radical a reduction in the size and scope of the "minimal state" is required to meet the challenge. A government that maintained only a monopoly on *legislating* and *adjudicating* rights, but left *enforcing* them up to private efforts, would be a very limited government indeed; it might very well have no police, no executive bureaucracy, no intelligence agencies, no border guards, and no armies. The microscopic state that resulted would be far more limited than Rand's "limited government," even more minimal than Nozick's "ultraminimal state." Sovereignty would be asserted by a properly limited government only insofar as general laws and rulings on specific legal disputes would be made under the authority of a single government. The microscopic state would have no authority to override or exclude private citizens from just efforts to protect their own rights, or the rights of others; its sovereignty would rest in its authority to act as a "final standard" on the definition and application of rights. In fact the closest historical analogue would be the constitution of *medieval Iceland*—a society most often discussed in libertarian literature for illustrations of what a functioning *anarchy* might look like. The Icelandic Free State was *not* an anarchy: there was a sovereign legislature (the *Althing*), which also served as a court of final appeal; but it remains interesting to anarchists because the legal order in Iceland functioned with no central executive. (For a detailed discussion of the constitution of medieval Iceland, see Byock 2001. Long 2002a sets out the both the continuities and departures from anarchist principles in the constitution of the Free State, and explains the eventual collapse of the Free State as the growth of the microscopic germs of government into bases of power for warlordism and civil war.)

In the "Letter to Grover Cleveland," Spooner argues that all legislation is either criminal, tyrannical, or idle:[24]

> Let me then remind you that justice is an immutable, natural principle; and not anything that can be made, unmade, or altered by any human power. ... Lawmakers, as they call themselves, can add nothing to it, nor take anything from it. Therefore all their laws, as they call them,—that is, all the laws of their own making,—have no color of authority or obligation. It is a falsehood to call them laws; for there is nothing in them that either creates men's [sic] duties or rights, or enlightens them as to their duties or rights. ... If they command men to do justice, they add nothing to men's obligation to do it, or to any man's right to enforce it. They are therefore mere idle wind, such as would be commands to consider the day as day, and the night as night. If they command or license any man to do injustice, they are criminal on their face. If they command any man to do anything which justice does not require him to do, they are simple, naked usurpations and tyrannies. If they forbid any man to do anything, which justice could permit him to do, they are criminal invasions of his natural and rightful liberty. In whatever light, therefore, they are viewed, they are utterly destitute of everything like authority or obligation. (1886, ¶¶ 4-7)

Minarchists usually agree that governments have no legitimate authority to command violations of individual rights, or to forbid acts permitted by individual liberty—the *motive* for limiting government was the idea that legitimate political authority only exists within the boundaries drawn by individual rights. But Spooner's point about laws that command justice or forbid injustice—prohibiting murder, theft, rape, etc.— may be harder to grasp. It is, after all, *true* that governments and defense associations are perfectly justified in enforcing those laws. But what must be appreciated here is that the obligation to follow those laws, and the right to enforce them, derives entirely from the *content* of the laws and not their *source*. The government is justified in enforcing those laws only because *anybody* would be justified in enforcing justice, *whether or not* self-styled legislators have signed off on a document stating "Murder is a crime most foul." The document itself is idle; it neither obliges nor authorises anyone to do anything they were not already obliged or free to do. The government is not so much making new *laws* that *impose* obligations, but (at best!) making *declarations* that *recognise* preexisting obligations—which could be objectively specified by anyone, with or without official approval from anyone.[25] Any right to override another's assessment would derive from objective and impersonal considerations of justice, demonstrated through argument or attested on the basis

---

24 See also Spooner's "Letter to Thomas F. Bayard" (1882a) and "Natural Law; or, the Science of Justice" (1882b) for close variations on the same challenge. Childs himself also anticipates something like this line of argument, and makes arguments that Rand's epistemological and ethical positions demands a similar conclusion. I've picked out Spooner's version of the challenge in the letter to Cleveland because it provides the most systematic exposition of the point.

25 If the government passed a resolution stating that the square of the hypotenuse in a right triangle is always equal to the square of the other two sides, then the resolution would say something *true*, and something that everyone is obliged to believe. But it would hardly justify the claim that we need a properly geometrical government to serve as the "final arbiter" of the properties of right triangles.

of expertise,[26] *not* from political prerogatives invested in the so-called legislature. Anyone, regardless of status, has the right to make correct declarations about justice, and override or ignore incorrect declarations. With no special prerogative to establish rights, and no special prerogative to enforce them (as per the Childs challenge), the claim of "sovereignty" for a "properly limited government" must involve either usurpation or idle pretense.

That said, I *do* think that there is one final straw for the minarchist to grasp, even after the Childs challenge and the Spooner challenge have been taken into account, relating to a lacuna in Spooner's account of the possible relationship between a piece of legislation and the background principles of justice. Spooner discussed three possible cases: (1) the legislation may demand something that *contradicts* what individual rights require—making it criminal; (2) it may demand something that *exceeds* what individual rights require—making it tyrannical; (3) it may demand something *identical* to what individual rights require—making it nugatory. Spooner's argument presumes that the "prepolitical" framework of individual rights determines *every* question of enforceable obligations, leaving no room for legislators to exercise legitimate prerogative. But while these options cover the bulk of both the criminal and the civil law, Spooner has overlooked one important possibility: there may be cases where the principle of self-ownership does not fully *specify* how to *apply* individual rights in the case at hand.

It may be that respect for individual rights requires that cars going opposite directions on a highway should drive on opposite sides—so that drivers will not needlessly endanger each other's lives. But self-ownership alone surely has nothing to say about whether motorists should drive on the *left* or the *right*. It requires that *some* rule be adopted, and that *once* adopted, each motorist obey it. But *which* rule to adopt is a question that needs to be settled by considerations other than individual rights. Medieval legal writers described similar cases as *reducing* the natural law (in the sense of making it more specific); the idea is to spell out the details for cases where the principles of natural justice underdetermine the correct application of individual rights. It may seem, then, that this ekes out a place for positive law-making in spite of the Spooner challenge: since there has to be *some* specification of how to apply rights in these cases, but more than one specification is compatible with the requirements of individual rights, a minarchist might think that you need a government to take on the prerogative of specifying which one to adopt.[27]

---

26 Spooner 1882b argues that the principles of justice are "usually a very plain and simple matter, easily understood by common minds" (Section IV ¶ 1), and that "Men [sic] living in contact with each other, and having intercourse together, *cannot avoid* learning natural law, to a very great extent" (Section IV ¶ 2). If so, then the "commands" of natural justice could all be understood as conclusions of arguments, without the need to appeal to the authority of experts. While I think that this is true of most if not all cases, nothing turns on it for the purposes of the challenge to legislative authority. If there are cases where understanding or applying the principles of justice requires expertise, then all those hard cases should be turned over to some expert for judgment. But it would be fallacious to infer from that that there must be some expert to whom all hard cases are turned over. In any case, the basis for the authority of the judgment would be acknowledged wisdom and judgment, not personal political position.

27 It's a dirty job, but *someone's* got to do it...

If the Childs challenge undermined the *executive* authority of the government, and the Spooner challenge undermined its *legislative* authority, you might think of this move as preserving *judicial* authority for a sovereign government. Sovereignty here means the right to serve as the final authority on setting out auxiliary principles for applying individual rights to specific cases where the requirements of self-ownership are vague or contingent. To be sure, the limits put on the scope of its authority by the Childs challenge and the Spooner challenge would be severe. The government would have no executive and no general legislature; it would have no special privileges to enforce and the scope of its law-making would be limited to ironing out minor details within a system of obligations almost entirely predetermined by the non-aggression principle. It would be a sort of "ultramicroscopic government," so small that its influence on the specification and protection of rights could barely be detected at all.

Although I think that the problem of reducing the natural law is one of the hardest problems for anarchist theory to resolve, I do not think that the minarchist is actually in a stronger position than the anarchist. The difficulty for the minarchist solution can be brought out with a final challenge, also from the works of Lysander Spooner. This second Spooner challenge is expressed most clearly in *No Treason* no. 1:

> The question still remains, how comes such a thing as "a nation" to exist? How do millions of men [*sic*], scattered over an extensive territory—each gifted by nature with individual freedom; required by the law of nature to call no man, or body of men, his masters; authorized by that law to seek his own happiness in his own way, to do what he will with himself and his property, so long as he does not trespass upon the equal liberty of others; authorized also, by that law, to defend his own rights, and redress his own wrongs; and to go to the assistance and defence of any of his fellow men who may be suffering any kind of injustice—how do millions of such men *come to be a nation,* in the first place? How is it that each of them comes to be stripped of his natural, God-given rights, and to be incorporated, compressed, compacted, and consolidated into a mass with other men, whom he never saw; with whom he has no contract; and towards many of whom he has no sentiments but fear, hatred, or contempt? How does he become subjected to the control of men like himself, who, by nature, had no authority over him; but who command him to do this, and forbid him to do that, as if they were his sovereigns, and he their subject; and as if their wills and their interests were the only standards of his duties and his rights; and who compel him to submission under peril of confiscation, imprisonment, and death?
>
> Clearly all this is the work of force, or fraud, or both.
>
> … We are, therefore, driven to the acknowledgment that nations and governments, if they can rightfully exist at all, can exist only by consent. (Section III, ¶¶ 1-6)

Spooner's aim in *No Treason* is, famously, to demonstrate that citizens are only obliged to recognise the sovereign authority when, and only for as long as, they genuinely, individually *consent* to recognise its authority. What I want to draw attention to are the *reasons* that Spooner suggests for the requirement. Here, Spooner questions the notion of a *political jurisdiction,* asking what *by what right* some gang calling itself "the government," *however* strictly limited, gains authority over otherwise unrelated people who never had anything to do with them? If there is some question of different ways in which rights could be applied, then what sort of process and what sorts of relationship justify the special claim that even an ultramicroscopic government would make to establish *their* judgment in preference to all the others?

Spooner suggests that genuine, individual consent can explain their authority over a jurisdiction. Suppose that Twain and Kearney have a dispute over how long land must be left unused before it can be reclaimed as abandoned property. If they both agree to turn the question over to Norton and defer to his judgment, then it's clear how Norton got jurisdiction over the case: Twain and Kearney *agreed* to bind themselves to his judgment. But suppose that Twain and Kearney never agreed to turn the question over to Norton, perhaps never even had anything to do with Norton at all. If Norton should insist that they should still defer to *his* judgment, because *he* is the Emperor, then Norton has the burden of explaining what binds Twain and Kearney to him in such a way that his judgment is more authoritative than anybody's arbitrary fiat. Even if the vague boundary between between Kearney's and Twain's claims needs to be made more precise, where does Norton, specifically, get the right to enforce *his* specification, except by consent of the disputing parties?

If consent is the standard, then the consent must be *genuine*. In particular, it must be possible to *refuse* consent, or to *withdraw* it later once given.[28] That means that consent cannot justify any government body claiming *permanent* and *irrevocable* sovereignty. If a court's jurisdiction depends on the consent of those who have put themselves under it, then each of those people must be individually free to take herself out of the jurisdiction and create or align herself with another jurisdiction. But *without* consent, it's hard to see what distinguishes the government's assertion of special authority from arbitrary fiat. If a community has settled on the rule of one year rather than two for abandonment, the government has no authority to arbitrarily override the settled conventions. If folks are divided over the right rule to follow, but have agreed to submit the dispute to some third party whom they trust more than the government, the government has no authority to butt in to enforce its own decision over the agreed terms. If folks are divided over the right rule to follow, and have not made any steps toward resolving the dispute, then the government has no authority to arbitrarily force *itself* on them as the arbiter.[29]

---

28 That does *not* mean that Twain can later renege and ignore Norton's decision, if he consented to let Norton decide the case. It *does* mean that Twain can later decline to let Norton decide any more cases for him. See note 18 on the failure of historical liberal theories to meet the criteria for genuine consent, including those that rely on claims of "tacit consent."

29 Perhaps under dire enough circumstances—if, for example, the dispute is not only unresolved but careening towards a violent feud—the parties to the dispute could rightfully be forced to the bargaining table by an impartial third party. I am not confident that this is true, but I am not confident that it is false, either. What I am confident of is that, *if* third parties ever have the right to force arbitration, then the right is possessed by *everyone*, and has nothing to do with the special prerogatives of a government to arbitrate. For the government to claim an *exclusive* or *superior* authority to intervene within an arbitrarily asserted jurisdiction might not usurp the natural liberty of the disputants. But if it did not, then it *would* usurp the natural liberty of other potential arbiters, who would have just as much of a right to intervene as the self-styled "government."

Liberty cannot coexist with government sovereignty, however "limited." The claim of sovereignty must be backed up by coercion at some point, given up or reduced to a vacuous arrangement of words, whether sovereignty is claimed over the *enforcement* of rights, the *definition* of rights, or the *application* of rights. Any way you slice it, government sovereignty means an invasion of individual freedom, and individual freedom means, ultimately, freedom from the State.

Equality

The standard against which I have been measuring minarchist governments in each of these three challenges is based on an intuitive notion of Liberty that I have taken more or less for granted. That might expose me to allegations that I've made my case by misapplying or inflating the concept of "liberty" beyond the conceptual or material context that gives it meaning. In my defense, I want to offer some remarks on the conceptual context within which I think the principles of self-ownership and individual liberty arise, and to consider two possible objections to the argument of the previous section. First, it might be held that I have demonstrated a genuine conflict between individual liberty and government authority, but that coercion is justified in the limited case of establishing government sovereignty, either because some other important value is at stake, or else because a little coercion is a necessary evil to avoid much greater or much worse coercion. Or, it might be held that I have only seemingly demonstrated a conflict between individual liberty and government authority by applying the concepts of liberty and coercion outside of the context within which they are meaningful: in this case, government authority could not be properly characterised as *either* "coercive" or "non-coercive," perhaps because (for example) notions such as coercion and freedom are only meaningful within a system of rights, and a system of rights is only meaningful in the context of a functioning legal system. I think that either charge reflects a failure to appreciate the conceptual relationship between the revolutionary demands for *Liberty* and *Equality*.

Attaching my controversial understanding of liberty to the standard of *equality* might seem less than prudent, if my interlocutor is a minarchist libertarian. Modern libertarians make demands for *individual liberty* with passion and urgency; their reaction to demands for *social equality* is more often tepid if not openly hostile. Criticism of social inequality is much more likely to be heard from the mouths of unreconstructed statists, and "egalitarianism" is hardly a term of praise in most libertarian intellectual circles. But I shall argue that equality, *rightly understood,* is the best *grounds* for principled libertarianism. When the conception of individual liberty is uprooted from the demand for social equality, the radicalism of libertarianism withers; it also leaves the libertarian open to a family of conceptual confusions which prop up many of the common minarchist arguments against anarchism.

My task, then, is to explain what I mean by "equality, rightly understood." I certainly do *not* intend to suggest that liberty is conceptually dependent on *economic* equality (of either *opportunity* or *outcome*), or on equality of *socio-cultural status*.[30] But the equality I have in mind is *also* much more *substantive* than the formal "equality before the law" or "equality of rights" suggested by some libertarians and classical liberals, and rightly criticised by Leftists as an awfully thin glove over a very heavy fist. Formal equality within a statist political system, pervaded with pillage and petty tyranny, is hardly worth fighting for; the point is to *challenge* the system, not to be equally shoved around by it. The conception of equality that I have in mind has a history on the Left older and no less revolutionary than the redistributionist conception of socioeconomic equality. It is the equality that the French revolutionaries had in mind when they demanded *egalité,* and which the American revolutionaries had in mind when they stated:

> We hold these truths to be self-evident, that all men [*sic*] are created equal, that they are endowed by their Creator with certain unalienable Rights, that among these are Life, Liberty and the pursuit of Happiness. (Jefferson 1776a ¶ 2)

Jefferson is making revolutionary use of concepts drawn from the English liberal tradition. Equality, for Jefferson, is the basis for *independence*, and the *grounds* from which individual rights derive.[31] Locke elucidates the concept when he characterises a "state of Perfect freedom"—the state to which everyone is naturally entitled—as

> *A State* also *of Equality*, wherein all the Power and Jurisdiction is reciprocal, no one having more than another: there being nothing more evident, than that Creatures of the same species and rank promiscuously born to all the same advantages of Nature, and the use of the same faculties, should be equal one amongst another without Subordination or Subjection ... . (1690, II. 4. ¶ 2)

The Lockean conception of equality that underwrites Jefferson's revolutionary doctrine of individual liberty is, as Roderick Long (2001a) has argued, equality of *political authority.* Jefferson and Locke denied, as arbitrary, the Old Regime's claim of a natural entitlement to lordship over their fellow creatures. Ranks of superior and inferior political authority were not established by natural differences in station or ordained by the will of God Almighty. Political coercion is the material expression of a claim of unequal authority: one person is entitled to dictate terms over another's person and property, and the other can be forced to obey. Declaring universal equality thus means denying all such claims of lordship, and, thus, asserting that everyone has authority over *herself*, and over herself *alone*. Equality is the context within which the principle of self-ownership, and thus the demand for individual freedom, takes root. This connection can be seen most explicitly in the second Spooner

---

30 I do, actually, think that the relationship between libertarianism and these forms of egalitarianism is more complex than many twentieth-century libertarians have suggested; but that's an issue for later discussion.

31 Jefferson makes this point even more explicitly, if less elegantly, in his original draft of the Declaration, where the same passage reads: "We hold these truths to be sacred and undeniable: that all men are created equal and independent; that *from that equal creation* they derive rights inherent and inalienable, among which are the preservation of life, and liberty, and the pursuit of happiness" (1776b ¶ 2, emphasis added).

challenge above. Spooner's demand to know how free and independent people are "compacted" together into a State against their will is intimately connected with the protest against *arbitrary* assertions of a right to dominate the affairs of others. Long points out that *neither* socioeconomic equality *nor* formal legal equality "calls into question the authority of those who administer the legal system; such administrators are merely required to ensure equality, of the relevant sort, *among those administered.* ... Lockean equality involves not merely equality *before* legislators, judges, and police, but, far more crucially, equality *with* legislators, judges, and police" (¶¶ 22-25). Whether or not Jefferson was right to treat the equality of authority as *self-evident*, a minarchist should hardly want to deny that it is *true*. The idea that legitimate governments must be constrained by the non-aggression principle *no less than* private citizens, and the *individualist* conception of rights, seem clearly rooted in the notion of equal authority.[32]

But whenever a minarchist brandishes equality of authority against statism, she also undermines her case for *any* form of State sovereignty. Considering liberty in light of equality systematically undermines both of the objections considered above, and justifies the unlimited demand for Liberty that I have employed. Insofar as the first objection depends on consequentialist calculation—holding that liberty can be sacrificed either in the name of other goods, or in the name of maximising the total amount of liberty going around—it necessarily conflicts with a demand for equal authority. The objection presupposes someone to do the consequentialist calculations, supposedly entitled to treat all goods, no matter *whom* they belong to, as common booty to be distributed. By claiming the right to volunteer not only her *own* liberty, but also *other* people's liberty for sacrificial duty, the consequentialist exempts *herself* from the standard of equality, pretending that she is entitled to stand over everyone and pass judgment on *their* liberty, taking some from Peter and rendering some to Paul in the name of the cause. Equality means that other people's lives and livelihoods are *not hers to give,* no matter the results she might get from it.[33]

---

32 The original conception of Equality from the revolutionary Left appreciates human plurality and supports an uncompromising *individualism* in politics—not the anonymising mass politics of the statist Left, in both its "progressive" and "radical" incarnations. Nozick expresses the point admirably: "Side constraints express the inviolability of other persons. But why may not one violate persons for the greater social good? ... But there is no *social entity* with a good that undergoes some sacrifice for its own good. There are only individual people, different individual people, with their own individual lives. Using one of these people for the benefit of others, uses him [sic] and benefits the others. Nothing more. What happens is that something is done to him for the sake of others. Talk of an overall social good covers this up. (Intentionally?) To use a person in this way does not sufficiently respect and take account of the fact that he is a separate person, that his is the only life he has. *He* does not get some overbalancing good from his sacrifice, and no one is entitled to force this upon him—least of all a state or government" (1974, 32-33).

33 The point here is not that deliberation about consequences is completely irrelevant to questions of justice. Like Roderick Long (2002b), I hold that, while deliberation about consequences cannot *trump* deliberation about rights, our understanding of the *content* of rights can be revised in light of consequences. (Thus, for example, consequentialist considerations can be important to determining the proper judgment in a case of reducing the

The second sort of objection conflicts with equality in a different way. It suggests, not that someone can legitimately *violate* one person's liberty in order to secure benefits for others, but that the force involved in establishing sovereignty cannot be assessed under standards of liberty at all, because the categorisation of force as *either* aggressive *or* defensive is only meaningful *within* the context of a functioning government legal order. Thus, Bidinotto's argument (1994) that the demand for liberty, when applied unconditionally outside the background context of a limited sovereign government, divorces rights-claims from the "final standard" to settle them, and degrades into a program for unrestrained tyranny and civil war.

But it is Bidinotto, not the anarchist, who strips the concept of liberty out of its proper context. The objection depends on a particular picture of the State and its laws, which is as metaphysically illusive as it is captivating. The State is imagined as a sort of titan standing *over* civil society, binding it to its will and acting on it from without. The constraints that a particular government imposes under the mantle of State authority may be tyrannical or just, but whether used properly or abused, the peculiar standpoint and the constraining force of the State seem necessary for any stable social order, and sufficient to decisively settle disputes just by being asserted. Since anarchy dispenses with the external constraints of the State, the minarchist feels that all rights-claims will be left, as it were, hanging in the air, with no final authority to ground them. It is this mystique of the State that Randolph Bourne set out to expose by distinguishing amongst the Nation, the State, and the Government:

> The State is the country acting as a political unit, it is the group acting as a repository of force, determiner of law, arbiter of justice. ... Government on the other hand is synonymous with neither State nor Nation. It is the machinery by which the nation, organized as a State, carries out its State functions. Government is a framework of the administration of laws, and the carrying out of the public force. Government is the idea of the State put into practical operation in the hands of definite, concrete, fallible men. It is the visible sign of the invisible grace. It is the word made flesh. And it has necessarily the limitations inherent in all practicality. Government is the only form in which we can envisage the State, but it is by no means identical with it. That the State is a mystical conception is something that must never be forgotten. Its glamor and its significance linger behind the framework of Government and direct its activities. (Bourne 1918, § 1 ¶¶ 8-9)

Equality of authority dulls the mystical glamor of State authority. The law is a human institution, and the legitimate authority of individual rights-claims does *not* need to be grounded in the dominance of a sovereign, or proclaimed from a standpoint *beyond* the fragile social relationships among fallible, mortal human beings. A good thing, too, since there *is* no Olympian standpoint for the State to occupy; governments are made of people with no more special authority than you

---

natural law.) But if our judgments about the requirements of justice can be revised in light of reflection on the consequences, the revision can (indeed must) go the other way, too. What *counts* as a "good consequence" also partly depends on what justice demands; in particular, if bringing about a situation S involves you in initiating force against an innocent person, then S is *not* a good consequence: being unjust is a defeater for an end counting as something worth pursuing. It is in this sense that rights act as "side constraints" (Nozick 1974, 28-33) on moral deliberation.

or I—even when they are speaking *ex cathedra* in the name of the State. Rights are grounded in the claims that each of us, as ordinary human beings, are entitled to hold each other to, and are implemented not by paper laws but by the concrete social and cultural relationships we participate in. Roderick Long (2007) shows that if the "final standard" demanded by Bidinotto is the *realistic* finality that comes from a broad consensus that an issue has been settled and should not be revisited, then it can be achieved through anarchist institutions no less than through a government; if the "finality" demanded is some sort of self-applying, self-grounding finality immune to even the *possibility* of further dispute, then that is not available even under a government, the mystique of State authority notwithstanding.[34] The choice is not between a system where disputes are never meaningfully settled and one where they are, but between one in which they are settled through a decentralised network of institutions holding each other in check, or through a centralised hierarchy forcing others to defer to it. And, as Long argues, anarchy actually provides a better hope for disputes to be settled *justly* than minarchy—especially when an arbitrator is herself a party to the dispute—because under anarchy the watchers are themselves watched, and are less able to force through unjust rulings simply in virtue of their dominant position.

The *context* of a concept is often conceived as a constraint on the concept, and context-dropping as a matter of applying the concept more *widely* than it should be applied. But dropping the context of a concept could make you go wrong in *either* of two ways: improper abstraction might *inflate* the application of the concept beyond its domain of significance; or it might *conceal* the concept's significance in cases where it *should* be applied. Understood in the context of Equality, the principle of Liberty becomes *more* radical, not less, challenging all forms of State mysticism with the standard of individual sovereignty. Dispelling the mystical conception of the State also reveals the need for concrete attitudes, practices and relationships to sustain a free society, not just paper laws to "limit" tyranny. Which brings me to *Solidarity*.

Solidarity

I have chosen the word "Solidarity" to stand for a family of cultural and political commitments usually associated with the radical Left, among them labor radicalism, populism, internationalism, anti-racism, gay liberation, and radical feminism. These commitments share a common concern with the class dynamics of power and a sensitivity to expressions of non-governmental forms of oppression. They demand

---

34 Government edicts have no more magical power to enforce themselves than decisions by anarchistic arbitrators. If someone is unhappy with the way a case was decided on final appeal, she can lobby Congress to change the law, or try to convince the President to appoint more congenial justices, or simply defy the ruling and try to find followers to stage a coup or a revolution.... See also Long 2006, which connects the mystical political conception behind the minarchist quest for legal finality with the mystical logical conception behind the metaphysical quest for a *self-applying rule*, as exposed by Wittgenstein's writing on rule-following.

fundamental change in the cultural and material conditions faced by oppressed people, and propose that the oppressed organise themselves into autonomous movements to struggle for those changes. They also emphasise strikes, boycotts, mutual aid, worker cooperatives, and other forms of collective action, both as a means to social transformation and also as foundational institutions of the transformed society once achieved. These shared concerns and demands have often been summed up in the call for "social justice"—a slogan assailed by Hayek (1978) and reflexively associated, by libertarians and state Leftists alike, with expansion of the anti-discrimination and welfare bureaucracies.

But solidaritarian ends can be separated from authoritarian means, and the relationship between Liberty and Solidarity has not always been so chilly. Nineteenth-century libertarians, particularly the individualist anarchists associated with Benjamin Tucker's magazine *Liberty*, identified with the cultural radicalism of their day—including the labor movement, abolitionism, First Wave feminism, freethought, and "free love." Indeed, while Tucker described his position as "Absolute Free Trade; ... *laissez faire* the universal rule" (1888, ¶ 21), he and his circle routinely identified themselves as *socialists*—not to set themselves against the ideal of the *free market*, but against *actually existing big business*. They argued that plutocratic control over finance and capital was the creature of, and the driving force behind, government economic regimentation and government-granted monopolies.[35] The Tuckerite individualists saw the invasive powers of the State as intimately connected and mutually reinforcing with the exploitation of labor, racism, patriarchy, and other forms of oppression, with governments acting to *enforce* social privilege, and drawing ideological and material support from existing power dynamics.[36] From their point of view, attacking statism alone, without addressing the broader social context, would be narrow and ultimately self-frustrating.

Today the leading intellectual force in the effort to connect libertarianism with a comprehensive vision of human liberation is Chris Sciabarra,[37] who has advanced the argument in a series of books and articles over the past two decades, most extensively in his "Dialectics and Liberty" trilogy (1995b, 1995a, 2000). Sciabarra persuasively advocates a *dialectical* orientation in libertarian social thought, which attends not only to the structural dynamics of statism but also to the extragovernmental *context* of statism in cultural, psychological, and philosophical dimensions. But unlike the nineteenth-century individualists, Sciabarra argues that dialectics pose a

---

35 See Tucker 1888 for an overview of the "four monopolies" that he believed to be at the root of both statism and the exploitation of labor: the land monopoly, the money monopoly, the tariff monopoly, and the patent monopoly. Chapter Five of Carson 2004 offers an excellent systematic overview of the views of Tucker and his fellow nineteenth-century individualists on the four monopolies.

36 Cf. Johnson and Long 2005, § 3.

37 This holistic picture of social power has been endangered and marginalised, but never completely eradicated, from libertarian theory in the twentieth century. During the late 1960s and 1970s it was partially and fitfully revived by the efforts of libertarians such as Murray Rothbard, Karl Hess, and Sam Konkin to make common cause with anti-imperialist and anti-authoritarian elements in the New Left. For the *locus classicus* of this approach in the late twentieth-century libertarian movement, see Rothbard 1965.

substantial *challenge* to libertarian anarchism. In *Ayn Rand: The Russian Radical*, he sympathetically interprets Rand's polemical defense of minarchism as a dialectical effort to transcend a false dualism between statism and anarchism (1995a, 278-83). In *Total Freedom* he devotes four chapters to a charitable but systematic critique of Rothbard's anarcho-capitalism, and the underlying conception of liberty as "universally applicable, *regardless of the context within which it is embedded or applied*" (2000, 218). Sciabarra argues that, at crucial junctures, Rothbard idealises the market and the State into dualistic, opposed spheres, related only through "the external, mutually antagonistic relationship between voluntarism and coercion" (2000, 355). This dualism leads Rothbard to romanticise market processes, proposing "the monistic, utopian resolution of anarcho-capitalism, in which the state's functions were fully absorbed by the market" (360). Thus Rothbard limits libertarianism to a narrow focus on structural and political questions, and exhibits a "lack of attention to the vast context within which [libertarian principles] might exist, evolve, and thrive" (355).[38]

Whether or not Rothbard himself is actually guilty of the "unanchored utopianism" Sciabarra attributes to him (2000, 202), Sciabarra's criticism identifies real strands of thought within the individualist anarchist tradition.[39] But in light of the discussion of Equality above, it seems that minarchists are actually far more prone to synoptic delusions and narrowly political reform than anarchists: the mystique of State authority depends on a picture of the State as an external constraint *on* civil society, whereas egalitarian anarchism highlights the fact that freedom is a matter of concrete relations *within* society. In any case, the best response to Sciabarra's challenge is to *exhibit* a dialectical anarchism, which connects anarchism with a systematic understanding and critique of the dynamics of social power, both inside and outside of the State apparatus. To aid in doing so, I'd like to set out some of the different possible relationships between libertarianism and "thicker" bundles of socio-cultural commitments, which would recommend integrating the two:

1. **Entailment thickness:** the commitments might just be applications of libertarian principle to some special case, following from non-aggression simply in light of non-contradiction.[40]
2. **Application thickness:** it might be that you could reject commitments without *formally contradicting* the non-aggression principle, but not without *in fact* interfering with its proper *application*. Principles beyond libertarianism alone may

---

38 Sciabarra is at pains to make clear that his critique does not aim at a *refutation* of anarchism as such; his emphasis is *methodological*, and for his critique "The essential issue is not whether anarchism or minarchism is preferable—to some extent, the jury is still out on many of the important questions raised by either side" (341). But he suggests that dialectics call for substantial revision to existing defenses of anarchism, stating in reply to a review that "I remain profoundly suspicious of anarchism and the non-dialectical premises that seem to inspire it" (2002, 394).

39 See Long 2001b for a detailed defense of Rothbard against Sciabarra's criticism. But if the anti-dialectical Rothbard did not exist, Walter Block has invented him.

40 An Aztec libertarian might urge, "*Of course* libertarianism has upshots for religious beliefs! It means you have to give up human sacrifice to Huitzilopochtli."

be necessary for determining where my rights end and yours begin, or stripping away conceptual blinders that prevent certain violations of liberty from being recognised as such.
3. **Strategic thickness:** certain ideas, practices, or projects may be *causal preconditions* for a flourishing free society, giving libertarians strategic reasons to endorse them. Although rejecting them would be logically *compatible* with libertarianism, it might make it harder for libertarian ideas to get much purchase, or might lead a free society towards poverty, statism or civil war.
4. **Grounds thickness:** some commitments might be *consistent* with the non-aggression principle, but might undermine or contradict the *deeper reasons* that *justify* libertarian principles. Although you could *consistently* accept libertarianism without the bundle, you could not do so *reasonably:* rejecting the bundle means rejecting the *grounds* for libertarianism.
5. **Conjunction thickness:** commitments might be worth adopting for their own sakes, *independent* of libertarian considerations. All that is asserted is that you ought to be a libertarian (for whatever reason), and, as it happens, you *also* ought to accept some further commitments (for independent reasons).

The two extreme cases, entailment thickness and conjunction thickness, can largely be set aside, since the "relationship" between libertarianism and the further commitment is either so tight (identity) or so loose (mere conjunction) as to make the point vacuous. But the three intermediate cases of application thickness, strategic thickness, and grounds thickness make deeper connections between libertarianism and a rich set of further commitments that naturally complement libertarianism.

Consider the conceptual and strategic reasons that libertarians have to oppose *authoritarianism*, not only as enforced by governments but also as expressed in culture, business, the family, and civil society. If libertarianism is rooted in the principle of *equality of authority,* then there are good reasons to think that not only political structures of coercion, but also the whole *system* of status and unequal authority deserves libertarian criticism. And it is important to realise that that system includes not only exercises of coercive power, but also a knot of ideas, practices, and institutions based on deference to traditionally constituted authorities. In the political realm, these patterns of deference show up most clearly in the honorary titles, submissive etiquette, and unquestioning obedience extended to heads of state, judges, police, and other visible representatives of government "law and order." Although these rituals and habits of obedience exist against the backdrop of statist coercion and intimidation, they are also often practiced voluntarily. Similar expectations of deference show up, to greater or lesser degrees, in cultural attitudes towards bosses in the workplace, and parents in the family. Submission to traditionally constituted authorities is reinforced not only through violence and threats, but also through art, humor, sermons, historiography, journalism, childrearing, etc. Although political coercion is the most distinctive expression of inequality of authority, you could—in principle—*have* an authoritarian social order without the exercise of coercion. Even in an anarchist society, everyone might voluntarily agree to bow and scrape when speaking before the (mutually agreed-on) town Chief. So long as the expectation of deference was backed up only by means of verbal harangues, social ostracism of "unruly" dissenters, culturally glorifying the authorities, etc., it would violate no-one's *individual liberty* and could not justifiably be resisted with force.

But while there's nothing *logically inconsistent* about envisioning these sorts of societies, it is certainly *weird*. If the underlying reason for committing to libertarian politics is rooted in the equality of political authority, then even strictly voluntary expressions of inequality are hard to *reasonably* reconcile with libertarianism. Yes, the meek could voluntarily agree to bow and scrape, and the proud could angrily but nonviolently demand obsequious forms of address and immediate obedience to their fiat. But why *should* they? Libertarian equality delegitimises the notion of a natural right to rule or dominate other people's affairs; the vision of human beings as rational, independent agents of their own destiny renders deference and unquestioning obedience ridiculous at best, and probably dangerous to liberty in the long run. While no-one should be *forced* to treat her fellows with the respect due to equals, or cultivate independent self-reliance and contempt for the arrogance of power, libertarians certainly can—and should—*criticise* those who do not, and *exhort* our fellows not to rely on authoritarian social institutions, for reasons of both grounds and strategic thickness.

General commitments to anti-authoritarianism, if applied to specific forms of social power, have far-reaching implications for the relationship between libertarianism and anti-racism, gay liberation, and other movements for social transformation. I have written elsewhere on the strategic and conceptual importance of radical feminist insights to libertarianism, and vice versa.[41] The causal and conceptual interconnections between patriarchal authority, the cult of violent masculinity, and the militaristic State have been discussed by radical feminists such as Andrea Dworkin and Robin Morgan, as well as radical libertarians such as Herbert Spencer and, more recently, Carol Moore.[42] Moreover, the insights of feminists such as Susan Brownmiller into the pervasiveness of rape, battery, and other forms of male violence against women, present both a crisis and an opportunity for the *application* of libertarian principles.

Libertarianism professes to be a comprehensive theory of human freedom; what supposedly distinguishes the libertarian theory of justice is that we concern ourselves with violent coercion no matter *who* is practicing it. But what feminists have forced into the public eye in the last 30 years is that we live in a society where one out of every four women faces rape or battery by an intimate partner,[43] and where women

---

41 Johnson and Long 2005.

42 Cf. Dworkin 1983/1993, 165-66; Morgan 1989; Spencer 185, Chapter XVI § 4; Moore 2006.

43 See Tjaden and Thoennes 2000 on the findings of the NIJ/CDC National Violence Against Women Survey in 1995-1996. Statistics on violence against women have been hotly contested, and some of these disputes have been taken up by libertarian authors such as Wendy McElroy. But most of the discussion has focused on the findings of a single study, Mary Koss's 1985 study of sexual assault amongst college women (which found that one in four college-aged women had suffered at least one act of rape or attempted rape in her lifetime). I think the criticisms of Koss are largely unfounded, but in any case Tjaden and Thoennes surveyed a broader sample, using more detailed questions, and definitions substantially more conservative than Koss; see pp. 3-12 for a discussion of the survey methodology. Detailed explanation and defense of the NVAWS figures, and of related feminist research into the prevalence and

are threatened or attacked by men who profess to love them, because the men coercing them believe they have a right to control "their" women. Male violence against women is nominally illegal but nevertheless systematic, motivated by the desire for control, culturally excused, and hideously ordinary. For libertarians, this should sound eerily familiar; confronting the reality of male violence means nothing less than recognising the existence of a violent political order working alongside, and independently of, the violent political order of statism.[44] Male supremacy has its own ideological rationalisations, its own propaganda, its own expropriation, and its own violent enforcement; although often in league with the male-dominated State, male violence is older, more invasive, closer to home, and harder to escape than most forms of statism. To seriously oppose all political violence, libertarians need to fight, at least, a two-front war, against both statism and male supremacy. It is, then, important to note how the ideological dichotomy between "personal" and "political" problems, so often criticised by feminists,[45] has tended to blank out systemic male

---

nature of gender violence is, as they say, beyond the scope of this chapter, but for an excellent discussion of Koss's findings that raises many salient general points, see Warshaw 1994, which includes both an analysis of the findings and a concluding methodological discussion by Koss.

44 Thus Susan Brownmiller writes that "Man's discovery that his genitalia could serve as a weapon to generate fear must rank as one of the most important discoveries of prehistoric times, along with the use of fire and the first crude stone axe. From prehistoric times to the present, I believe, rape has played a critical function. It is nothing more or less than a conscious process of intimidation by which *all men* keep *all women* in a state of fear" (1975, 15). Libertarian critics often dismiss Brownmiller's and similar analyses on the grounds that not all men are rapists and not all women are raped, but this badly misunderstands Brownmiller's point. Brownmiller is concerned with the *systemic role* of rape, considered as a social fact that affects all men and all women, whether or not the particular man commits rape or the particular woman suffers it. The fact that rape is so prevalent—even more prevalent than Brownmiller realised in 1975—and the constraints that the threat of rape imposes on *all* women in ordinary life systematically structures the social relationships between men and women, as Brownmiller details throughout her book. Similar remarks could be made about other pervasive forms of violence against women, such as wife beating. The systemic violence of male dominance ought to be recognisable to libertarians as a politically coercive order, even though it is usually carried out in "society," independently of the State apparatus; as Catharine MacKinnon writes, "Unlike the ways in which men systematically enslave, violate, dehumanise, and exterminate other men, expressing political inequalities among men, men's forms of dominance over women have been accomplished socially as well as economically, prior to the operation of the law, without express state acts, often in intimate contexts, as everyday life" (1989, 161).

45 See Hanisch 1969/1978 for the original formulation of the idea that "the personal is political:" "So the reason I participate in these meetings is not to solve any personal problem. One of the first things we discover in these groups is that personal problems are political problems. There are no personal solutions at this time. There is only collective action for a collective solution." It must be stressed that for Hanisch and other radical feminists, "collective action" and "political action" do not necessarily entail *State* action. The point is to recognise the conditions faced by individual women as expressions of an overarching system of social power, rather than sweeping it under the rug of the "private." Cf. Johnson and Long 2005, § 2.

violence from libertarian analysis. And also how the writings of some libertarians on the family—especially those identified with the "paleolibertarian" political-cultural project—have amounted to little more than outright denial of male violence. Hans-Hermann Hoppe, for example, goes so far as to indulge in the conservative fantasy that the traditional "internal layers and ranks of authority" in the family are actually bulwarks of "resistance vis-a-vis the state" (Hoppe 2001, § IV). Those "ranks of authority" in the family mean the *pater familias*; but whether father-right is, at a given historical moment, in league with or at odds with State prerogatives, the fact that it is so widely enforced by the threat or practice of male violence makes enlisting it in the struggle against statism look much like enlisting Stalin to fight Hitler—no matter who wins, we all lose.

Considerations of grounds and strategy also suggest important connections between anarchism and the virtue of *voluntary mutual aid between workers*, in the form of community organisations, charitable projects, and labor unions. Once again, the underlying *reasons* for valuing Liberty also give good reasons for committing to voluntary *solidarity* with your fellow people. One could in principle believe that everyone ought to be free to pursue her own ends while *also* holding that nobody's ends actually matter except her own.[46] But again, while the position is possible, it is *weird*; one of the best reasons for being concerned about the freedom of others to pursue their own ends is a certain generalised respect for the importance of other people's lives and the integrity of their choices, which is intimately connected with the libertarian conception of Equality. That says nothing in favor of *forcing* you to participate in welfare schemes,[47] or robbing Peter to pay Paul; but it does say something for working with your neighbors in *voluntary* cooperative efforts to improve your own lives or the lives of others. It's likely also that networks of voluntary aid organisations would be *strategically* important to individual flourishing in a free society, in which there would be no expropriative welfare bureaucracy for people living with poverty or precarity to fall back on. Projects reviving the bottom-up, solidaritarian spirit of the independent unions and mutual aid societies that flourished in the late nineteenth and early twentieth centuries, before the rise of the welfare bureaucracy, may be essential for a flourishing free society, and one of the primary means by which workers could take control of their own lives, without depending on either bosses or bureaucrats.[48]

---

46 Perhaps that's what Max Stirner believed.

47 Quite the contrary; respect for your fellow human beings entails that you must respect each person's perfect *right* to refuse or to withdraw her support, and *vice versa*—and that anyone who tries to *force* the unwilling to participate in their collective project is nothing more than a sanctimonious highwayman.

48 During the late nineteenth and early twentieth century, before the rise of the modern Welfare State, there was in fact a vast and growing network of mutual aid societies in which low-income workers pooled their resources to gain affordable healthcare, small-scale credit, lifelong education, information about wages and conditions in workplaces, worker-run hiring halls, labor bargaining, strike relief, personal and cultural connections, old-age pensions, life insurance, and many other important services which were later co-opted and colonised by the emerging welfare bureaucracy. Sometimes the independent, government-free societies withered due to obsolescence; in other cases—particularly radical labor unions such as the

If twentieth-century libertarians have mostly failed to emphasise the potential for cooperative mutual aid, the failure can be traced to two related confusions, born of undialectical analysis and the failure to integrate Liberty with Solidarity. The first conflates the principles of mutual aid with government coercion in the name of "social welfare"—most dramatically in the visceral hostility most twentieth-century libertarians expressed towards labor unionism. Libertarian critics have often condemned unions as "bands of thugs,"[49] the government-privileged foot soldiers of a stagnant, interventionist political economy. Currently existing labor unions do use coercive means to organise—in the United States, employers are forced to enter into collective bargaining with unions that gain National Labor Relations Board recognition, and non-violent means of opposing unionisation drives, such as retaliatory firing, are legally prohibited. The official, government-privileged union establishment also *has* for decades sought more government planning and economic intervention. But treating the existing union establishment as representative of the essential features of organised labor disregards the historical process by which unions were co-opted, captured, and domesticated by the expanding State bureaucracy during the 1920s-1950s. The process was achieved with the collaboration of one conservative faction *within* the labor movement, represented most visibly by the "business unionism" of the AFL, which gained leverage over its many competitors and seats in the back-rooms of power through the new system of patronage.[50] It would be hard to discover from the writings of anti-union libertarians that labor unions existed before the Wagner Act of 1935, or that around the turn of the century one of the most vibrant wings of organised labor were the radical, anarchist-led unions, most famously the I.W.W., which rejected all attempts to influence or capture State power.[51] They argued that putting economic power into the government's hands deprived *workers* of control over their own fate, and wasted unions' resources on bureaucracy and partisan maneuvering. Although they worked for incremental improvements in wages and conditions, they ultimately hoped to win not reforms of the existing capitalist system, but *workers' ownership of the "means of production"*—the land, factories, and tools they labored with—not through the political means of expropriation (as the Marxists suggested), but through the economic means of free

---

Industrial Workers of the World—they were destroyed by violent government persecution. See Beito 2000 for an excellent discussion in the context of the rise and fall of voluntary "fraternal society" or "friendly society" lodges. Reconnecting with this history would have direct strategic benefits for libertarians, insofar as similar voluntary associations are likely to be an important part of any healthy free market. Besides those direct benefits, it may also be worth considering the likelihood that mutual aid projects based on free association and self-help could help divorce well-meaning Leftists from the mystique of the welfare state. (Even if it does not cure their souls, it may at least give them something less destructive to do with their time and resources.)

49 Most recently by Walter Block (2006), in his working paper criticising "thick libertarianism," whether allied with Left-wing or Right-wing cultural politics.

50 See Buhle 1999, especially Chapter 1 and pp. 119-36, on the consolidation of establishmentarian unionism and the "tripartite" system of managerial planning between the government, the captains of industry, and the labor bosses of the official unions.

51 Cf. *Ibid.*, 65-70.

association, agitation, direct action, voluntary strikes, union solidarity, and mutual aid between workers, which would "build a new society within the shell of the old." The emerging new society, far from the central planning boards of state socialism, would be a world of independent contractors and worker-owned co-ops, organised from the bottom up by the workers themselves.

It was only through the political collaboration of the establishmentarian union bosses and the "Progressive" business class—in the form of violent persecution of the radicals, such as the Palmer raids, and government patronage to establishment unions through the NLRB—that the centralised, statist unionism of the AFL-CIO rose to dominance within the labor movement.[52] Union methods are legally regulated and union demands effectively constrained to modest (and easily revoked) improvements in wages and conditions—with issues such as workers' voice in the workplace, let alone control of the means of production, dropped entirely. The only real power remaining to effect more substantial changes comes through their power as organised blocs for lobbying and electioneering. If unionism is today mostly statist, then it is because unions are largely what the State has made them, through the usual carrots and sticks of government interventionism.

General Motors has benefited *at least* as much from government patronage as the UAW, yet libertarian criticism of the magnates of state capitalism is hardly extended to business as such in the way that criticism of existing unions is routinely extended to any form of organised labor. The difference in treatment is no doubt closely connected with the emphasis many twentieth-century libertarians placed on defending capitalism against the attacks of state socialists. While they were right to see that existing modes of production should not be *further* distorted by even greater government regimentation, this insight was often perverted into the delusion that existing modes of production would be the natural outcome of an *undistorted* market. The confusion has been encouraged by systematic ambiguity in the term "capitalism," which has been used to name at least *three* different economic systems:

1. The free market: any economic order that emerges from voluntary exchanges

---

52 Under the smothering patronage of the Wagner/Taft-Hartley labor bureaucracy, official unions gained new political privileges that made them the most effective vehicles for workers' short-term goals, allowing them to out-compete the unsubsidised unions. But the price of government privileges were government controls: the NLRB system constrained union goals to mediated settlements with management, and in 1947 the Taft-Hartley Act pulled official union tactics firmly into the regulatory grip of the managerial State. Union methods are legally restricted to collective bargaining and limited strikes. Strikes cannot legally be expanded to secondary or general strikes, and any strike can be—as many strikes have been—broken by the arbitrary fiat of the President of the United States. Obvious violations of the freedom of contract—such as the ban on union hiring halls and "closed shop" contracts—strip officially recognised unions of effective tactics and sap their resources. The emphasis on collective bargaining and bureaucratic mediation favors centralised union bureaucracies over more decentralised, democratic forms of organisation. Thus both the internal culture of the post-Wagner union establishment and the external controls of federal and state regulations have conspired to enrich a select class of professional unionists while hamstringing the labor movement as a whole and limiting progress for rank-and-file workers.

of property and labor, free of government intervention and other forms of systemic coercion.

2. **The corporate State:** government intervention favoring cartelised big business, through subsidies, tax-funded infrastructure, central banking, production boards, eminent domain seizures, government union-busting, etc.

3. **Alienation of labor:** a specific form of labor market, in which the dominant economic activity is production in workplaces strictly divided by class, where most workers *work for* a boss, in return for a wage, surviving by renting out their labor to someone else. The shop, and the tools and facilities that make it run, are owned by the boss or by absentee owners to whom the boss reports, not by the workers themselves.

Since government intervention always ends with the barrel of a gun, free market "capitalism" and corporate state "capitalism" cannot coexist at the same time and in the same respect. "Capitalism" in the *third* sense—the alienation of labor—is a category *independent* of "capitalism" in either of the first two senses. There are many ways that a labor market might turn out; it could be organised into traditional employer-employee relationships, worker co-ops, community workers' councils, or a diffuse network of shopkeeps and independent contractors. Unflinching free marketeers might advocate *any* of these, or might be indifferent as to which prevails; interventionist statists might also favor traditional employer-employee relationships (as under fascism) or any number of different arrangements (as under state communism). Once these three senses are disentangled, it is important to see how twentieth-century libertarian defenses of "capitalism" against interventionist critique have fallen into a second conflation, between economic defenses of (1) the free market, and (2, 3) the way that big business operates in the unfree market that actually exists today. This confused approach, aptly dubbed "vulgar libertarianism" by Kevin Carson,[53] obscures the ways in which actually existing businesses benefit from pervasive government intervention, and blinds "capitalist" libertarians to the affinity between anti-statist models of labor organising and libertarian defenses of free markets.

Disentangling free market economics from the particular market structure of alienated labor reveals some good reasons to think that there are serious *economic* problems with bureaucratic, centralised corporate commerce that rose to dominance in the nineteenth and twentieth centuries under the auspices of "Nationalist" and "Progressive" interventionism.[54] Central planners face the knowledge problems

---

53 "Vulgar libertarian apologists for capitalism use the term 'free market' in an equivocal sense; they seem to have trouble remembering, from one moment to the next, whether they're defending actually existing capitalism or free market principles. So we get the standard boilerplate article in *The Freeman* [on sweatshop labor] arguing that the rich can't get rich at the expense of the poor, because 'that's not how the free market works'—implicitly assuming that this *is* a free market. When prodded, they'll grudgingly admit that the present system is not a free market, and that it includes a lot of state intervention on behalf of the rich. But as soon as they think they can get away with it, they go right back to defending the wealth of existing corporations on the basis of 'free market principles'" (Carson 2004, 142).

54 For an extensive discussion of the nature of the corporate state and the role of government patronage in the formation of actually existing capitalism, see especially part two of Carson 2004 and Kolko 1963.

identified by Mises, Hayek, and Rothbard whether those planners are government or corporate bureaucrats.[55] If workers are often deeply unhappy with the regimented, authoritarian structure of corporate workplaces, then there is also reason to believe that many would happily dump the bosses off their backs in favor of more autonomous forms of work, as those become widespread, successful, and economically reliable. Thus there is reason to think that in a free market less hierarchical, less centralised, more worker-focused forms of production would multiply and bureaucratic big business would wither under the pressure of competition.[56] Since the cooperative, bottom-up model of labor unionism offers one of the best existing models for practically asserting workers' self-interest, and ultimately replacing boss-centric industry with decentralised, worker-centric production, there are good reasons for libertarians to integrate wildcat unionism into their understanding of social power.

Solidaritarian considerations may also shed some light on the standing debate amongst libertarians over secession and constitutional centralism. Liberty in the abstract demands a universal *right* of secession; to keep any one person or any group of people under a government that they wish to exit requires you to violate their individual liberty in at least one of the three ways challenged above. But voluntarily organised protection agencies, arbiters, etc. could still claim wide or narrow jurisdictions, and could organise their administrative and juridical functions into rigid hierarchies or take a more "horizontal," decentralised approach. Affirming a *right* of secession does not answer the constitutional question of which free arrangement libertarians ought to prefer. But the same solidaritarian considerations that tell against centralisation and hierarchy in making widgets should tell even more strongly against centralisation and hierarchy in political power. The pretensions of the powerful threaten a free society when it is hard to defend yourself physically against abuses of the power entrusted to defense associations, or intellectually against the allure of State mysticism. And there are good *prima facie* reasons to suppose that people will be better able to resist both threats by devolving power from centralised seats of power down to the local level, with arbitration and enforcement handled face-to-face through diffuse networks of local associations, rather than mediated through powerful, bureaucratised hegemons.

Centralists may object that the historical record is more complex, and less favorable to decentralism, than *prima facie* considerations would suggest. While a centralised political power has more resources and a wider scope to enforce coercive demands, local powers are often more subject to parochial prejudices, and can often enforce them with force that is less diffuse, closer to home, and therefore

---

55 It is important to remember that the calculation problem, as variously formulated, has to do either with the lack of market pricing or with the dispersal of idiosyncratic knowledge, not essentially with the use of coercive means. Political coercion is one of the most effective ways to stifle negotiation and shove people with idiosyncratic knowledge out of the way. But it is not the only way; voluntary structures can block the flow of knowledge no less than coercive ones. Cf. Rothbard 1962, Chapter 10, Section F on the calculation problems that would be faced by One Big Cartel, even without government intervention.

56 See Long 2005 for an economic analysis of the trade-offs involved in increasing the size of firms and the economic factors that would tend towards greater decentralisation in a free market.

more intense than anything a mighty but remote central government could muster. American history seems to illustrate this point dramatically with the case of the Confederacy, in which the opponents of federal power urged secession in order to strengthen and perpetuate the absolute tyranny of chattel slavery.[57] But what is needed here is a *more radical* decentralism, dissociated from the humbug of "states' rights." Decentralist libertarians are perfectly *justified* in supporting the white Southerners' right to secede, and condemning the bayonet-point Unionism of the Civil War—provided that they *also* support *black slaves' rights to secede from the Southern states*, and condemn the bayonet-point paternalism of the Southern slavelords. The approach here is to condemn the federal war against secession, while also supporting the efforts of black Southerners to free themselves, through escape or open rebellion.[58] The problem with the Confederacy was not the defiance of *federal* authority, but the elevation of *state* authority over the objections of poor whites and black slaves: too much, not too little, centralised power. Nothing other than pure mysticism limits secession to states or provinces: provincial governments enjoy no more sovereign authority over their citizens than the federal government does, and the same principles that justify the withdrawal of states from the federal union also justify counties or cities withdrawing from State governments, and neighborhoods or *individual* citizens withdrawing from local governments, or from any government anywhere.

Liberty, understood in the context of Equality and Solidarity, calls for political revolution against all forms of government, no matter how "limited," and overweening centralisation of power even in non-coercive institutions. But "revolution" itself takes on a different character when the obscuring haze of State mysticism has been dispelled. If "revolution" means the process of dissolving the legal authority of a government, then revolution is quite easy to achieve. You have no obligation to obey any government longer than you choose to remain under it; once you have declared your intent to withdraw from the State, no government on earth has the authority to force you to recognise its authority over you—let alone to force you to

---

57 Whether or not Southern secessionism was closely linked with slavery is—God help us all—still a matter of considerable controversy in libertarian intellectual circles. But see Hummel 1996 for a persuasive argument that while the *Federal government's* motives in pursuing the Civil War had little to do with freeing slaves, the *Confederate states'* motives for seceding were dominated by the desire to perpetuate and expand race slavery.

58 The most dramatic historical example of this line of argument can be found in the work of Lysander Spooner, who penned *No Treason* (1867-1870) as a defense of the moral right of the Southern states to secede from the Union, but also published a "Plan for the Abolition of Slavery" (1858), which called on slaves and non-slaveholding whites to launch a guerrilla war against Southern slaveholders, with aid and comfort provided by Northern abolitionists. Thus in *No Treason*, Spooner stated that "The result—and a natural one—has been that we have had governments, State and national, devoted to nearly every grade and species of crime that governments have ever practised upon their victims; and these crimes have culminated in a war that has cost a million of lives; a war carried on, upon one side, for chattel slavery, and on the other for political slavery; upon neither for liberty, justice, or truth" (No. II, § X ¶ 2). Hummel 1996 offers an excellent historical defense of a similar view of the secession crisis and the Civil War.

pay taxes or regiment your behavior. If a government's orders invade your rights—and all governments' orders eventually do—then you have every right to withdraw from, ignore, defy, or resist it however seems best to you. Earlier, I stated that this essay's purpose was political revolution, then stated it was merely to convince you to become an anarchist. But it should now be clear that I was not moving the goalposts. If you become an anarchist, then you have already *completed* the revolution: no government on earth has any *legitimate authority* to bind you to any obligation that you did not already have on your own. It's a mistake to think of the State as holding you under its authority while you struggle to escape; at the most, it has *power*, not *authority* over you. As far as your former government is concerned, you have the moral standing not of a subject, but of the head of a revolutionary state of one.

Of course, that leaves the question of how best to *defend* your revolutionary state from counter-revolutionary invasion. Declaring yourself independent really is enough to release you from any obligation to your former government—but try telling *that* to the judge. Still, the first task is to recognise your situation for what it is. Minarchism, by leaving the myth of legal authority unchallenged, concedes moral dignity to the statists that they have not earned. The point is to challenge not only the *abuses* of government authority, but the normal *uses* of that authority—to see the taxmen, policemen, hangmen, and Congressmen who invade your liberties not as unruly representatives of a State with authority over you, but a sanctimonious gang of robbers, swindlers, and usurpers bringing *war* upon you. Once you have recognised that, you can begin to think intelligently about the best cultural and material arrangements for defending against them. I have already discussed a few of the particulars above; the rest is another discussion for another essay.[59]

Bibliography

Barnett, Randy. 2004. *Restoring the Lost Constitution: The Presumption of Liberty*. Princeton: Princeton University Press.

Beito, David T. 2000. *From Mutual Aid to the Welfare State: Fraternal Societies and Social Services, 1890-1967*. University of North Carolina Press.

Bidinotto, Robert J. 1994. "The Contradiction in Anarchism." <http://tinyurl.com/4zdpf>

Block, Walter. 2006. "Libertarianism is unique; it belongs neither to the right nor the left: a critique of the views of Long, Holcombe, and Baden on the left, Hoppe, Feser and Paul on the right." Mises Institute Working Paper. <http://www.mises.org/journals/scholar/block15.pdf>

Bourne, Randolph. 1919. "The State." <http://fair-use.org/randolph-bourne/the-state/>

Brownmiller, Susan. 1975. *Against Our Will: Men, Women, and Rape*. New York: Simon and Schuster.

---

[59] A project like this one cannot be undertaken without accumulating debts. My own are too numerous to give an accounting of them all; but in particular I would like to thank Laura Breitenbeck and Roderick Long for patience, inspiration, collaboration, encouragement, and detailed and very helpful comments.

Buhle, Paul. 1999. *Taking Care of Business: Samuel Gompers, George Meany, Lane Kirkland, and the Tragedy of American Labor*. New York: Monthly Review Press.

Byock, Jesse L. 2001. *Viking Age Iceland*. New York: Penguin Books.

Carson, Kevin A. 2004. *Studies in Mutualist Political Economy*. Fayetteville, AR: self-published. <http://www.mutualist.org/id47.html>

Childs, Roy A. 1969. "Objectivism and the State: An Open Letter to Ayn Rand." In Joan Kennedy Taylor. Ed. 1994. *Liberty Against Power: Essays by Roy A. Childs, Jr.* San Francisco: Fox and Wilkes. 145-56. <http://www.lewrockwell.com/orig4/childs1.html>

Dworkin, Andrea. 1983. "I Want a Twenty-Four Hour Truce During Which There Is No Rape." In *Letters from a War Zone* (1993). Brooklyn: Laurence Hill Books. 162-71. <http://www.nostatusquo.com/ACLU/dworkin/WarZoneChaptIIIE.html>

Hanisch, Carol. 1969. "The Personal is Political." In Redstockings (ed.) (1978), *Feminist Revolution*. New York: Random House. 204-05.

Hayek, Friedrich A. 1978. *Law, Legislation, and Liberty, Vol. 2: The Mirage of Social Justice*. Chicago: University of Chicago Press.

Hoppe, Hans-Hermann. 2001. "Secession, the State, and the Immigration Problem." <http://www.lewrockwell.com/orig/hermann-hoppe3.html>

Hummel, Jeffrey R. 1996. *Emancipating Slaves, Enslaving Free Men: A History of the American Civil War*. Peru, IL: Open Court Publishing.

Jefferson, Thomas. 1776a. "Declaration of Independence." <http://www.yale.edu/lawweb/avalon/declare.htm>

Jefferson, Thomas. 1776b. "Original Rough Draft of the Declaration of Independence." <http://www.ushistory.org/declaration/document/rough.htm>

Johnson, Charles, and Roderick T. Long. 2005. "Libertarian Feminism: Can This Marriage Be Saved?" <http://charleswjohnson.name/essays/libertarian-feminism/>

Kolko, Gabriel. 1963. *The Triumph of Conservatism: A Reinterpretation of American History, 1900-1915*. Chicago: Quadrangle Books.

Locke, John. 1690. *Second Treatise of Government*. <http://etext.library.adelaide.edu.au/l/locke/john/l81s/>

Long, Roderick T. 2001a. "Equality: The Unknown Ideal." Presented for the Philosophy of Liberty Conference at the Ludwig von Mises Institute in Auburn, AL, Saturday, September 29, 2001. <http://www.mises.org/story/804>

Long, Roderick T. 2001b. "The Benefits and Hazards of Dialectical Libertarianism," in *The Journal of Ayn Rand Studies*, Vol. 2, No. 2 (Spring 2001). 395-448.

Long, Roderick T. (2002a. "Privatization, Viking Style: Model or Misfortune?" <http://www.lewrockwell.com/orig3/long1.html>

Long, Roderick T. 2002b. "Why Does Justice Have Good Consequences?" Alabama Philosophical Society Presidential Address, Orange Beach, AL (26 October 2002). <http://praxeology.net/whyjust.htm>

Long, Roderick T. 2005. "Freedom and the Firm," at *Austro-Athenian Empire* (December 4, 2005). <http://praxeology.net/unblog12-05.htm#04>

Long, Roderick T. 2007. "Market Anarchism As Constitutionalism," this volume.

Long, Roderick T. 2006. "Rule-Following, Praxeology, and Anarchy," forthcoming in *New Perspectives on Political Economy*, Vol. 2, No. 1.

MacKinnon, Catharine A. 1986. *Toward a Feminist Theory of the State*. Cambridge, MA: Harvard University Press.

Moore, Carol. 2006. "Woman Vs. The Nation-State" (revised edition). Originally published in *Liberty*, November 1991. <http://www.carolmoore.net/articles/woman-v-nationstate.html>

Morgan, Robin. 1989. *The Demon Lover: On the Sexuality of Terrorism*. New York: W. W. Norton.

Nozick, Robert. 1974. *Anarchy, State, and Utopia*. New York: Basic Books.

Rand, Ayn. 1964. *The Virtue of Selfishness: A New Concept of Egoism*. New York: New American Library.

Rothbard, Murray N. 1962. *Man, Economy, and State*. Auburn, AL: Ludwig von Mises Institute. <http://www.mises.org/rothbard/mes/>

Rothbard, Murray N. 1965. "Left and Right: The Prospects for Liberty." <http://www.lewrockwell.com/rothbard/rothbard33.html>

Sciabarra, Chris M. 1995a. *Marx, Hayek, and Utopia*. Albany, NY: SUNY Press.

Sciabarra, Chris M. 1995b. *Ayn Rand: The Russian Radical*. University Park: Pennsylvania State University Press.

Sciabarra, Chris M. 2000. *Total Freedom: Toward a Dialectical Libertarianism*. University Park: Pennsylvania State University Press.

Sciabarra, Chris M. 2002. "Dialectical Libertarianism: All Benefits, No Hazards," in *The Journal of Ayn Rand Studies* Vol. 3, No. 2 (Spring 2002). 381-400.

Spencer, Herbert. 1851. *Social Statics: or, The Conditions essential to Happiness specified, and the First of them Developed. Online Library of Liberty.* <http://tinyurl.com/93188>

Spooner, Lysander. 1858. "To the Non-Slaveholders of the South: A Plan for the Abolition of Slavery." <http://praxeology.net/LS-PAS.htm>

Spooner, Lysander. 1867-1870. *No Treason*, Nos. 1, 2, and 6. <http://www.lysanderspooner.org/notreason.htm>

Spooner, Lysander. 1882a. "A Letter to Congressman Thomas F. Bayard: Challenging His Right—And That of All the Other So-Called Senators and Representatives in Congress—To Exercise Any Legislative Power Whatever Over the People of the United States." <http://praxeology.net/LS-LB.htm>

Spooner, Lysander. 1882b. "Natural Law; or, the Science of Justice." <http://praxeology.net/LS-NL-1.htm>

Spooner, Lysander. 1886. "A Letter to Grover Cleveland on His False Inaugural Address: The Usurpations and Crimes of Lawmakers and Judges and the Consequent Poverty, Ignorance, and Servitude of the People." <http://www.lysanderspooner.org/LetterToGroverCleveland.htm>

Tjaden, Patricia, and Nancy Thoennes. 2000. *Full Report of the Prevalence, Incidence, and Consequences of Violence Against Women: Findings from the National Violence Against Women Survey*. Washington, DC: Office of Justice Programs. Research Report NCJ 183781. <http://www.ncjrs.gov/pdffiles1/nij/183781.pdf>

Tucker, Benjamin R. 1888. "State Socialism and Anarchism: How Far They Agree, and Wherein They Differ." <http://praxeology.net/BT-SSA.htm>

Warshaw, Robin. 1994. *I Never Called It Rape: The Ms. Report on Recognizing, Fighting, and Surviving Date and Acquaintance Rape*. New York: HarperCollins.

Wolff, Robert Paul. 1970. *In Defense of Anarchism*. Berkeley: University of California Press.

Index

A
abortion, and rights 52
Afghanistan 50, 55
al Qaeda 33, 36, 53
American Civil Liberties Union 138
American Founders vii, 79
American Philosophical Society 32
anarchism
    as constitutionalism 139–41
    dialectical 176
    double standard on 140
    examples 50
    force, position on 89
    individualist, meaning 155fn1
    see also anarchy; market anarchism
anarcho-capitalism *see* market anarchism
anarcho-libertarianism 18–19, 59–62, 63
    government, rejection of 64–5
anarchy
    case for 112
    and conflict resolution 173
    definitions 111, 112
    disorder, association with 111
    Locke's arguments against 134–7
    Rand on 43
    see also market anarchism
Anderson, Terry 100
anti-authoritarianism, libertarian stance 177–8
assault and battery, evolution of rules 115–16
authority, and deference, example 159–60
Axelrod, Robert, *The Evolution of Cooperation* 94

B
Barnett, Randy vii, 96–8
Barry, Brian, review of Nozick's *Anarchy, State, and Utopia* 145
Bastiat, Frédéric vii
Benson, Bruce vii, 98
    The Enterprise of Law 21, 74

Berlin Wall 8
Berman, Harold 115
Bidinotto, Robert 164, 172
Block, Walter 60, 78
    on government 80–84
    critique 80–84
    on libertarianism 79–80
book censorship, Polish-Lithuanian Commonwealth 31–2
Bourne, Randolph, on the state 172–3
Brownmiller, Susan 178

C
capitalism, economic systems 182–3
Carson, Kevin 183
Childs, Roy 44, 60
    critique of Rand 160–61, 164–5
    on government use of force 46
    "Open Letter to Ayn Rand" 160
Cicero 19
common law
    and conflict resolution 118
    as customary law 113–14
    evolution 114–16
    and fraud 119
    as spontaneous cooperation 93–4
    vs government legislation 126
Confederacy, secession, motives 184–5
conflict resolution 97, 108–9
    and anarchy 173
    in Anglo-Saxon times 101, 114
    and common law 118
    defense agencies 147–8
    and the legal system 133
    in minarchism 142
    moot forum 114
    non-monopolistic 100–101
    Polish-Lithuanian Commonwealth 29
    pre-federal American west 100
    without courts 120–21
    see also cooperation
constitution

as behavior patterns 140, 141
  meaning 140
constitutional republic
  formation 35
  human rights, need to uphold 36
constitutionalism, anarchism as 139–41
contractual relations, and law 18
cooperation
  and need for state 93
  and Pavlov strategy 94–5
  and prisoner's dilemma 93, 94
  spontaneous, common law as 93–4
  see also conflict resolution
cooperative organization
  formation, in market law 34–5
  transformation, to constitutional republic 35
courts
  government provision 120–22
  as public goods 128
Cowen, Tyler, definition of state 65
crime
  and defense agencies 50
  misattributions of 25–6
  nature of 25
  and police 124–5
  prevention
    government role 138
    and property rights 97–8
  see also punishment

D
De Jasay, Anthony 141
Declaration of Independence 65–6, 67
defense, morality of 72
  see also national defense; self-defense
defense agencies
  competition possibilities 80–81, 164
  conflict resolution 147–8
  and crime problem 50
  government approved 163
  limitations 47, 161
  in market anarchism 18–19
  monopolistic tendencies 18–19, 89–90, 95–6
  Polish-Lithuanian Commonwealth 28–9
deference, and authority, example 159
Den Uyll, Douglas J. 60
Descartes, René, *Meditations*
  dream argument 8
  problem of skepticism 8, 12
Din Torah custom 29
dispute resolution *see* conflict resolution
double standard
  on anarchism 140
  and the state 7–8, 9, 12, 13–14
dream argument, in Descartes' *Meditations* 8
Dworkin, Andrea 178
Dykes, Nicholas 46, 53, 54, 60

E
egoism 39, 44
enterprises, and need for property rights 75, 82
equality 169–74
  as *egalité* 170
  Jefferson on 170
  and libertarianism 170
  liberty (individual), relationship 170–72
  Locke on 170–71
  and self-ownership 171
exploitation, and morality 12

F
Filmer, Robert 142
force
  anarchist position on 89
  government use 65, 67, 71–2, 88, 158, 160–61
    Childs on 46
  market in 27
  need for, and politics 68
  use of, and rights 45
fraud, and common law 119
free market, von Mises on 138–9
free riding
  and public goods 127
  Schmidtz on 100
freedom, need to create 56
Friedman, David vii
  on government 139

G
Gadsden Purchase boundary line 8
government
  anarcho-libertarianism, rejection by 64–5
  authority, basis 168–9

Block on 80–84
  critique 80–84
claims 158
consent to, argument 133fn1
constitutional vii
courts, provision of 120–22
and crime prevention 138
definition 39–40, 64
  contestability 78–9
  Rand's 39fn1
features 158–9
force, use of 65, 67, 71–2, 79, 88, 158, 160–61
  Childs on 46
Friedman on 139
funding
  citizenship fee 48–9
  contract fees 41, 42, 43
  Rand on 41–2, 43, 79
  sources 40–41
law
  accessibility 118–19
  provision 66–8
  uniformity 116–17
legislation, vs common law 126
Machan on 88
market regulation 125–7
minimal functions 40
  prospects for 110
  see also minarchism
objectivist view 39–40, 47–8, 52, 55
police, supply of 122–5
and property rights 40
public goods production 127–30
and rights 39, 65–6, 67
role, Rand on 40, 160–61
taxation, as mark of 78
and warfare 146
Weber's definition vii
see also minarchism; state
governments, competition between 72–4

H
happiness
  measurement of 22
  pursuit of 22–3
harmony of interests, principle 23–4
Hasnas, John 60, 111–31
  definition of state 65

Hayek, Friedrich
  Law, Legislation, and Liberty 88, 93, 101
  thesis/nomos concepts, distinction 88
Hill, P.J. 100
Hobbes, Thomas 89, 93, 113, 142
Hoppe, Hans-Hermann vii
Hoppe, Hermann 179
Hospers, John 19, 60
Hughes, Howard 19
Hume, David
  critique of Locke 3
  on obedience to the state 3–4, 5, 6
  "Of the Original Contract" 3
Hunt, Lester H. 3–14

I
Iceland, medieval, market law example 27, 54, 164fn23
individual rights
  in market law 34
  and self-ownership 167
individualism
  ethical 156
  libertarian 156
Innocence Project 25
Institute for Justice 138
interest groups
  and market anarchism 147
  and minarchism 146–7
international law, adjudication problems 76
international relations, and market anarchism 54
irrationality, consequences 50

J
Jefferson, Thomas 19
  on equality 170
Johnson, Charles 155–88
Jordan 53

K
Kalkstein, Christian Ludwig von 31
Kelley, David 46, 60, 68
  "The Necessity of Government" 45

L
labor movement, and solidarity 156fn4, 174
labor unions, libertarian hostility to 180–82

law
  American, sources 18
  common law sources 109
  and contractual relations 18
  customary, development 101, 113–15
  as enterprise 74–7
    adjudication problems 75–6
    limitations 77
  obedience to 4
  objective 40
  and property rights 17
  uniformity, and government role 116–17
  see also common law; market law
Law Merchant, uniformity 135–6, 149
laws
  origins of 17–19
  Spooner on 165–7
Lebanon 50, 53, 54
Lee, John Roger 15–20, 68
legal finality
  impossibility of 143–5
  market anarchism, lack 142–3
legal services provision
  government 66–8
  market anarchism 135
  minarchism 135
  non-monopolistic 70, 99
legal system, and conflict resolution 133
Lester, Jan 60
liberal democracies, features 62
libertarian rights theory 156
libertarianism vii
  anti-authoritarianism, commitment to 177–8
  application "thicknesses" 176–7
  Block on 79–80
  definitions 15, 103–4, 156fn3
  dialectical 156
  and equality 170
  governmental 18
  minarchist position 61, 63–4
  negative rights vii, 104, 156
  non-aggression principle 156
  principle 106
  and property rights 106
  Rothbard on 175
    Sciabarra's critique 175–6
  see also anarcho-libertarianism
libertarians

expectations 77–8
labor unions, hostility to 180–82
minimal-state 89
liberty (individual) 157–69
  definition 157
  equality, relationship 170–72
  government sovereignty, incompatibility 169
  and legal right 160
  and revolution 155, 185–6
  and right of secession 184
  and self-ownership 157, 169
  solidarity, relationship 174–5, 179–80
Liberty (periodical) vii, 174
licensing agency, minarchist state as 148
  objections to 148–50
life, sustainment of 22
Locke, John vii, 19, 79
  arguments against anarchy 134–7
    critique of 134–7
  on equality 170–71
  justification for the state 3
  on the political realm 5–6
  state, social contract argument 3, 6
Long, Roderick T. 60, 133–54, 171, 173

M
Machan, Tibor R. 21, 59–84
  on government 88
  on the state 91–2
  works
    Human Rights and Human Liberties 91
    The Market for Liberty 80
Mack, Eric 60
market anarchism
  features vii, 18
  incoherence of 18–19
  and interest groups 147
  and international relations 54
  legal finality, lack 142–3
  legal services provision 135
  limitations 46–7
  objectivist arguments against 45–53
  private defense agencies 18–19
  Rand on 43–4, 49, 51
  societies, examples of 54–5
market anarchists, Rand on 53
market law

conclusions 33–4
cooperative organization, formation 34–5
individual rights in 34
medieval Iceland 27, 54, 164fn23
Polish-Lithuanian Commonwealth 28–33
Milosevic, Slobodan 76
minarchism 157
   authority to act 106–7
   challenges to 160–69
   claims 158–9
   conflict resolution in 142
   definition vii
   inevitability of 59–60
   and interest groups 146–7
   legal services provision 135
   as licensing agency 148
      objections to 148–50
Mises, Ludwig von vii
   on the free market 138–9
Molinari, Gustave de vii, 141
monopoly
   coercive, examples 69–70
   tendencies, defense agencies 18–19, 89–90, 95–6
   "monopoly of force" argument, state 4, 65, 69fn31, 122, 133, 158fn8
Moore, Carol 178
moot forum, conflict resolution 114
moral rules 10–11
morality
   and exploitation 12
   state, comparison 10–12
Morgan, Robin 178
mutual aid 180
   see also solidarity

N
Narveson, Jan 60, 103–10
nation, Spooner on 167–8
national defense 50, 112
   as public goods 129–30
natural justice 109
natural law
   making specific 167
   and natural rights 19–20
natural rights
   and natural law 19–20

   tradition 19
nature, state of
   pre-political representation 9
   state derivation from 9
nomos concept, Hayek 88
Nowak, Martin 94
Nozick, Robert 18–19
   Anarchy, State, and Utopia vii, 59
      Barry's review 145
   on core philosophical problems 12–13, 14
   on the minimal state 89–90, 95–6, 107, 162–4

O
objectivism
   market anarchism, arguments against 45–53
   political principles 39
   and rationality 49–50
   view of government 39–40, 47–8, 52, 55

P
Paterson, Isabel vii
Pavlov strategy, and cooperation 94–5
Peikoff, Leonard 47
Pinochet, Augusto 76
Plato, on division of labor 87
plutocracy 138–9
police
   and crime 124–5
   governmental 122–5
   non-governmental 121–2
   as public goods 127–8
Polish-Lithuanian Commonwealth
   book censorship 31–2
   conflict resolution 29
   corruption 30
   defense agencies 28–9
   market law, example 28–33
   national defense 29
   partition by invaders 32–3
   religious
      diversity 30
      intolerance 31
   Unitarians in 30–31
   von Kalkstein abduction of 31
political realm

Locke on 5–6
  moral explication of 8–9
  skepticism, need for 9
political system
  function 27
  need for 27
politics
  foundation of 24–6
  and need for force 68
Potocki, Jan, *Essai de Logique* 32
prisoner's dilemma, and cooperation 93, 94
property rights
  and crime prevention 97–8
  for enterprises 75, 82
  example 15–17, 19, 20
  and government 40
  and libertarianism 106
  need for law on 17
  prerequisites 19–20
'prudent predator' 24
public goods
  courts as 128
  definition 127
  and free riding 127
  national defense as 129–30
  police services as 127–8
  production, need for government 127–30, 134fn3
punishment
  objective standard, need for 26
  see also crime

R
Rand, Ayn vii
  on anarchism 43
  concept of rights 23
  on funding government 41–2, 43, 79
  on market anarchism 43–4, 49, 51
  on market anarchists 53
  objective politics 21–2
  on property status, of radio spectrum 53–4
  on role of government 40, 160–61
    Childs's critique 160–61, 164–5
  on taxes 40–41, 67
  works
    Atlas Shrugged 35, 39, 50, 55–6
    The Fountainhead 50

    "The Nature of Government" 43–4, 45
Rasmussen, Douglas B. 60
rationality
  and disagreements 51–3
  and objectivism 49–50
realm, meaning 5
  see also political realm
Reed, Adam 21–37
revolution, and liberty (individual) 155, 185–6
rights
  and abortion 52
  assertion of, problems 164
  basis of 173
  and government 39, 65–6, 67
  human, need for constitutional republic to uphold 36
  individual, in market law 34
  need for agreement on 35–6
  negative (libertarian) vii, 104, 156
  prerequisites for 19–20
  Rand's concept 23
  scope 19fn7
  and use of force 45
  see also individual rights; natural rights
Roman Empire 143–4
Rothbard, Murray N. vii, 59, 60, 67, 78
  on libertarianism 175
    Sciabarra's critique 175–6
  Power and Market 97
  on the state 91, 97

S
Sanders, John 60, 67
Schmidtz, David 100
  on free riding 100
Sciabarra, Chris 156
  Rothbard, critique of 175–6
  on statism 175
  works
    Ayn Rand 175
    Total Freedom 175
The Scotsman 21
Scruton, Roger 109
secession
  Confederacy, motives 184–5
  right of, and liberty (individual) 184
Sechrest, Larry 41

self-defense
  collective 89
  morality of 72
self-ownership 97
  and equality 171
  and individual rights 167
  and liberty 157, 169
  unconditionality of 157
Shariah Law 21, 33
Sigmund, Karl 94
skepticism
  in Decartes' *Meditations* 8, 12
  in political realm, need for 9
Skoble, Aeon James 87–102
Smith, Adam vii
social contract, argument for state, Locke's 3, 6
social justice 174
social living, need for 87
society
  features 4
  Plato on 87
  rationale for 87
  spontaneously ordered 112
  and the state 4
solidarity 174–86
  concept, scope of 174
  and the labor movement 156fn4, 174
  liberty, relationship 174–5, 179–80
  see also mutual aid
Somalia 50, 55
sovereignty
  aggression, need for 161
  liberty, incompatibility 169
  meaning 167
Spencer, Herbert 65, 178
Spooner, Lysander 60
  on laws 165–7
  on nation 167–8
  works
    "Letter to Grover Cleveland" 165
    No Treason 167
standard, definition 26
state
  arguments for 104–5
  Bourne on 172–3
  definitions 74–5
    Cowen's 65
    Hasnas's 65
    development, conditions for 141
  and the double standard 7–8, 9, 12, 13–14
  justification, need for 3
  Locke's social contract argument 3, 6
  Machan on 91–2
  minimalist form 75, 157
    Nozick on 89–90, 95–6, 107, 162–4
  "monopoly of force" argument 4, 65, 69fn31, 122, 133, 158fn8
  morality, comparison 10–12
  mystique of 172–3, 174
  need for, and cooperation 93
  obedience to, Hume on 3–4, 5, 6
  Rothbard on 91, 97
  rules made by 11
  and society 4
  state of nature, derivation from 9
  Weber's definition 65
  see also government
statism, Sciabarra on 175
Stewart, Martha 119

T
Tannehill, Morris & Linda vii, 60
taxation
  alternatives to 40–41
  as mark of government 78
  Rand on 40–41, 67
  as theft 7
  as use of force 43
Taylor, *The Possibility of Cooperation* 95
Teller, Edward 19
thesis concept, Hayek 88
Thomas, William 39–57
Thoreau, Henry 110
trader principle 23, 24
Tucker, Benjamin vii, 60, 174
Turkey, role of military 144

U
Unitarians, in Polish-Lithuanian Commonwealth 30–31
US Constitution 143
utilitarianism 5

V
values
  beneficial 23

irrational 24
obtaining 23

W
Wagner Act (1935) 181
warfare, and government 146
Warren, Josiah 60

Weber, Max
    definition of state 65
    government, definition vii
welfare provision 145–6
Wolff, Robert Paul 159
women, violence against 178–9

Made in the USA
Middletown, DE
15 November 2021